NEWMAN

Towards the Second Spring

Also by Michael Ffinch

Voices Round A Star
The Beckwalker
Selected Poems
Westmorland Poems
Simon's Garden
The Dame School at Raisbeck
A Portrait of the Howgills and the Upper Eden Valley
A Portrait of Kendal and the Kent Valley
A Portrait of Penrith and the East Fellside
G. K. Chesterton

NEWMAN
Towards the Second Spring

Michael Ffinch

SAN FRANCISCO   IGNATIUS PRESS

First published in Great Britain in 1991 by
George Weidenfeld and Nicolson Limited
91 Clapham High Street, London SW4 7TA

Cover illustration by Jenny Powell

Published 1992 by Ignatius Press, San Francisco
and HarperCollins London
ISBN 0-89870-388-3
Library of Congress Catalogue number 91-76069

Contents

Contents

Acknowledgments

Every student of Newman will inevitably owe a considerable debt to the Fathers of Newman's own Oratory at Birmingham, and in particular to the great work carried out by Fr Henry Tristram and Fr Stephen Dessain in their earnest desire to place Newman's Letters and Diaries before the public. This work has been continued more recently by Fr Ian Ker and Fr Thomas Gornhill SJ together with the Oratory Archivist, Mr Gerard Tracey: to all these Newman scholars I wish to acknowledge my indebtedness. I should also like to thank the Birmingham Oratory for its kind permission to quote from Newman's correspondence and to reproduce certain photographs in its keeping.

I have received much help and encouragement during the writing of this book and I should like to express my thanks in particular to Mr Lawrence James, Mgr Frederick Miles, Fr Jeremy Davies, Mr Martin Blake, Dr Laurence Catlow, Mr Andrew Maynard, Miss Lucy Ffinch, Mr and Mrs Christopher Tinker, Mr Shaun Maclaughlin, Fr Peter Allen, Canon William Jackson, Fr Thomas Walsh, Mrs Veronica Ffinch, Mr John Saward, Mr Graeme Soffe, Miss Judy Medrington, Mr Peter George, Mr Edward Wild, Mr Alexander Ffinch, Miss Candida Brazil, Mrs Elspeth Griffiths, Mr Edward Bierley, Mr Richard Thomas, Mr and Mrs Matthew Fullerton, Mr and Mrs Gordon Stuart, and Mr and Mrs John Robotham.

I should like to express my thanks to Messrs Bevan, Thornton and Hollett for obtaining necessary books; to the Headmaster of Sedbergh School, Dr Roger Baxter, for permission to use books from the School Library; to the Kendal Branch of the Cumbria County Library, and to the British Library for their invaluable help.

Lastly, I should like once again to thank my wife, Patricia, for her support and encouragement.

Illustrations

John Henry Newman by Sir William Ross, 1845   (Keble College, Oxford)

The Newman family, after a drawing by Maria Giberne   (The Misses M. and E. Miller)

John William Bowden   (Macmillan & Co.)

Henry Wilberforce   (Macmillan & Co.)

John Keble by George Richmond, 1863   (National Portrait Gallery)

Edward Pusey   (National Portrait Gallery)

Ambrose St John   (Birmingham Oratory)

Rev Frederick Faber   (Longmans, Green & Co.)

Contemporary skit on Littlemore and Oscott   (Longmans, Green & Co.)

Father Dominic Barberi   (Birmingham Oratory)

Rev George Spencer   (Longmans, Green & Co.)

John Henry Newman   (Burns, Oates and Washbourne Ltd.)

Cardinal Wiseman   (Longmans, Green & Co.)

Bishop Ullathorne   (Longmans, Green & Co.)

Henry S. Manning   (Burns, Oates and Washbourne Ltd.)

Dr Gentili   (Longmans, Green & Co.)

St Mary's, Oscott College   (Longman's, Green & Co)

The Oratory, King William Street, London   (Longman's, Green & Co.)

John Henry Newman by William Thomas Roden   (Manchester Art Gallery)

Foreword

It is surely necessary for every Christian to seek the unity for which Christ prayed. Happily, the Ecumenical Movement has already done much to make Christians aware of the damage their divided state has done. Certainly it has brought theological differences out into the open, and revealed significant, and in some cases surprising, agreement in many areas, but, sadly, through prejudice and misunderstanding damage is still being done.

However, there can be no unity among Christians until they can agree about the nature of the Church. They must first answer the vital question: What is the Church that Christ founded and promised he would never abandon? Does such a Church exist? Has it ever existed, or is it something of the future, an ideal towards which all Christians are hopefully moving? In providing a satisfactory answer the life and work of John Henry Newman is of considerable assistance, since this was the question he set out with all his energy to answer, in the tireless search for which, following his conscience, he moved from a position of extreme Evangelicalism towards Anglicanism, until his reception into the Catholic Church.

Now it may well be thought presumption, since Newman himself described the circumstances of his conversion adequately in his *Apologia Pro Vita Sua*, one of the finest examples of autobiographical writing in the language, that anyone should choose to write about it again. Surely, the facts are sufficiently well known. The only answer is that the present situation among Christians demands a further look.

It is important to emphasise at the outset that my book is not a biography in the accepted sense; rather, it is an attempt to place Newman's spiritual pilgrimage in the context of the religious revival of the nineteenth century, and in particular to show how his conversion to Catholicism and his establishing of the Oratorian Congregation in England played an important part in the emergence of the Catholic Church after many years of injury and isolation. Because of this, I have chosen to follow Newman's advice to the author of a life that he should make use of his subject's letters and writings but refrain from as much comment and speculation of his own as possible. Towards the end of the book I have intentionally allowed Newman's voice to be heard more and more strongly, and I have ended the narrative at an important moment in the English Catholic Church's history, the year 1852, when after the recent restoration of the Catholic Hierarchy Newman preached his famous sermon, 'The Second Spring', at St Mary's, Oscott during the First Provincial Council of Westminster.

There are many themes in the book besides the important one of Newman's spiritual development, but perhaps among the most significant is one essential to it: Newman's growing devotion to the Real Presence in the Eucharist. It was his discovery and understanding of this mystery that may be said to have led him into the Catholic Church just as much as the polemics in which he engaged. It amazed him that as an Anglican he had travelled through Italy and Sicily without once being aware that Our Lord was present in every church he had visited. After his conversion to Catholicism, when he was living in a house where the Blessed Sacrament was reserved, he would speak of the 'incomprehensible blessing to have Christ in bodily presence in one's house ... to know that He is close by – to be able again and again through the day to go to Him'.

It is, of course, largely, if not entirely, owing to the Movement Newman and his friends began at Oxford in 1833 that the Blessed Sacrament is reserved in some Anglican churches today, but it is the exception rather than the rule, the formularies do not encourage it. Newman in his controversial Tract 90 did his best to argue that the Anglican Articles of Religion were open to a 'Catholic' interpretation, but in later life, although he continued to believe in most cases this was still possible, he came to see that in the question of the Mass and the Real Presence, they repudiated the central and most sacred doctrine of the Catholic religion.

It may suit the Prince of this World that Christians remain divided, but as Newman came to see so clearly, the moment of consecration is not symbolic: the Presence of Our Blessed Lord in the Most Holy Sacrament of the Altar binds us together, safeguards against error and destroys all pain.

Michael Ffinch
Dodding Green

PART I

The Search for Truth

1

Childhood, Oxford and the Bitterest of Blows

$$\boxed{1801-20}$$

On 3 April 1833, the Wednesday in Holy Week, Monsignor Nicholas Wiseman, the young Rector of the English College in Rome, was informed that Mr Severn, an artist well known in the city, had called with two travellers from England. These were clergymen of the Established Church, Oxford dons of about Wiseman's own age. They could have expected a warm welcome, for Wiseman was known to enjoy such visits; he had already gained a reputation as a scholar who enjoyed debate, and it was not long since he had been requested personally by the Pope to preach a series of public sermons for the benefit of the increasingly large crowd of English visitors and residents in Rome. In fact, the two clergymen had attended one of these sermons, but this was to be their first meeting.

Wiseman's five years as Rector of the Venerabile, as the place was affectionately called, had continued the College's reconstruction begun by his predecessor, Dr Gradwell, after the ravages of Napoleon's troops. When Gradwell had returned to England as a bishop, it had seemed natural that Wiseman, his Vice-Rector, should succeed him in spite of his comparative youth. Wiseman was described at about that time as 'tall, slight, apparently long-necked, with features rather pointed and pale, and demeanour very grave',[1] and Severn's keen eye might well have noted the contrast between him and the lean, bespectacled figure of the elder of the two Englishmen, Mr Newman; though it was the younger, Mr Froude, who seemed to engage more of Wiseman's attention. The main reason the two had sought an introduction as related by Froude is surprising.

'We got introduced to him to find out whether they would take us in on any terms to which we could twist our consciences, and we found to our dismay that not one step could be gained without swallowing the Council of Trent as a whole.'[2]

3

The Council of Trent! What in the Lord's name were these two clergymen up to? Both staunch champions of the Established Church; Protestants, surely? How could they even contemplate 'twisting their consciences' to accept any accommodation between their Church and the accursed Rome? Did they mean to bend their knees to the Pope? Had they forgotten totally the Reformation? Did they doubt that Rome had erred? They could have no doubt that was true. Nevertheless, it was all something of a mystery, and the visit excited Wiseman greatly. Could it be that Oxford was about to experience the same sort of awakening as had lately stirred some Cambridge men, men like George Spencer and Ambrose Phillipps? Whatever it meant, this introduction had as much effect on Wiseman as on the others; but what Severn, or anyone else at the time could not have foreseen was that this simple meeting was the first between two future Cardinals of the Catholic Church, and that each had been chosen to play a major part, though acting out widely differing roles, in the renewal of the Faith in England, the renewal that Newman himself would call the 'Second Spring'.

In Wiseman's case future high office in the Catholic Church might have been expected, he had all the right credentials, but hardly in Newman's. He had come to Rome quite by chance, a hasty decision brought about by Hurrell Froude's ill-health. It was true he had found Rome a delightful place and he would regret leaving it. It was 'so calm, so quiet, so dignified and beautiful' and he knew nothing like it but Oxford, but it was a false charm. As he wrote back home to a friend: 'Nothing could make the Queen of the Seven Hills any thing but evil,'[3] and it surprised him to find clergymen like himself so inconsistent as to praise what God had cursed.

As for Froude, Wiseman confirmed all his worst fears. 'We found to our horror that the doctrine of the infallibility of the Church made the acts of each successive Council obligatory for ever, that what had once been decided could never be meddled with again; in fact, that they were committed finally and irrevocably, and could not advance one step to meet us, even though the Church of England should again become what it was in Laud's time, or indeed what it may have been up to the atrocious Council.'[4] This altogether hardened Froude's attitude to Roman Catholics and it made him wish for the overthrow of their system. From this moment he would fix his allegiance to the 'ancient Church of England', by which he meant the Church of King Charles I and the Non-Jurors.

However, the two had found Wiseman 'too nice a person to talk nonsense about', and a further meeting was arranged. Newman's diary for Saturday, 6 April includes the entry: 'Called on Dr Wiseman with Froude and had a long talk with him.'[5]

Before they left, Wiseman said he hoped they might visit Rome for a second time, and asked how long they intended to remain in the city. Newman said he did not know for they had work to do in England. What he did not know was that Wiseman himself felt he had work to do in England also. In later life he recalled that the visit of Newman and Froude had marked a turning point in his life and that from that time he entered a 'new state of mind'.

'From the day of Newman and Froude's visit to me,' he wrote, 'never for an instant did I waver in my convictions that a new era had commenced in England ... to this grand object I devoted myself ... the favourite studies of former years were abandoned for the pursuit of this aim alone.'[6]

Perhaps Wiseman, like some others in Rome, was wondering who exactly this Mr Newman was.

The Newman family came from the Fen Country. John Henry Newman's grandfather had moved from Swaffham Bulbeck in Cambridgeshire to London where he worked as a grocer. He used to refer to himself as a 'coffee man', but little is known about him except that he died intestate in the July of 1799. Three months later, his son, a partner in a banking firm and also named John, married Jemima Fourdrinier, the only daughter of a family of Huguenot descent that had been very successful in the paper business. As it happened, Jemima had also lost her father a few months before her marriage, but it is likely he had already sanctioned her considerable dowry of £5,000. John Henry, their eldest child, was born in the City of London on Saturday, 21 February 1801 at 80 Old Broad Street.

By all accounts John Newman had done very well by his marriage, for Jemima made an excellently loyal wife and mother, and the fact that she came from a higher position in the social scale than the Newmans spurred on her husband to keep her in the proverbial manner to which she was accustomed and, if possible, even better. At the time the prospects of Harrison, Prickett and Newman of No 1, Mansion House Street seemed good. The new-born baby was baptised in the Church of St Benet Fink on 9 April; his two godfathers were an uncle, and Richard Ramsbottom, MP, with whom John Newman was later to go into partnership.

The Newmans remained at Old Broad Street for a very short time, for their second son Charles was born at their new house in Southampton Street in June 1802. There were to be six children in all; after Charles came Harriett (1803), Francis (1805), Jemima (1808) and Mary (1809). Besides the town house, the family had taken Grey's Court, at Ham. This 'square-set Georgian House' had extensive grounds, and, although he was only there for a relatively short while, it was to haunt Newman's imagination: 'I know more about it than any house I have been in since, and I could pass an examination in it. It has ever been in my dreams,'[7] he wrote. It was at Ham in 1805 that he 'lay abed with candles in the windows in illumination for the victory at Trafalgar'.[8] Two years later the family left the house for good.

Newman recalled that when he was at school he dreamed about the Ham house as if it were Paradise. In the May of 1808 he had been sent as a boarder to a school in Great Ealing where there were some two hundred pupils, though by the time Newman left eight years later the number had risen by a further hundred. A success story indeed, and the school included among its pupils at different times Thomas Huxley, W.S. Gilbert, William Makepeace Thackeray and Captain Marryat, while Louis Philippe, formerly King of France, used to come over from Twickenham to give lessons in geography and mathematics. The master was Dr George Nicholas of Wadham College, Oxford. At Great Ealing School, Newman proved to be an exceptional pupil.

> As a child, he was of a studious turn, and of a quick apprehension; and Dr
> Nicholas, to whom he became greatly attached, was accustomed to say, that
> no boy had run through the school, from the bottom to the top, so rapidly
> as John Newman. Though in no respect a precocious boy, he attempted
> original compositions in prose and verse from the age of eleven, and in prose
> showed a great sensibility and took much pains in matters of style. He devoted
> to such literary exercises and to such books as came his way a good proportion
> of his play-time; and his school-fellows have left on record that they never,
> or scarcely ever, saw him taking part in any game.[9]

The Doctor had the reputation for 'getting boys on', but, to begin with, although he managed the academic work happily enough, Newman had been too immature to cope with the other boys' teasing. 'O, Sir, they will say such things! I can't help crying,'[10] he informed the master. However, he was soon to settle down, and when his parents considered moving him to Winchester, he pleaded with them to be allowed to remain at Ealing, where his two brothers joined him.

Newman's chief enjoyments at school were acting and music, and he became an active member of the Spy Club, producing a weekly paper in imitation of Addison's *Spectator*, and appointing himself Grand Master of a special Order within the Club. Not content with writing 'The Spy', he also initiated an opposing weekly, the 'Anti-Spy', in which he contested the opinions of the former, proving not only his ability to see clearly both sides of an argument but also revealing his remarkable gift for writing concise English prose. Throughout his life Newman was meticulously careful to preserve documents and many of his early pocket books remained among his treasures, as did his school text books. The entries in the pocket books are brief and to the point, but among them are several that catch the eye particularly with the benefit of hindsight.

1810. May 4th. Heard for the first time the cuckoo. Dreamed that Mary was
dead.
1811. Jany 27th. Sunday—went to Westminster Abbey, and R.C. Chapel.

Of the latter entry Newman recalled that it had been Warwick Street Chapel
in the company of his father who had wanted to hear a particular piece
of music. All Newman bore away from it was 'the recollection of a pulpit
and a preacher, and a boy swinging a censer'.[11]

Newman's religious background was fairly typical for the time; his parents
were nominally members of the Established Church, though his father considered himself a 'man of the world', a Freemason, and a member of the
Beef-steak Club where the 'chief wits and great men of the nation' were
said to gather. His mother was more religious. Of a 'mildly Calvinistic' frame
of mind, she brought up her children to take great delight in reading the
Bible and they were taught the Catechism, but, as Newman confessed later,
he had no formed religious convictions until he was fifteen. The great change
came about through the interest taken in him by the classics master, Revd
Walter Mayers, who, as Newman later put it, 'was the human means of
this beginning of Divine faith in me'.[12] From Mayers Newman accepted the
concept of a definite Creed; he received into his intellect 'impressions of
dogma, which, through God's mercy, have never been effaced or obscured'.[13]
Above all, it was the many books to which Mayers introduced him, rather
than his conversations and sermons, that had most influence. This Newman
considered as his First Conversion, and the ideas he gained from Mayers
were 'all of the school of Calvin'. At about the same time another important
realisation came to him.

> I am obliged to mention, though I do it with great reluctance, another deep
> imagination, which at this time, the autumn of 1816, took possession of me,
> – there can be no mistake about the fact; viz. that it would be the will of
> God that I should live a single life. This anticipation, which has held its ground
> almost continuously ever since – with the break of a month now and a month
> then, up to 1829, and after that date, without any break at all, – was more
> or less connected in my mind with the notion, that my calling in life would
> require such a sacrifice as celibacy involved; as, for instance, missionary work
> among the heathen, to which I had a great drawing for some years.[14]

The Newman family needed all the religious consolation possible, for about
the same time, in the winter after the Battle of Waterloo, the fortunes of
Mr Newman's banking business took a turn for the worse. On 8 March
1816 the doors of Ramsbottom, Newman and Ramsbottom were closed.
A difficult time followed during which the family moved from Southampton
Street to Alton, in Hampshire, where Mr Newman worked in the brewing

business. From that time onwards, although the bank's creditors were paid in full, the family never completely recovered its stability.

So it was that in the spring of 1817, with his new-found religious principles and intentions, and with eyesight which his studies had begun to affect, Newman waited the few months before moving from Ealing to Oxford.

Newman's name is so firmly linked in most people's minds with Oxford that it comes as a surprise to learn that, but for the happy guiding of Providence, he might have gone to Cambridge. Even on the morning he left home with his father there seems still to have been doubt as to which university to head for. Should the post boy direct the chaise towards Hounslow, or for the first stage on the road to Cambridge? The matter was decided by the timely arrival of the Curate of St James's Piccadilly, Revd John Mullins, who had taken an interest in the boy's education, and who persuaded Mr Newman to make speedily for Oxford.

Mullins's hope had been to find young John a place at Exeter, his own College, but on arrival there was no vacancy and so he 'took the advice of his Exeter friends to introduce him to Dr Lee, President of Trinity, and at that time Vice Chancellor'.[15] Newman matriculated as a commoner. On informing Dr Nicholas of the outcome of his Oxford visit, the news was met with the enthusiastic reply, 'Trinity? a most gentlemanlike College; I am much pleased to hear it.'[16]

Newman did not take up residence at Trinity until early in the following June when he was offered 'borrowed apartments'. He had already missed most of the year and the undergraduates were about to leave for the long vacation. With his natural shyness Newman felt this some advantage. He was very ill at ease for the first day or two; his eyes were giving him trouble once more, and he could not see to read. He was depressed and, knowing no one, he felt very solitary. After a few days his eyes slowly improved and he was able to study, breaking off for an hour's walk.

On 16 June he informed his father: 'I am not noticed at all, except by being stared at. I am glad they do not wish to be acquainted with me, not because I wish to appear apart from them and ill-natured, but because I really do not think I should gain the least advantage from their company.'[17] A generous attempt to make the new arrival feel at home in College was made but not appreciated. 'They drank and drank all the time I was there,' Newman complained, 'for I am sure I was not entertained with either their drinking or their conversation.'[18] The summons to prayer came as a blessing and brought the half hour ordeal to an end. 'I really think, if any one should ask me what qualifications were necessary for Trinity College, I should say there is only one, – Drink, drink, drink.'[19]

One might assume from this that Newman was a prude, but the assumption would be false. In another letter home he praises the College dinner: 'Fish, flesh and fowl, beautiful salmon, haunches of mutton, lamb etc and fine, very fine (to my taste) strong beer, served up on old pewter plates, and mis-shapen earthenware jugs.'[20] He wishes his Mama to know there were goose-berry, raspberry, and apricot pies, and Harriett must be told he had seen the fat cook!

It was not to be very long, however, before Newman found a friend in John William Bowden. Although their initial meeting had been brief, since Bowden left Oxford for the vacation on 19 June, during the following terms the two became inseparable; eating, reading and walking in each other's company and seeing as much as possible of each other during the vacations. In fact, they were so often seen together that men used to mistake their names and call them by each other's. The friendship lasted and Bowden remained one of Newman's inner circle of friends. 'One whom to have known is to have loved and to hold in perpetual remembrance', Newman wrote of him, 'with whom passed almost exclusively my Undergraduate years.'[21] In later life Newman recalled how Bowden had been sent to call on him the day after he came into residence, and how he had introduced him to the College and the University. 'He is the link between me and Oxford. I have ever known Oxford in him.'[22]

Newman was present at the ceremony at which Robert Peel, at the time Chief Secretary for Ireland, was made a Doctor of Laws. 'I had a very good place in the theatre,' he told his father. He thought his brother Charles would have enjoyed the noblemen's dresses, 'as also the I-do-not-know-what-they-were, very fat men, I suppose DDs, in red robes, or scarlet, and the Proctors with sheepskins.'[23] Peel's elevation had been in recognition of his successful opposition to Catholic emancipation and Oxford acknowledged his services to Protestantism even further by making him her Member of Parliament.

At home these early letters from Oxford were received with a certain anxiety, but Mrs Newman was thankful that John was showing such strong principles, such as might be able 'to stem the torrent of folly and impropriety'. 'I must echo what your father says,' Mrs Newman continued. 'Change of society, even if agreeable, is trying to a feeling mind.'[24]

For a short time Newman had the College to himself, and when one evening, with half a dozen servants waiting upon him, he feasted alone on veal cutlets and peas, so awesome did the occasion seem he could hear the noise he made chewing throughout the empty hall. When another man came in and sat opposite, because they had not been introduced, they preserved an ami-cable silence and conversed with their teeth.

Anxious to have his course of reading organised, Newman attempted to see the President. A servant showed him into the parlour, saying the doctor would be ready in a minute. After waiting for an hour and a half, Newman rang the bell, but discovered that Dr Lee was out. The following day the doctor told him that all matters of study were left to the tutors. It looked as though he might have to retreat home without any information about the one matter uppermost in his mind, except for the chance sight of one of the tutors, dressed in top-boots and on horseback, on his way into the country. Newman dashed out into the road and abruptly accosted him, asking him which books he should read during the vacation. The tutor treated him kindly, explaining that he himself was now leaving Oxford for the vacation, but that a colleague still in College would be able to help, as proved to be the case. But for this fortunate meeting Newman might have had little to do except sit and console himself with his violin.

Music was to play an important part in Newman's time as an undergraduate. For the first weeks he had hired a violin while his own was being repaired, and, during that hot June, he composed some couplets on the subject of music.

> His list of blessings worthily to crown
> God sent his sweetest gift, sent Music down.
> – Soul of the world! – for thy harmonious force
> Restrains all nature in its proper course ...[25]

In the coming years he would join other musical friends, taking the first violin part in quartets by Haydn or Mozart. On one occasion an enthusiastic don, 'a very good-natured man, but too fond of music', kept him playing quartets for five hours at a stretch so that his arms and eyes hurt, and his head and back grew stiff. Newman developed a passion for Beethoven, 'the gigantic nightingale', as he called him, and he used to participate in weekly concerts, given privately to a music club formed next door at St John's College.

On 29 June 1817 what Newman called his 'first solitary term of three weeks' came to an end.

Newman returned to Oxford in the following October. Among the many items his scout bought for him in the town were an egg-saucepan and spoon, a shaving pot, several decanters, two dozen wine glasses and an earthen slop pan. He was unable to have a bath because the ceiling had collapsed and the bath was being repaired, but he still owed the College for the few baths he had had during the hot weather in June. To begin with his eyes were giving little trouble, though on the first Sunday he had a dizzy spell during the service in the University Church of St Mary's and had to be helped back to his rooms. His tutor, Mr Short, had advised him which lectures to attend: 'one in Tacitus every morning but Thursday; one in Cicero on Wednesday, and Mathematics three times a week'.[26] Newman did not think this enough: 'of course, they begin with little to see what I can do.'[27] Still, apart from his friendship with Bowden, he stood somewhat aloof from the rest of the College. His mother wrote hoping he was not over-exerting himself. 'Remember all extremes as bad, and that a steady permanent attention is most prudent, because compatible with health,'[28] she advised. However, 'Mr Newman and his fiddle' had been noticed; on one occasion later in the term he was invited to a wine party and asked to bring his violin, but the gathering was too riotous for him to play and he departed leaving one or two others to play their flutes.

Towards the end of November the University was plunged into mourning, as was the whole nation, for Princess Charlotte, who had died after giving birth to a stillborn son. The Proctors would not allow anyone to appear unless in black: 'Black coat, black waistcoat, black trowsers (*sic*), black gloves; black ribbon, no chain to the watch; no white except the neckcloth and the unplaited frill,'[29] Newman informed his mother.

Soon it became obvious to his tutors that he was an exceptional scholar. When at Easter 1818 his father came to Oxford to take John Henry home, Mr Short greeted him like a long-lost friend. 'O, Mr Newman, what have you given us in your son,' or some such words. Short's interest was increasing, to the extent that he gave his student extra books to read and encouraged him to sit for a College scholarship. In this Newman was successful and he was elected a scholar on 18 May 1818. The award was for nine years at £60 a year, after which, if there were no other Fellow from his county at the College, Newman would have stood the chance of being elected Fellow 'as a regular thing for five years without taking orders'. What was certain was that his tutors, and Newman himself, expected that he would reach the highest academic distinction, and for the next two years he worked assiduously towards gaining First Class Honours in his Final Examination.

Both term-time and vacations were from that time onwards spent in study. Besides the classical authors, he read Gibbon twice, as he informed Bowden during the vacation of 1819.

Herodotus, Thucydides and Gibbon have employed me nearly from morning to night. A second perusal of the last historian has raised him in my scale of merit. With all his faults, his want of simplicity, his affectation and his monotony, few can be put in comparison with him, and sometimes when I reflect on his happy choice of expressions, his rigorous compression of ideas, and the life and significance of every word, I am prompted to exclaim that no style is left for historians of an after day. Oh, who is worthy to succeed our Gibbon? Exoriare aliquis! and may he be a better man.[30]

Newman himself was one to succeed him, and he was a better man. 'I seldom wrote without an eye to style,' he said with reference to his earliest efforts at composition, 'and since my taste was bad my style was bad. I wrote in style as another might write in verse, or sing instead of speaking, or dance instead of walking. Also my evangelical tone contributed to its bad taste.'[31] However, as Newman's taste developed, so did his literary style. Together with Bowden he produced *The Undergraduate*, a magazine that ran for several issues until its authorship became known; once the secret was out all Newman's enthusiasm diminished, and he felt ashamed of his effort. 'What imprudence have I committed? I had told no one. I never felt such a dreadful shock. The whole day I was so weak I could hardly walk or speak.'[32] Another joint venture was 'The Huguenot', a poem about the Massacre of St Bartholomew; but such enjoyments might hinder his progress towards success in Schools. During one Christmas vacation he made 'a very full analysis or abridgment of the whole of Thucydides'; during the long vacation of 1819, he read at the rate of nine hours a day. As the months drew on to his examination he increased the pace, during twenty out of the twenty-four weeks reading up to twelve hours a day, and if for any reason he read for less, he would make it up the following day, sometimes reading for some fifteen hours. 'I stayed in Oxford during the vacations, got up in Winter and Summer at five or six, hardly allowed myself time for my meals, and ate, indeed, the bread of carefulness.'[33]

His tutors in College continued to have high hopes; for some years they had had no success in the Honours list. In Newman they appeared to have a dead certainty. Just before the exam Bowden wrote to his friend: 'By the time you receive this, I conclude you will have completed your labours in the schools and covered yourself and the college with glory.'[34] But only shame was to follow, for Newman had burnt himself out: when he discovered he was called to the examination a day earlier than expected he went completely to pieces. On 1 December he wrote in anguish home to his father.

> It is all over; and I have not succeeded. The pain it gives me to be obliged
> to inform you and my Mother of it I cannot express. What I feel on my
> own account is indeed nothing at all, compared with the idea that I have
> disappointed you; and most willingly would I consent to a hundred times
> the sadness that now overshadows me if so doing would save my Mother
> and you from feeling vexation. I will attempt to describe what I have gone
> through; but it is past away, and I feel quite lightened of a load. – The
> Examining Masters were as kind as it was possible to be; but my nerves quite
> forsook me and I failed. I have done every thing I could to attain my object,
> I have spared no labour and my reputation in my College is as solid as before,
> if not so splendid. – If a man falls in battle after a display of bravery, he
> is honoured as a hero; ought not the same glory to attend him who falls
> on the field of literature?[35]

It was the bitterest of blows. When the class list was posted Newman's name did not appear at all on the mathematical side of the paper, and in classics he was placed well down in the Second Class. However, his performance gained him his BA and his father sent him the £15 necessary for the fee and he graduated on Tuesday, 5 December 1820.

In reply to his letter Mrs Newman assured him: 'We are more than satisfied with your laudable endeavours ... Every body who knows you, knows your merit; and your failure will increase the interest they feel in you.'[36] She concluded with a reminder of something Newman had written to his sister Jemima some weeks before he sat for the exam. That letter had revealed not only a remarkably mature attitude to circumstance, but also a trust in Providence consonant with a highly developed state of spiritual awareness.

> I am doing my part, but God chooseth the event and I know he will choose
> for the best. It therefore is not only my duty but my privilege to take no
> thought of the morrow; for thinking of the event and its uncertainty would
> only tend to make me anxious and care worn and sad. But now striving to
> feel that, whether I pass a good or bad examination, God will be bestowing
> what is best for me, I may rest calm and joyful. I will not therefore ask for
> success, but for 'good'; I dare not ask for success, for it might prove fatal
> to me. Do you therefore, dearest sister, wish for me to obtain that which
> is best for me, and not for me to gain high honours here; for then, whether
> I succeed or fail, I shall have the comfort of feeling assured that I have obtained
> real advantage and not apparent.
>
> > Still raise for good the supplicating voice,
> > But leave to Heav'n the measure, and the choice.[37]

The measure was harsh indeed, and the choice hurt deeply.

2

A Fellow of Oriel College

$$\boxed{1822\text{--}28}$$

Determined not to let his failure distress him too deeply Newman continued to work as hard as ever. He would learn the choruses of Aeschylus by heart. Music would be a consolation, and he thought of setting one or two of the choruses as he learnt them. Recently the first symphony of Haydn had made a great impression on him. He had a concerto of his own to write, as he informed Jemima, besides a treatise on astronomy to complete. Nevertheless, the trauma of the examination had alarmed him. He had never experienced anything like it before. 'My memory was gone, my mind altogether confused,'[1] he wrote to Mayers. It was as if a surgical operation were day after day being carried out upon him; he had dragged himself through the examination from Saturday to Friday, and after all was obliged to withdraw from the contest, but he still believed God was leading him through life in the way best adapted for His glory and his own salvation. 'I trust I may have always the same content and indifference to the world, which is at present the prevailing principle in my heart – yet I have great fears of backsliding.'[2]

After some time spent with his father at Cheltenham and London over Christmas, Newman returned to Oxford on 12 February 1821. A few days earlier he had visited Drury Lane for the opera *Artaxerxes*, which was perhaps his last visit to the theatre. His scholarship had not expired and the College welcomed him back; both Dr and Mrs Lee were particularly kind. Newman decided to attend anatomy and mineralogy lectures, and during the term he rode out to Abingdon to look at a fine collection of minerals, and determined to visit the British Museum collection at the earliest opportunity. He wrote the mineralogy lectures up in simple and direct form so that his young sisters could enjoy them.

It seemed unlikely that he would be able to keep his rooms after July, but he was decided about staying at Oxford. In April he wrote to his tutor of his intention to take in pupils, but the future at this time remained uncertain. No longer was a career at the Bar likely, for he had been entered at Lincoln's Inn in the summer of 1819. After his failure in the examination, his father acquiesced to his son's growing desire to be ordained, though the matter was not finally decided until January the following year.

In fact, Newman moved out of College earlier than was expected. During either the Trinity or Summer Term he lodged at a house opposite Balliol College where he remained until 5 July. Returning in October after the long vacation he took rooms well known to him, since they had been formerly occupied by Bowden, at Seal's Coffee House, at the corner of Holywell and Broad Street, his main room looking down the street. There he would remain until the Easter of 1822. On 1 November Mr Newman's financial affairs reached breaking point and the unhappy man was declared bankrupt. Realising the desperate situation in which the family was now placed, and the effect the strain might have on his father's health, John Henry wrote home declaring his intention to take the education of his brother, Francis, upon his own shoulders, in spite of the fact that he as yet had only one pupil. At about the same time the 'audacious idea' entered his mind that he would pursue the object of ambition of all rising men at Oxford at that time and stand for a Fellowship at Oriel.

Francis spent much of the autumn of 1821 at Oxford, studying under his brother's tuition in preparation for his matriculation. Although in theory the plan was a sensible one, in practice matters did not work out, as Newman confessed to his mother. 'While with Frank at Oxford I have felt a spirit of desperate ill-temper, and sullen anger rush on me.'[3] So violent had he become on occasion that he would tremble from head to foot and he thought he might fall down under excess of agitation. Aware of the friction between the brothers, in spite of his many difficulties their father thought it might be better if Frank remained at home after Christmas and gave up all idea of Oxford; this prompted a letter from John full of praise for Frank's ability. He wrote that Frank was amazingly advanced for his age in both classics and mathematics. He was quite unsuited to go into business, if that were the alternative to staying at Oxford. 'He is in my opinion very quick as to things, and very slow as to persons; he is more expert at mathematical, than moral evidence. To speak from my own judgment, it seems to be taking him from the very thing which is naturally adapted to him.'[4]

The letter made Mr Newman reconsider, and Frank did return to Oxford where he remained, gaining a scholarship to Worcester College in the November of 1822, taking a Double First in 1826, after which he was elected a Fellow of Balliol. On learning of his brother's success in the Worcester scholarship Newman admitted that Frank was a better Greek scholar and a much better mathematician than he, but later in life he used unfairly to cite Frank as an example of the dangers of Protestantism. 'Whether or not Anglicanism leads to Rome,' he wrote to Jemima, 'so far is clear as day, that Protestantism leads to infidelity.'[5] However, he could well afford to be magnanimous in the autumn of 1822, for by that time his own life had taken a decided turn for the better: he was now a Fellow of Oriel.

The House of the Blessed Mary the Virgin in Oxford, founded in 1326 by King Edward ii, and one of the University's oldest colleges, soon became known as Oriel. At the beginning of the nineteenth century it was not only leading the colleges in a reformed system of examination and degrees for undergraduates soon to be followed by the others, but also it drew its Fellows from the University at large. The reform had been introduced by John Eveleigh, who was Provost of Oriel until 1814. By electing College Fellows by examination Eveleigh had been able to attract the brightest candidates from all the other colleges, so that soon Oriel became the most desired of prizes.

Newman, as we have seen, had made up his mind to try for Oriel in the November of 1821, but it was not until the first week of the following February that he called on the Provost of that college to ask leave to stand. The Provost, Dr Copleston, requested that the College see Newman's birth certificate. Newman, perhaps realising he was a little young, made it known at Trinity that he had no chance on the first attempt, but that he was 'simply standing for the sake both of knowing the nature of the examination for the sake of next year, and being known to the examiners'.[6] Certainly those at Trinity did not try to dissuade him, although few thought he had much chance of success; Newman, they considered, was likely to remain an 'under-the-line' man. One of the Fellows of Trinity, William Kinsey, later to become Vice-President of the College, wrote to Newman's father in the middle of March to assure him that John was not overdoing things, or overfagging, as he had done before his Schools. 'He wisely determines not to calculate upon success at Oriel, for there the struggles of the best have failed, and the odds are always fearfully against contending candidates. Knowing as I do the many opponents he will have to encounter, men of celebrity for talent and reading, I, with all my eager desire for his success, do not permit myself to be at all sanguine as to his beating the field.'[7]

As for the candidate himself, it seems he had a strong intuition that he would do well. 'I do not know how it happens,' he wrote to his friend James Tyler, 'but I certainly feel very confident with respect to Oriel ... God keep me from setting my heart upon it.'[8] But his heart was set on it. The candidates began the examination on Saturday, 6 April and were supplied with sandwiches, fruit, cake, jellies and wine to help them on their way. A blazing fire warmed them, and they were given plenty of time to complete the papers.

On the following Friday Newman learnt of his success. For the rest of his life he considered that Friday the turning point, 'of all days most memorable'. It raised him, he said, 'from obscurity and need to competency and reputation'.[9]

Unknown to him his papers had aroused great excitement at Oriel, and three days into the exam Dr Copleston had sent a deputation round to Trinity to make inquiries in the strictest confidence 'about his antecedents and general character'. Mr Short had been so elated that he sent for Newman, whom, he was alarmed to discover, had more or less decided to withdraw from the contest, but without betraying any secrets managed to persuade him to continue, while offering him a share in the lamb cutlets and fried parsley he was having for dinner.

Newman had every right to feel pleased with himself and although big-headed, the dramatic account of how he received the good news must have given him great pleasure to compose when he remembered the occasion some fifty years later.

> The Provost's Butler, to whom it fell by usage to take the news to the fortunate candidates, made his way to Mr Newman's lodgings in Broad Street, and found him playing the violin. This in itself disconcerted the messenger, who did not associate such an accomplishment with a candidateship for the Oriel Common Room; but his perplexity was increased, when, on his delivering what may be supposed to have been his usual form of speech on such occasions, that 'he had, he feared, disagreeable news to announce, viz. that Mr Newman was elected Fellow of Oriel, and that his immediate presence was required there,' the person addressed, thinking that such language savoured of impertinent familiarity, merely answered 'Very well' and went on fiddling. This led the man to ask whether perhaps he had not mistaken the rooms and gone to the wrong person, to which Mr Newman replied that (it) was all right. But, as may be imagined, no sooner had the man left, than he flung down his instrument, and dashed down stairs with all speed to Oriel College.[10]

As he hurried past St Mary's and crossed over the High Street towards his new college his eagerness was noticed. Tradesmen bowed low to him, for the news had evidently spread quickly. Friends congratulated him. At Trinity there was great excitement over the success of one of their college; bells began tolling from three different towers, for which Newman later had to pay; and the few undergraduates remaining in college revising for their degree reproached him for having spoilt their day's reading.

The move to Oriel was immediate. On the same Friday morning Newman found himself in the small tower room where on the Tuesday he had undergone the torturous ordeal of his viva voce. The occasion was scarcely less daunting. He did not so much mind the presence of the Provost, since he already felt relatively at ease with Copleston; many of the assembled Fellows he knew little about, but he felt like a young school boy in the presence of his hero when he confronted Keble. 'When Keble advanced to take my hand,' he told his mother, 'I quite shrank and could have nearly sunk into the floor, ashamed at so great an honour.'[11] The enthusiastic hand-shakings over, the group moved into the chapel, where with two others he was installed. Later, at six o'clock, he dined in Hall for the first time, and the following day he took his place in the Common Room.

It was not long before his new colleagues realised that Newman was more than usually shy, and all efforts at drawing him out proved fruitless. In view of the brilliant talker he later became this seems surprising, but the change was brought about slowly, and the beginning of it was due to Richard Whately, an Oriel Fellow, who had recently married and was living out of college. The future Archbishop of Dublin took young Newman under his wing. In Whately he found a warm and generous heart, a gentle and encouraging instructor, and for a shy person his easy optimism was infectious. Whately was one for whom all geese were swans, and he taught Newman to think and to open his mind, in short, to use his reason; so impressed was he by Newman's mind that when in 1825 he was appointed Principal of St Alban Hall he asked that Newman might be his Vice-Principal and Tutor. However, the friendship was not to last, since as time went on their ways diverged so far from each other that they ended in complete estrangement. 'I like you,' Whately once said, 'for you do not, as others, only agree with me, but you differ.'[12]

No less important to Newman's development during his early months at Oriel was the influence of another Fellow, Edward Hawkins, who became the Vicar of St Mary's in 1823, and succeeded Dr Copleston as Provost in 1828. Dr Hawkins spent much time with Newman during the long vacations. 'I can say with a full heart that I love him, and have never ceased to love him,' Newman wrote. 'He was the first who taught me to weigh my words, and to be cautious in my statements. He led me to that mode of limiting and clearing my sense in discussion and in controversy, and of distinguishing between cognate ideas, and of obviating mistakes by anticipation, which to my surprise has been since considered, even in quarters friendly to me, to savour of the polemics of Rome.'[13] Newman found Hawkins's exact mind impressive, though he often felt the sharpness of it when Hawkins snubbed him severely after reading the young prelate's early sermons. Above all, Newman owed to Hawkins his understanding of the doctrine of tradition, the understanding that the Scriptures were never intended to teach doctrine, but only to prove it.

Newman continued to take responsibility for his brother's education. In November 1822, he assured their parents that they had no need to worry. Francis was incurring no great expense. No bill was owing except the tailor's and the hatter's. Board and lodging was all paid for, and a whole year had passed at Oxford without any inconvenience or trouble. In the same month Frank entered Worcester, though he would not take up residence in college until the following summer. 'It seems as if I should have the requisite sum to pay for him, when he comes to reside,'[14] John wrote home. He now had four private pupils.

On 4 June 1823 he took his MA. He enjoyed the countryside round Oxford; his last hack horse bill had amounted to £2 19s. Several times a year he visited his parents. During the summer he spent four weeks at Strand-on-the-Green and six weeks in London. In October he returned to Oxford and, having joined the Bible Society, he decided to learn portions of Scripture by heart. 'The benefit seems to me incalculable,' he informed his sister Harriett. 'It imbues the mind with good and holy thoughts. It is a resource in solitude, on a journey, and in the sleepless night.'[15] If only his sisters and Francis could join him in incessant supplications for all who were dear to them, what may not be expected. He knew already there was little point in including his younger brother, Charles.

On the eve of All Saints' Day, Oxford was veiled in snow; a fierce gale had torn trees out of the earth in all directions. The Cherwell burst its banks and nearly overflowed Christ Church water walk. Newman now had rooms in the High Street, a little walk away from Oriel. He would have to paddle in his thin shoes and silk stockings down to dinner in college. He was pleased that the Regius Professor of Divinity, Dr Lloyd, had chosen him as one of eight to whom he would give private lectures. He was already well aware that 'those who pursued the truth were playing with edged tools, if instead of endeavouring perseveringly to ascertain what the truth is, they considered the subject carelessly, captiously, or with indifference.'[16]

Newman was ordained to the diaconate on Trinity Sunday, 13 June 1824, in Christ Church. He felt like a man thrown suddenly into deep water. 'At first, after the hands were laid on me, my heart shuddered within me; the words "for ever" are so terrible. It was hardly a godly feeling which made me feel melancholy at the idea of giving up all for God. At times indeed my heart burnt within me, particularly during the singing of the Veni Creator.'[17]

Ten days later he preached his first sermon at Worton. In the next week on a visit to London he called in at the Church Missionary Society to ask what qualifications would be necessary to become a missionary. His college had other plans for him and offered him the position of curate at St Clement's Church. Newman hesitated for a time, but after consulting both Mayers and Edward Bouverie Pusey, a newly elected Fellow of his college who was to play a major part in his life, he accepted. The parish of St Clement's was situated beyond Magdalen Bridge, on each side of the London Road, and on Sunday, 4 July Newman preached there and administered his first baptism.

From now on he would be exceedingly busy, for besides his pupils he would have some 2,000 parishioners for whom he was in part responsible. He undertook his duties meticulously, making a list of names and addresses and visiting each house in turn. His diary gives a clear outline of his many tasks and engagements: there were many sick to be visited, a church to be rebuilt, and almost immediately he began to stand in for other clergy. At the same time news came from home that his father's health was declining. Although the sad, broken man rallied a little in the late part of the summer, by September he was fading fast. On the night of 25 September Newman travelled to town by coach. He arrived to find his father 'very ill', but the sick man recognised him and tried to put out his hand to bless him; in the evening he said his 'last and precious words'. Throughout the next two days the doctor came and went many times and the end came on the evening of 29 September. That night the three brothers slept in the parlour in their clothes. After attending to his father's papers and informing his uncles of the family's loss, Newman remained at home until after the funeral, returning to Oxford on 2 October, convinced that no man could be a materialist once he had seen a dead body. It was the first he had seen, the first of the very many he would see during the years of his priesthood.

Newman was to work in the parish of St Clement's for a little less than two years. He was ordained to the priesthood on 29 May 1825, Trinity Sunday, the anniversary of his diaconate. Besides his parish duties he now had the responsibility of being Vice-Principal of St Alban Hall under Whately, and Junior Treasurer of his college.

In the summer of 1825 Mrs Newman brought the three girls to stay at Oxford. The Whatelys being away, they were able to occupy the Principal's House at St Alban Hall. John saw as much of them as he could, dining with them or walking in the afternoons. The visit did his mother much good, and he was able to report favourably to his aunt, Elizabeth Newman; but his chief worry at the time concerned his brother Charles, whose case he found 'truly lamentable'. Charles he saw as 'rushing along a dark and dangerous cavern, thinking he must find light at the end of it'.[18] In fact, Charles and his problems were to remain a burden to him for the rest of his life. For several whole days towards the end of the month he busied himself answering Charles's questions; his state of mind, Newman thought, led him to see in false colours every thing he looked upon. Charles had even accused him of having doubts about Christianity.

On Sunday, 7 August his mother was present when Newman administered the Sacrament of Holy Communion for the first time. During those same weeks he was researching for his essay on miracles for the *Encyclopaedia Metropolitana*, a task he did not complete until early in the following year, and he had begun work on a life of Apollonius of Tyana, 'a crafty old knave'. When his family returned to Strand towards the end of September, he took his own holiday, visiting the Bowdens at Southampton, leaving his St Clement's responsibilities in the hands of friends.

The Bowdens took him sailing round Freshwater beyond the Needles in a yacht; with John he explored the Hampshire countryside and crossed over to the Isle of Wight in the steamer. These were familiar haunts to him; at the age of fifteen he had attempted to circumnavigate the island in an open boat in the midst of a persevering drizzle and a dangerous sea. This time, in relative safety, he could only wish that the English language had more adjectives to express his admiration as he gazed at the beauty of the water and land beyond the Needles towards St Catherine's Point. The Bowdens had received him warmly, and there was music almost every evening with Newman playing the violin and Bowden the bass.

When in the January of 1826 it was known that Richard Jelf would leave Oxford for Berlin to take up his appointment as tutor to the young Prince George of Cumberland, Newman was asked to take his place as one of the four College Tutors. This was a great honour, and the position would improve his financial situation considerably as the post carried an annual income of between £600 and £700. However, it would mean he would have to give up his curacy at St Clement's and resign as Vice-Principal of the Hall. He moved into Jelf's vacated rooms on the first floor in the front quadrangle, near the chapel. Of all Oriel rooms these were those that Newman had always hoped for and, on 21 March with his books 'in disorder all over the room', he made himself at home, mindful, as he informed Harriett, 'There is always the danger of the love of literary pursuits assuming too prominent a place in the thoughts of a College Tutor, or his viewing his situation merely as a secular office, a means of future provision when he leaves College.'[19]

Easter fell early that year. On the Saturday Newman's diary recorded that the Fellowship examinations had begun. On Easter Day he completed his sermon and attended prayers and Holy Communion in the Oriel Chapel and then walked across Magdalen Bridge to St Clement's to take the services for the last time as curate. During the next few days he spent some time with both the Provost and Keble; Jelf came to say farewell. On the following Wednesday the viva voce for the Fellowships was held, and on the Thursday evening the College Fellows deliberated until two in the morning. On Friday it was announced that both the successful candidates were, in fact, commoners of the College, Richard Wilberforce and Richard Hurrell Froude. 'Froude is one of the acutest and clearest and deepest men in the memory of man,'[20] Newman informed his mother. 'I hope our election will be "in honorem Dei et ad Sponsae Suae Ecclesiae salutem", as Edward the IInd has it in our Statutes.'[21] It was indeed, but no one could have foreseen that the friendship soon to develop between Newman and Froude would change both of their lives and deal a mortal blow to the English Reformation.

Froude was two years younger than Newman. Always known to his family and friends by his second name, Hurrell, the family name of his grandmother, he was the eldest son of the Archdeacon of Totnes who lived at Dartington in Devon. Educated for a time at Ottery, and later at Eton, Froude entered Oriel College in 1821 where he was tutored by Keble, his devoted friend from whom he learnt his High Churchmanship. It was Newman's opinion that Froude was 'formed' by Keble, but in turn the pupil's mind also reacted on the tutor.

The younger man admitted to being shy of Newman at first and the two did not really get to know each other well until 1828, when Froude had become a Tutor at the College. Even then he would give a few odd pence, he said, if Newman were not a heretic, an opinion he must have inherited from Keble who had always regarded Newman with suspicion. Yet it was Froude who brought the two together. 'Do you know the story of the murderer who had done one good thing in his life?' he wrote later. 'Well, if I was ever asked what good deed I have ever done, I should say I had brought Newman and Keble together.'[22]

It may seem strange that this friendship had needed such a catalyst but, although he was seen on occasion at Oxford, Keble had given up his post as Tutor in 1823 and retired to the country in order to follow his father's example and concentrate on parish work. Keble's attitude to Newman up to this time was influenced by what he thought him to be: a dyed-in-the-wool Evangelical, Low Church in the extreme, one who might well take his inspiration from liberal-minded men such as Whately, and Thomas Arnold, another Oriel Fellow. Newman, in Keble's somewhat blinkered view, was never likely to sympathise with a more Catholic interpretation of the Book of Common Prayer, or believe in the Real Presence. So, although Newman for his part had admired Keble from the very first, his admiration was not reciprocated until Hurrell Froude 'brought them together'.

In the June of 1827 Keble published his *The Christian Year* anonymously. This series of devotional poems based on the Liturgy had been written at various times since 1819. For Newman they seemed the most soothing, tranquillising, subduing work of the day; 'if poems can be found to enliven in dejection, and to comfort in anxiety; to cool the over-sanguine, to refresh the weary, and to awe the worldly; to instil resignation into the impatient, and calmness into the fearful and agitated.'[23] Such were the general sentiments the poems aroused. Arnold had written as early as 1823, after seeing some of the poems in manuscript, that nothing equal to them existed in the language; 'the wonderful knowledge of Scripture, the purity of heart, and the richness of poetry'[24] he had never seen paralleled. Froude's was the only dissenting voice: he found the verses addressed too much to matter-of-fact people, and they did not do enough to sober down into practical piety those whose feelings were acute, and who were inclined to indulge in a dreamy, visionary existence. As the poems had been published anonymously, he was afraid the author might be taken for a Methodist. Today, the poems are seldom read, if at all, and one would probably agree with Froude. However, the earliest poem, 'The Purification', contains several well-known lines included in the hymn 'Blest are the pure in Heart'.

> Still to the lowly soul
> He doth himself impart,
> And for his cradle and his throne
> Chooseth the pure in heart.

Six weeks of the long summer vacation Newman spent in Hampstead where he had agreed to take on the parochial duties for his friend Edward Marsh. He had also offered to take Henry Wilberforce and C.P. Golightly under his wing as private pupils. Marsh had offered his house as accommodation, but on arrival Newman's party, which included his mother and his youngest sister, Mary, found the place in such a filthy state, so 'full of bad vermin', that they had to leave. On informing Marsh of the fact, the 'meek, gentle, amiable man' wrote that it was one of the trials of his life and it had to be borne.

At this time the family was preoccupied with setting up a house in Brighton, which Mrs Newman could live in during the winter months and let during the season. Lack of money was a constant problem, and it soon became obvious that Newman's Aunt Elizabeth was in a desperate situation financially. Writing from Oxford towards the end of October, John Henry showed grave concern for the poor woman but said that he could not personally give any bill or bond which might make him legally answerable. 'I could not do this consistently with my duty to myself as a clergyman, who must have nothing (if possible) to do with mere worldly matters.'[25] However, on 5 November he was sending his mother the halves of five twenty-pound notes, the other halves he would send by the same coach two days later. 'I have been a good deal plagued in various ways,' his mother wrote to Harriett, 'but yet

I hope the main things go on right. I have had various communications with dear John Henry: he is, as usual, my guardian angel.'[26]

Guardian angel or not, the whole matter was causing Newman great distress, adding to a general state of debility that had worried his friends for months. His punishing schedule of reading had been taking its toll. When he had arrived at Ulcombe, in Kent, to spend a fortnight with Samuel Rickards and his family, Mrs Rickards had been shocked to see how tired and drawn he looked. 'If he improves in looks at Ulcombe, how delightful it will be.'[27] But by November matters stood far worse and with the Schools imminent there was no hope of rest. Pusey had been forced to take a rest and had gone to Brighton to regain his health, which put more responsibility on to Newman's shoulders. To crown it all news came that Dr Copleston had been appointed Bishop of Llandaff which raised the prospect of an immediate vacancy in the headship of Oriel. 'This completed my incapacity,'[28] Newman wrote. For two nights he thought or dreamed of nothing else; a weekend which should have brought some rest only increased his anxiety. On the Saturday he had begun to droop and on Sunday he felt the blood collect in his head; on the Monday he found his memory and mind gone and while he was examining a candidate for the first class he felt so ill he had to leave the room. His doctor advised an immediate leaching of the temples. On the Wednesday Robert Wilberforce took Newman to his home at Highwood for a two-day holiday. Newman became worse and the consultant, Mr Babington, said it was a determination of blood to the head arising from over exertion of the brain, with a disordered stomach. The patient could certainly not return to Oxford, but must remain at the Wilberforces' for a week and then go on down to Brighton.

> Now I must give some account of the mode in which this attack manifested itself. I was not in pain exactly; nothing acute, nothing like a rheumatic headache; but a confusion, an inability to think or recollect. Once or twice indeed, when my head was on my pillow, I felt a throbbing so distressing, though it was not violent, to make me sensible I had never experienced a real headache. It was not pain, but a twisting of the brain, of the eyes. I felt my head inside was made up of parts. I could write verses pretty well, but I could not count. I once or twice tried to count my pulse, but found it quite impossible; before I had got to 30, my eyes turned round and inside out, all of a sudden.[29]

On 14 December Newman took the coach to Brighton. The wind and rain swept into his face, but he was able to keep his head and shoulders and, in particular, his feet, relatively dry. Three days later he was already feeling very much better and, when the two men walked over the Downs, he was pleased to find Pusey's condition had also improved. No doubt the topic uppermost in their minds was the forthcoming College Election brought about by Copleston's departure. The two candidates were Hawkins and Keble. Newman was strongly in favour of the former. As Robert Wilberforce indicated to Froude, 'Hawkins was more suited to the task of cleansing that Augean stable – the meeting of Heads'; besides he was a 'man of business'. However, Keble had his supporters too. 'I have a kind of feeling that Keble will infuse his spirit wherever he is known, and if every one had his spirit what would there be left to desiderate?'[30] Wilberforce added. Froude was firmly in support of Keble. As far as Newman was concerned, Keble would have been the certain choice had they been electing an angel rather than a mere Provost. In any event Hawkins was elected, something Newman lived to regret. His elevation meant that in the following March the University church, St Mary's, was offered to Newman.

In January the Newman family was plunged into grief. Mary, whose health had been delicate for some time, died suddenly. During her short illness she had been consoled by Keble's verses. 'She told us she had been enabled to repeat mentally some she had committed to memory, during hours of acute suffering. No one can fully enter into their meaning but those who have been in deep affliction,'[31] Newman informed their author, who coincidentally had not long before lost his own sister.

Newman had loved Mary with a special affection for she was the youngest of the family, and her loss following so closely on his own illness was a serious blow. For the next few months he grieved deeply, and even to the end of his life he continued to feel his loss. 'I have as vivid feelings of love, tenderness, and sorrow, when I think of dear Mary, as ever I had since her death,'[32] he wrote in 1877. Two months after her death he wrote to Harriett, the sister who, as he put it, alone knew his feelings and responded to them: 'It draws tears to my eyes to think that all at once we can only converse *about* her, as about some inanimate object. But she "shall flourish from her tomb". And in the meantime, it being but a little time, I would try to talk to her in imagination, and in the hope of the future, by setting down all I can think of about her.'[33]

In May, in company with Froude and Wilberforce, Newman rode over to Cuddesden for dinner. 'It is so great a gain to throw off Oxford for a few hours so completely as one does in dining out, that it is almost sure to do me good.'[34] As he rode along through the countryside, the fresh leaves, the scents and the varied landscape reminded him of the 'transitory nature of this world'. He wished 'it were possible for words to put down those indefinite vague and withal subtle feelings which quite pierce the soul and make it sick'.[35] It was not only Mary's sudden death, for his earliest mentor, Walter Mayers, had also died unexpectedly, and Newman, at the widow's request, had travelled to Worton to preach the Funeral Sermon and conduct the burial. But on this May evening 'Dear Mary seemed embodied in every tree and hid behind every hill. What a veil and curtain this world of sense is! beautiful but still a veil.'[36]

> Meanwhile, where last on earth she trod,
>   This grace to faith is given,
> There to discern the house of God,
>   There find the gate of heaven.[37]

3

The Vicar of St Mary's

1828–32

Newman was instituted as Vicar of St Mary's on 14 March 1828 by the Bishop of Oxford, and inducted about a week later by Henry Buckley, a Fellow of Merton College. The excitement of his new appointment brought him a great sense of relief, 'like the feeling of spring weather after winter'.[1] The University church was by no means new to him; he had read the prayers on numerous occasions in Hawkins's absence, and he had preached there. For his health at this time the doctors had ordered him to take as much exercise as possible. Riding was the obvious choice, and from now on the cost of hiring hacks for the purpose was recorded carefully in the list of his expenses. It was not long before he was telling his mother how he had learnt to jump, 'a larking thing for a don',[2] and relating to her the exhilaration he felt at going quickly through the air.

Sunday, 6 April was Easter Day. In the morning Newman assisted the Provost at Holy Communion and preached in the College chapel. In the afternoon the two swopped places, Hawkins assisting Newman and preaching in St Mary's. In the evening the two were joined for dinner by Pusey.

Besides his duties at St Mary's, there were also frequent visits to be made to Littlemore, a small hamlet in the cure of the parish, some three miles outside Oxford on the south-south-east side. There was no church there and on Sundays the parishioners were expected to walk into the city for the service. Soon the new vicar became a familiar sight as he walked or rode out towards the small run-down group of houses he came to love. At a later date he would settle his mother at Littlemore, and spend more and more time there himself. 'My ride of a morning is generally solitary, but I almost prefer to be alone,'[3] he told Harriett.

As he had done at St Clement's he visited every family in the vicinity and brought what comfort he could to the sick and dying. Such parish duties were a release from the rigours of academic work, and he admitted to nursing a secret wish for 'a small cure of a few hundreds a year and no preferment as this world calls it'. Yet he knew such a wish was a desire for idleness. 'I do not think that I shall have this obscurity because I wish for it.'[4]

An undergraduate seeing Newman at about this time described him striding along the Oxford road, 'with large head, prominent nose, tortoiseshell spectacles, emaciated but ruddy face, spare figure, whose leanness was exaggerated by the close-fitting tail-coat then worn'.[5]

Early in May a letter came from Bowden announcing his forthcoming marriage to Elizabeth, the musical daughter of his next door neighbour, Sir John Swinburne. 'She is particularly fond of Beethoven,' he wrote. 'In point of family, connections, fortune, the match is every thing that the world calls desirable.'[6] Recording the receipt of the letter in his diary Newman added an exclamation mark. One thing was fast becoming clear to him: he would not find *himself* in a similar situation, Beethoven or no. Although at that time he had made no binding resolution, he felt strongly he had been called to remain celibate. He would hear from Froude of the 'high severe idea of the intrinsic excellence of Virginity', but it was not until 1829 that he made up his mind finally upon the matter.

It was during the summer of 1828 that he began to read the early Fathers of the Church chronologically, starting with St Ignatius of Antioch, the bishop martyr who had died mauled by lions in the arena at Rome in AD 107. In three days at the beginning of July, Newman read all Ignatius's epistles and began to make notes. He intended to stay in Oxford for much of the vacation; he could spend more time at Littlemore, and St Mary's would be at its fullest with visitors; besides he had to prepare the children for Confirmation. Nevertheless, he was able to visit Brighton later in the month, where he bathed in the sea on most days or walked on the Downs; friends were entertained to tea or dinner. By August he had returned to Oxford. The plan was that at the end of the month his mother and sisters would stay at Joseph Dornford's cottage, at Nuneham, while Dornford, another Oriel Fellow, was away. Newman was now reading Justin's *Apologia*. He intended to spend much time at Nuneham himself and had hired a special horse for a month. Soon Henry Wilberforce had come to stay, and the two would ride into Oxford on most days, taking interesting scenic routes through the country. During that time Newman developed acute toothache and had to take medicine. Besides making notes on Justin, he read aloud to his pupil the latest book: *Death-Bed Scenes, and Pastoral Conversations* by John Warton DD, in four volumes.

Great pains were taken over his instructing of Wilberforce, who read diligently but for not so many hours as his tutor would have liked. It was doubtful whether the young man would 'master a first class list in time'. However,

Newman himself confessed to being a slow reader and was sympathetic on that account. He need not have worried, for there was time enough, and when Henry came to be examined two years later he gained his First in Classics. It must be said that Newman tended to keep his pupils to himself, something which, to Hawkins's way of thinking, was nothing less than favouritism, and did the College no good.

Towards the end of September Newman was speaking of himself as an indefatigable equestrian, but his reading of the early Fathers was not going as smoothly as he had hoped. He would have to shut himself up for a month or so, when his health allowed. In fact, the task occupied his thoughts for the next two years; in one letter he talks of 'hungering' for Irenaeus and Cyprian.

When his work on the history of the early Church became known it was suggested that he might put together a popular ecclesiastical history, but Newman was not interested. 'I never would undertake to write lightly on any subject which admits to being treated thoroughly. I think it is the fault of the day,'[7] he wrote to Dr Jenkyns, the Oriel Fellow who had suggested it. 'Now this probably will be a great objection to my engaging in a professedly popular work. Not that it is necessary to compose a long treatise; but more time, I feel, ought to be given to the subject than is consistent with the despatch of booksellers, who must sacrifice everything to regularity of publication and trimness of appearance. An Ecclesiastical History, for example, whether long or short, ought to be derived from the original sources, and not to be compiled from the standard authorities.'[8]

Writing of a different kind was to occupy much of his time. In September his friend and fellow music enthusiast, Blanco White, had been appointed editor of the *London Review*. 'My friends must stand by me, especially my Oriel friends,'[9] he wrote. He implored Newman to sharpen his pen and give him an article on any subject he liked excepting Divinity, for he was expecting a flood of that. Newman set to work on an article entitled 'Poetry with reference to Aristotle's Poetics', which so pleased White that he implored its author to write for him constantly. 'You want an outlet for your mind and heart, which is running over where there is no call for their riches. Tell the world what you feel and think. Talk with the people of England through my journal, and let me have the benefit of their delight.' The letter ended with an 'Adieu, my Oxford Plato.'[10]

Such a letter was encouragement, although Newman did not hold out much success for the magazine, and he was not surprised when the venture folded after the second issue. For all his enthusiasm White was not a wise editor and lacked the good health and enterprising mind necessary to the task. In Newman's opinion he had an insufficient knowledge of the English public and, with such bookish and academical contributors, on which its fate depended, the review was dull.

In the second week of April 1829, the House of Lords carried a bill for the Emancipation of the Roman Catholics from their Civil Disabilities, and on 16 April, 'hating the bill and sobbing as his gouty hand signed', King George IV returned it. Two months earlier at Oxford, Convocation had voted 3 to 1 in favour of petitioning against the Catholic claims and much opprobrium was directed towards Peel, who had changed his mind about emancipation and had been one of the chief supporters of the measure, though he had resigned his seat for Oxford. Newman was indifferent to the bill: as far as he was concerned the clamours of the Catholics were but the accidental development of the jealousy Ireland must feel towards a country which had stolen her parliament and independence. He did not see it as a religious question and he did not think the Church, by which he meant the Church of England, would be injured in any way, but, as he told Rickards, emancipation was the symptom of a systematic hatred of our Church borne by Romanists, Sectarians, Liberals and Infidels. He voted against the petition, but was concerned that Peel should not be re-elected 'for want of a better man', since he did not wish for a rat as a member.[11] When he wrote to Jemima on 8 February he revealed more of his attitude to the Catholic Question.

I began my Littlemore evening catechetical lecture last Sunday. I am now about an hour from it, and I am not fatigued ... I was much struck with this evening's 1st lesson – it seemed to apply to the Church. You know I have no opinion about the Catholic Question; and now that it is settled, I shall never perhaps have one – But still its passing is one of the signs of the Times, of the incroachments of philosophism and indifferentism on the Church. Is not the age evil? the chapter applies – and those words 'our holy and beautiful house' seemed to mean York Minster, the conflagration of which at this moment was a sort of ominous emblem of what was to come.[12]

During the next few weeks Newman's letters kept his family and friends informed of the latest developments. It was the first public event he had been concerned with, and he thanked God from his heart both for his cause and its success when Peel, persuaded to stand again for the University by 'meddling individuals', failed to win his seat. For Newman this proved the independence of both the Church and Oxford; 'Oxford has never turned with the turn of fortune,' he wrote. But he was angry that the Provost, without consulting the Oriel Fellows, had gone up to London and 'engaged himself (and the College) to the Government party'.[13] It was the beginning of an ever-widening gap that would develop between Hawkins and the senior members of the College.

Without realising it Newman had also upset Whately, another staunch Peelite, who considered Newman's part in the election a sign of his withdrawing from the intellectual aristocracy of Oxford which was for the most part firmly on the side of Liberalism. He invited Newman to dinner and placed him in the midst of the least intellectual men he could muster, Tory-minded, heavy port drinkers, the 'two bottle orthodox' as they were suitably called. Whately had revealed his vengeful intentions by warning Newman beforehand and placed him 'between Provost this and Principal that',[14] and then asked him if he were proud of his friends. Newman realised that Whately thought he had abandoned his circle of influence because of a desire to head a party himself. Although this was not strictly true, it could certainly be seen that Newman attracted people to him, and Whately could not have failed to notice the devotion shown by younger probationer Fellows like Robert Wilberforce and Hurrell Froude. Later Newman admitted that Whately had been right in discerning around him the signs of an incipient party, but that he had not been conscious of it himself. Nevertheless, these were the first signs of 'that movement afterwards called Tractarian'.[15]

When Newman spoke of the Church at this time it was only the Church of England he had in mind: he was anti-Catholic. Like all members of the Established Church, he thought Rome was wrong and had veered off into extravagant error far removed from the divinely revealed truths confirmed by the early Fathers and defined by the first five General Councils. The more he studied the history and doctrine of the early Church the more he became convinced that, although Rome may have erred, so had the Church of England, whose clergy were predominantly Low Churchmen unlikely to withstand the spirit of the age, a spirit of 'latitudinarianism, indifferentism, republicanism, and schism, a spirit which tends to overthrow doctrine'.[16] As Newman expressed it, the talent of the day was against the Church. However, he believed there was a promise of permanence in the Church, and in its Sacraments there were such means of heavenly grace that he did not doubt that the Church would live on even in the most irreligious and sceptical times.

Much of Newman's time was taken up by College duties; he was still the Treasurer. Froude had been appointed his Junior, which brought the two closer together. Evidently Froude caused Newman some irritation when a book went missing. 'The fact is that I have not been in the habit of locking up your book,' Froude wrote, addressing his letter to *Suavissime N*, 'and I believe you will find it in the place under the largest of my book cases.'[17] If it could not be found there, Froude suggested, it might be in the right hand drawer of his side sofa, and he gave Newman permission to open the drawer 'by any means which most readily present themselves – a poker or any thing else'.[18] In April two new Fellows were elected, both Oriel men, John Christie and Thomas Mozley, whom Newman described as a singularly able man in a letter to Harriett. Perhaps those simple words took root, for Harriett would later accept Mozley's proposal of marriage.

The diary entries at this time reveal Newman's strenuous effort to keep all aspects of his life active: his relationship with the College and the parish, his pupils, and his large circle of friends and acquaintances. Underlying every week was the sermon he would preach on the following Sunday. Often he would begin work on it as early as Tuesday, but frequently did not complete the task until an hour or two before the service. No doubt there was nothing unusual in this, although it does show how seriously he prepared himself for the important task. He was already gaining a reputation as a preacher. What distinguished him from other preachers was not only his clarity of thought and his remarkable command of the English language, but the way he set out to instruct his congregation, guiding it carefully through every possible difficulty or perplexity. He explained, exhorted, and to those who heard his quiet, rather high-pitched voice, he spoke with authority.

On 24 May 1829, for instance, he explained to the congregation in St Mary's that religious faith was rational and not the extravagant fiction that some were beginning to claim it to be.

> There are serious men who are in the habit of describing Christian Faith
> as a feeling or principle such as ordinary persons cannot enter into; a
> something strange and peculiar in its very nature, different in kind from every
> thing that affects and influences us in matters of this world, and not admitting
> any illustration from our conduct in them. They consider that because it is
> a spiritual gift, and heavenly in its origin, it is therefore altogether superhuman;
> and that to compare it with any of our natural principles or feelings, is to
> think unworthily of it.[19]

Newman went on to argue that many who wished to excuse their own irreligious lives spoke of the Christian Faith as extravagant and irrational, as if it were a mere fancy or feeling which some persons had and others had not, and which, accordingly, could only, and would necessarily, be felt by those who were disposed that certain way. It was true, he said, that the object on which Faith fixes our thoughts, the doctrines of Scripture, were most marvellous and exceeding in glory, unheard and unthought of elsewhere, and that it was also true that no mind of man will form itself to the habit of Faith without the preventing and assisting influences of Divine Grace. Yet it was not at all true that Faith itself, that is, Trust, was a strange principle of action. To say Faith was irrational was even an absurdity.

He continued by pointing out how people thought it perfectly rational to trust memory or to rely on the words of others. In fact, trust played an essential part in all human endeavour; the world could not go on without trust.

> Consider how men in the business of life, nay, all of us, confide, are obliged

to confide, in persons we never saw, or know but slightly; nay, in their hand-
writings, which, for what we know, may be forged, if we are to speculate
and fancy what may be. We act upon our trust in them implicitly, because
common sense tells us, that with proper caution and discretion, faith in others
is perfectly safe and rational. Scripture, then, only bids us act in respect to
a future life, as we are every day acting at present.

Sometimes he uses a humorous image. 'There is a chance (it cannot be
denied),' he said, 'that our food today may be poisonous, – we cannot be
quite certain, – but it looks the same and tastes the same, and we have
good friends around us; so we do not abstain from it, for all this chance,
though it is real.'[20]
Then Newman came to the main point of his argument, which was that
if men trusted their senses and their reason, why did they not trust their
consciences? 'Is not conscience their own? Their conscience is as much part
of themselves as their reason is; and it is placed within them by Almighty
God in order to balance the influence of sight and reason.' Men did not
obey their consciences because they loved sin and wished to be their own
masters, 'therefore they will not attend to that secret whisper of their hearts,
which tells them they are not their own masters, and that sin is hateful and
ruinous'.
The sermon ended, as one would expect, on an encouraging note.

For ourselves, let us obey God's voice in our hearts, and I will venture to
say we will have no doubts practically formidable about the truth of Scripture.
Find out the man who strictly obeys the law within him, and yet is an
unbeliever as regards the Bible, and then it will be time enough to consider
all that variety of proof by which the truth of the Bible is confirmed to us.
This is no practical inquiry for us. Our doubts, if we have any, will be found
to arise after disobedience; it is bad company or corrupt books which lead
to unbelief. It is sin which quenches the Holy Spirit.
    And if we but obey God strictly, in time (through His blessing) faith will
become like sight; we shall have no more difficulty in finding what will please
God than in moving our limbs, or in understanding the conversation of our
familiar friends. This is the blessedness of confirmed obedience. Let us aim
at attaining it; and in whatever proportion we now enjoy it, praise and bless
God for His unspeakable gift.[21]

Newman had been speaking for about fifteen minutes. It was the one
hundred and ninety-sixth sermon he had preached.

At the beginning of the Lent Term, Newman's new plan for conducting
tutorials and preparing undergraduates for their Finals was put into operation.

As Senior Tutor he knew he could assess the plan's success and make necessary alterations as the scheme proceeded. However, he was soon to discover he had made one vital error of judgment in not informing the Provost of the precise nature of his revisions. Certainly this was because he knew Hawkins would find his plan too radical, but there might have been a greater chance of gaining his agreement had Hawkins been involved from the start.

Newman's scheme was, in fact, the one still used today when each tutor has a number of pupils for whom he is responsible. But the system that had for so long prevailed at Oriel was almost the opposite: the tutors were little more than lecturers and hardly knew the young men personally. Obviously Newman was right, but he was not prepared for such drastic action from the Provost. Not that Hawkins acted in any hurry: at the start of the next term when the tutors informed him how the new system was working, they were 'much surprised and disconcerted at the rude way in which he received the intelligence'.[22] It seemed that Hawkins did not even wish to discuss the matter. It was the beginning of what Newman described as the gradual mode of removing him from his post as Senior Tutor, and many months later Hawkins crushed the scheme altogether by refusing to let the 'rebel' tutors have any fresh pupils to teach. Newman's conscience was quite clear on the matter; as far as he was concerned, preparing candidates for the Schools was a University and not a College responsibility, so that he felt justified in his defiance, though it lost him the work he treasured most, the careful and affectionate fostering of young men's minds.

There was a certain vindictiveness in Hawkins's action, for he knew that, besides loving the work, Newman really did need the tutor's salary, unlike Froude who had private means. Also Hawkins had it in mind, if possible, to drive some sort of a wedge between Newman and Froude, thinking the younger man's influence dangerous. In this he failed, for as a result of the tension the two men became more and more closely associated.

On 11 September 1829 Newman had written to Froude outlining his hope for the parish.

> I mean ultimately to divide the duty of St Mary's from Littlemore, and wish the person I gain to take Littlemore at once, having nothing to do with St Mary's . . . I shall begin my stir about a chapel, which, when (if) built will be his. Till then I fear I must confess he will be without public duty. As to vacations, I do not suppose there will be much difficulty in arranging them. I would divide the residence with him. At least you can give your counsel.

Newman's hope was that Froude might agree to become his assistant, but when he eventually answered Newman's letter from Keswick he was doubtful if he were the right choice. He did not think he could devote enough time to Littlemore during the term-time and he preferred to be at home during the vacation. 'You see I am a double minded man unstable in all my ways – so I advise you not to count on me but to look about for some surer person.'[23] He went on to suggest two possible names, Grenfell and Isaac Williams, who did later take the post. However, Froude suggested that Keble should be consulted. If Keble advised him to accept Newman's offer he could answer for him 'without further communication'.[24]

Newman's 'stir about a chapel' was to have no immediate result, again owing to Hawkins's opposition. Littlemore remained without a chapel until 1835. 'I think I am right in saying,' Newman recalled, 'that the Provost always steadily threw cold water on the building'.[25]

Adding to his burden of responsibilities was the post Newman had accepted as joint secretary to the Oxford branch of the Church Missionary Society, a position to which he had been elected in March 1829. It was not long before the new secretary realised he needed to be vigilant: preachers were delivering sermons on the Society's behalf whose doctrine differed from that professed by the Society. In February 1830 he produced a privately printed letter, which bore the lengthy title, 'Suggestions respectfully offered to Individual Resident Clergymen of the University on behalf of the Church Missionary Society', in which he argued that the Society should be brought under the influence of the Bishops.

Newman circulated the letter himself, but it caused great offence. The result was that the Oxford members were anxious to get rid of him, and a month later at the next annual meeting they succeeded, though he remained an ordinary member for a further four years, and at one time thought of becoming one of its missionaries. He was still, as he later recalled, on the whole Protestant in doctrine, 'with a growing disposition towards what is called High Church'.[26] In his letter he had listed the 'evils existing in the proceedings of the Society', the last of which gives an indication of how far the author's sympathies had moved away from Calvinism. 'The doctrine held by some of its active directors, though not acknowledged perhaps by the individuals themselves to be Calvinistic, still are more or less such practically, whatever dispute may be raised about the exact meaning of words and phrases.'[27] It was essential, Newman argued, that the Society should become closer to the Church and not be a rival to it, thus it was essential that the clergy, and in particular the senior clergy, should become more active lest,

> If with an unwise timidity we let things take their course, it will insensibly
> be familiarised to the principles and practices of schism, and be lost to us
> with its resources, actual success, prospects for the future, its piety and activity;

in the process of its separation, perplexing and enfeebling the Church, which has already enemies enough without our providing others for her.[28]

Newman made no comment on something which later would have disturbed him, the fact that in its missions abroad the Society, part of the Established Church, employed seventeen Lutherans. These were early days.

The letter was of little significance compared with the work Newman commenced at about this time, his first important writing, which was eventually given to the public as *The Arians of the Fourth Century*.

Newman's involvement with the theological wrangles of the early Church may be seen as the natural development of his chronological reading of the Fathers, but he had begun to write this particular book in answer to an invitation by Messrs Rivington who wanted a study of the Council of Nicea for their Theological Library. It soon became obvious to Newman that what he had produced was, as he put it, 'little fitted for the objects with which that publication had been undertaken'.[29] In his desire to explain the origins of the Arian business as fully as possible he had gone too deeply into his subject, and some of his opinions, though now accepted as correct, seemed paradoxical at the time. When the book came out independent of the series in the autumn of 1833, Dr Burton, the Divinity Professor at Oxford, told the author disparagingly: 'Of course you have a right to your opinion.'[30]

The Arian Heresy takes its name from Arius, the priest of the Catholic church of Bucalis, a suburb of Alexandria. By repute Arius was a persuasive preacher, which no doubt accounted for his popularity, but his unorthodox doctrine of the Trinity presented the Church with its first great doctrinal crisis. Although there had been instances of false teaching almost from the start, as may be seen from St Paul's many warnings, Arius's doctrine, an attempt to rationalise a mystery, threatened the Church at the very heart – its belief in the mystery of the Incarnation, that God had become Man. To put it as simply as possible for beginners, Arius taught that Jesus, the Second Person of the Trinity, had been created by the Father and therefore, although endowed with divine power, was not God coequally and coeternally. To use Arius's famous phrase, 'There was a time when the Son was not.' Newman expressed the fundamental error of Arianism for the more adventurous like this:

> The Son of God was a creature, not born of the Father, but, in the scientific language of the times, made 'out of nothing.' It followed that He only possessed a super-angelic nature, being made of God's good pleasure before the worlds, before time, after the pattern of the attribute Logos or Wisdom, as existing in the Divine Mind, gifted with the illumination of it, and in consequence called after it the Word and the Wisdom, nay inheriting the title itself of God;

36

and at length united to a human body, in the place of its soul, in the person of Jesus Christ.[31]

A sceptic might well wonder what all the fuss was about. Certainly when Gibbon came to write of it, his irony was as pointed as ever; but even Carlyle, who had little time for orthodoxy, admitted that, had Arianism won, Christianity 'would have dwindled away into a legend'. It is important therefore to realise that had Arianism prevailed the civilisation which the Catholic Church was to build up would never have developed; all would have been fundamentally different, for an Arian world would have been more like a Muslim world or, as Hilaire Belloc suggested, seeing the nature of Greek and Roman society, an Arian world might well have nurtured something like an Oriental Calvinism.

An intricate subject at the best of times, but while in many passages it makes for heavy, not to say dull, reading, Newman's *Arians of the Fourth Century* succeeds not only because it set out the matter succinctly and clearly for his contemporaries, but also because it reveals to those readers interested in the growth of his mind his understanding of the necessity of creeds and the Church's need to develop doctrine. While he knew that the early Church, before the dogmatic definitions, might have been the ideal state of things, he accepted that as much as we may wish it, we cannot restrain the rovings of the intellect. It had been vital at that time for the Church to speak out, in order to exclude error. How many people who say the Nicene Creed realise why those strange words are included, 'God from God, Light from Light, True God from True God, begotten not made, of one substance with the Father'? They were put there to knock Arianism on the head.

However, Newman upset some people at Oxford because he broke with accepted opinion in that he traced the origin of the heresy to the school of Antioch rather than Alexandria. Although Arius was its chief exponent, the error, Newman argued, had existed in various forms for many years and Arius had been trained at Antioch; only on his arrival in Alexandria had he made the idea popular.

Newman writes with greatest assurance once his hero Athanasius enters the stage, for Athanasius was to fight Arianism to the bitter end. As a young deacon he accompanied his bishop to the Council of Nicea in the year 325, only to see the error become more popular after it was condemned. Then as Bishop of Alexandria he endured misunderstanding, exile and imprisonment, but triumphed at the last, though he died before Arianism was finally and irrevocably condemned at the Council of Constantinople in 381. 'After a life of contest, prolonged, in spite of the hardships he encountered, beyond the age of seventy years, he fell asleep in peaceable possession of the Churches for which he had suffered.'[32] Thus Newman describes the death of Athanasius, but it is perhaps not strange that one of the best passages in the book relates the stunning end of Arius himself at his moment of glory as he prepared, at the Emperor's insistence and after a dubious recantation, to be received back into the Church.

> For seven days previous to that appointed for his re-admission, the Church
> of Constantinople, Bishop and people, were given up to fasting and prayer.
> Alexander, after a vain endeavour to move the Emperor, had recourse to
> the most solemn and extraordinary form of anathema allowed in the Church;
> and with tears besought its Divine Guardian, either to take himself out of
> the world, or to remove thence the instrument of those extended and
> increasing spiritual evils, with which Christendom was darkening. On the
> evening before the day of his proposed triumph, Arius passed through the
> streets of the city with his party, in an ostentatious manner; when the stroke
> of death suddenly overtook him, and he expired before his danger was
> discovered.[33]

With Athanasius to thank for the information, how Newman must have enjoyed writing that. 'Under the circumstances,' he continued, 'a thoughtful mind cannot but account this as one of those remarkable interpositions of power, by which Divine Providence urges on the consciences of men in the natural course of things, what their reason from the first acknowledges, that He is not indifferent to human conduct.'[34]

4

Rome, How Shall I Name Thee?

$$\boxed{1832\text{--}33}$$

It had been obvious since the early months of 1832 that Hurrell Froude's health was failing. 'I am afraid I cannot disguise from myself that within this ten day I have had an attack on my lungs,'[1] he had informed Newman in February, going on to explain that he did not think it very serious. However, his doctor advised caution: the patient might return to Oxford, but he must wear more clothing and renounce wine for ever. 'The prohibition extends to beer – quo confugiam,'[2] Froude wrote from Dartington. The doctor had perhaps recognised the first symptoms of the consumption that would sap the young man's energy over the next few years, so that he would be forced to spend much time in a warmer climate. It was this necessity that took him, and Newman also, to Italy during the next winter.

The idea of the journey had been Archdeacon Froude's. Although he intended to accompany his son, it would be better if he had another, younger companion. Newman hesitated when he was invited. 'It quite unsettled me and I have had a disturbed night with the thought of it,'[3] he told Froude. Yet the advantages of accepting were obvious. It would, as Froude had said, 'set him up'. He needed a rest, certainly; the writing of his Arian book had worn him out, but it might be difficult to leave his parish for such a long time. There had been a cholera epidemic, though mercifully his people had been spared, and he felt he could not be away for Easter; then there were his mother and sisters to be considered. He was no longer employed as a tutor at Oriel, but he was expected to become Dean in the next academic year. Ideally he would like to postpone the journey, rather than decline the invitation altogether. In the end all his 'many hindrances' seemed less important than being in Falmouth ready to embark by the end of the first week in December.

The coach journey from Exeter struck him by its mysteriousness. It was a beautiful night, clear, frosty, and bright with the full moon, a sight too beautiful to be over-vexed that the buckle of his new carpet bag had broken, his portmanteau had been cut, and the purse Harriett had lent him had torn, and his fellow-travellers were mostly irksome. Newman had upbraided 'an unpleasant kind of man' who was talking great nonsense 'with improprieties in his speech' to 'a silly goose of a maidservant stuck at the top of the coach.'[4] Yet, it seems that the fellow had shown reverence for the cloth, saying that he had several relations himself who were clergymen.

On his arrival at the port Newman sat down and described the episode in a letter to his mother. 'It is so odd, but for the greater part of the time the man thought I had attacked him under personal feeling – so much has the idea even, the vision, faded away from men's minds of the fact of persons censuring others (whether rightly or wrongly yet) because they think they ought to.'[5]

The packet boat *Hermes* sailed out of Falmouth with the three clergymen aboard a little after midday on 8 December. By evening they had lost sight of the Lizard and as he was going down to dinner Newman felt 'seasickish', a condition that was to continue until the Monday morning. 'Never certainly had I ailment more easy to be borne,'[6] he informed Harriett, but he went on to describe the feeling in some detail. All three had had difficulty in reading the Service on the Sunday morning, the Archdeacon being the most affected. Luckily the Bay of Biscay was very calm. Some forty miles from land they saw a shark eating a dead horse. During the next few weeks they rested, read and talked. Froude read prayers aloud and Newman composed verse and wrote many letters. It was decided to remain with the ship until it reached Corfu. Brief stops were made at Cadiz, Gibraltar and Algiers and Christmas Day was spent in the harbour at Malta in quarantine.

In spite of the obvious excitement of seeing new places, Newman's thoughts had been concentrating on England. He had ample time to ponder over his recent problems. The dispute with Hawkins had been a great trial; yet, had he still the responsibility of teaching, he would never have been able to leave Oriel. At least he had the satisfaction of knowing his system had worked; the undergraduates had been more successful in the Schools. He wondered how his friends were. There had been talk at one time of George Ryder, one of Froude's pupils, joining them on the journey. How was his own Henry Wilberforce, who instead of returning to Oxford after gaining his First, as Newman had hoped, had retired to Yorkshire consumed with passion for one or two of the young ladies he had met. The young man needed occupation, and a good deal of bodily exercise. Newman had offered advice. 'It is dangerous to experimentalize, but I confess it seems a sensible thing for a conscience-stricken sinner to inflict some penance on himself as a continual humiliation – abstinence from some pleasure or convenience, which it is in the power to enforce – or other privation, which may keep his sin in remembrance and withdraw him from temptation.'[7] The important thing was to have the vigilance to stop the evil in the beginning, for, 'when once it outruns its first moments, it is incurable, like the dreadful plague which has visited us'.[8] Such a problem in his young friend's life made Newman yet more certain that celibacy, although a high state of life to which the multitude of men cannot aspire, and one that did not make a man any better than anyone else, was nevertheless the noblest of states.

Another young man he would have recalled was Henry Manning, of Merton College, some seven years his junior. Newman had invited him to dine in Hall, and the two had taken to walking together. Then Manning had made an excuse to call off an invitation he had previously accepted. Perhaps the two were not destined to be very close friends.

On Sunday, 30 December the *Hermes* sailed past Ithaca, arriving at Corfu on the same evening. The passengers stayed there for a week, exploring the island by day, but returning on board at night. To begin with the weather had been appalling, 'incessant violent rain'. 'To fancy Homer and Thucydides here,'[9] Newman wrote to Harriett. It was extraordinary to reflect that the place looked precisely the same in their times.

On several evenings the three clergymen had been entertained to dinner on the island by members of the garrison. At the Artillery mess 'the officers were the same gentlemanly persons as at Gibraltar',[10] in contrast with the Commander of Forces, General Sir Alexander Woodford and his wife, neither of whom Newman liked very much, though the General had a fine pepper tree in his garden and his geraniums were superb. He had produced a ring belonging to his family which the Earl of Derby on the scaffold had given to his chaplain, and a gold coin from Agincourt. The only person who stood out from the 'number of dandy officers, aides-de-camps etc, brimfull of the indifference, which is now the characteristic of high society,'[11] was one who seemed to Newman to have good in him, a German scholar who passionately loved Weber's music and offered to transcribe some Greek airs. He was a man superior to and feeling his superiority to the generality of soldiers, yet Newman could not help thinking that this officer was substituting refinement and elegance for genuine religious feeling.

How different from what he was used to was the formidable round table with neither top nor bottom, with a Greek to wait, service of plate, dishes all handed round and no conversation. The olive trees on the island had reminded him of the willows in Christ Church walk.

The town they found picturesque in the Venetian style. They visited the church of St Spiridion, the patron saint of the island, and one of the Nicene Fathers. The saint's body was in its reliquary, though Newman was cynical of its authenticity; 'doubtless it is not his body',[12] he wrote to his sister. There was so much superstition. But this was the Greek Church; Newman had yet to see Rome.

The three travellers left Corfu on the *Hermes* and sailed to Malta where they spent the best part of a month, much of the time in quarantine. Newman had not anticipated the strange feeling that overcame him as he watched the ship set off back to England. 'It was a kind of home, as having conveyed me from England – it was going back thither – and as it went off, I seemed more cast upon the world than ever I had been – and to be alone.'[13] He had been closely confined with the Froudes now for five weeks. While the father and son sketched or painted he wrote poetry or tried to learn Italian. He had managed to hire a violin, which, bad though it was, sounded grand in the spacious halls of the Lazaretto, the large building put up by the Knights of Malta as a place of quarantine for the Turks. 'Many a savage and dirty fellow has been here, I dare say, but they can leave no trace behind them,'[14] he told Jemima. The system of quarantine was, in his view, the most absurd of all conceivable humbugs, but the British were obliged by other powers to keep it up. 'Nobody touches nobody – yet it would not I suppose do us much harm if we did.'[15]

The window of Newman's room in the Lazaretto looked out over the room used for fumigating letters. It was like being in prison; he was locked in his room at night, though he was allowed, if he wished, to go about the harbours in a small boat during the day.

On 23 January 1833 the required seventeen days' quarantine officially ended, but Newman had such a bad cough he did not feel well enough to accompany the Froudes to the palace for dinner. Instead, he dined alone comfortably in the rooms they had taken in Valetta. His 'ailment of the chest' was to continue to be a problem, while Froude's health seemed to be improving. Luckily, a doctor on the island was able to recommend a simple remedy: 'fifty drops of antimonial wine three times a day', Newman informed his mother. 'My morning's dose has made me feel (not qualmish but) languid till breakfast time – but otherwise I have had no inconvenience from the medicine at all – and it is wonderfully efficacious.'[16] As a result of his sickness the only places in Malta he was able to visit were those easily accessible in the town, the only exception being St Paul's Bay which he went to by water.

How he wished they had gone straight across to Ancona from Corfu and quarantined there: they could have been in Rome before the winter was out, but it would have been a tedious journey. There were no steam packets in the Adriatic at that time of year and a sailing vessel would almost certainly have taken too much time. Nevertheless, had they adopted that course, as they had been strongly tempted to do, they could always have spent time in Sicily after Rome. In the event, when they left Malta for Naples the steamer only stopped briefly at Messina and Palermo, though at the latter they were able to spend the best part of two days ashore. After passing an uncomfortable night plagued by mosquitoes at Calatafimi they visited Egesta on muleback, the mules' bells singing and clinking in the dark. There Newman was shocked to find children sleeping in holes dug into the walls, which 'smelt not like dog kennels but a wild beast's cage, almost overpowering us in our rooms upstairs'.[17] He had never known what human suffering was like until he came to Sicily, but the weather during all this time was magnificent and the experience of the landscape pierced his heart 'with a strange painful pleasure'. He paid a brief visit to the remains of a small Greek town, with its single temple on a circular hill, simple and unadorned. It fixed its faith as a solitary witness on the heights where it could not be hid. 'Such was the genius of early Greek worship, grand in the midst of error.'[18]

Lent began on 20 February. At Naples, 'a place singularly enjoyable as regards animal pleasure',[19] it rained. Visits were arranged to Herculaneum, Pompeii and Cumae. On the following Sunday Newman preached at the Ambassador's Chapel and administered Holy Communion. Exactly a week later he received the Sacrament in the English Chapel in Rome and on the same day stood gazing up into the dome of St Peter's.

> Far sadder musing on the traveller falls
> At sight of thee, O Rome,
> Than when he views the rough sea-beaten walls
> Of Greece, thought's early home.[20]

At Rome, 'the most wonderful place in the world',[21] Newman found he was close to people he knew. A few doors away from his apartments (six rooms, kitchen, servants' rooms, and walk on the housetop), members of the Wilberforce family were lodging. During their time in the city the Archdeacon and his party were entertained and guided round the sites. They were able to catch up with news from home as it was possible now to obtain English newspapers. However intoxicating the eternal city seemed to be aesthetically, Newman was intent on keeping matters in proportion: Rome must be viewed as a place of religion. He was not as enamoured of the Roman Church as Hurrell Froude, although even he was soon to become less enchanted. It was true that this was the city to which England owed the blessing of the Gospel. But there was so much wrong: superstition; the obvious wealth of the churches, many built from the sale of indulgences, so that Newman could not help but think of it as a cruel place. But there was more to be seen and thought of daily. 'It is a mine of all sorts of excellences, but the very highest.'[22] Expressing his thoughts in verse he wrote,

> O that thy creed were sound!
>   For thou dost soothe the heart, thou Church of Rome,
> By thy unwearied watch and varied round
>   Of service, in thy Saviour's holy home.[23]

Newman did not explain how an unsound creed could so soothe the heart, but he was quite certain he could not tolerate for an instant 'the wretched perversion of the truth'[24] which Rome sanctioned. 'By no means short of some terrible convulsion and through much suffering can this Roman Church, surely, be reformed ... the blood of the martyrs, which was shed on her soil, rather cries out against her, than hallows her,'[25] he wrote to Pusey. Yet he was equally certain that his own Church was at the mercy of bad men who had not faith. Men such as Arnold were opening the door to alterations of doctrine through his plan for Church reform. 'We have heard of Arnold's pamphlet, the contents of which seem to be so atrocious that I am quite unable to talk calmly about it.'[26]

Of course, Newman knew there were good men to be found in both churches, and in the Greek Church too. The parable uppermost in his mind was the Parable of the Tares: he felt the force of this particularly on the Feast of the Annunciation when, separating himself from the Froudes, he had managed to enter the Church of Sta Maria sopra Minerva where the Pope was presiding at a Mass in honour of the Virgin. Newman was disgusted to see young girls kissing the Pope's foot before receiving a present from him, 'considering how much is said in Scripture about the necessity of him that is greatest being as the least'.[27] Nor could he endure the Pope's being carried in on high. 'And yet as I looked on, and saw all Christian acts performing, the Holy Sacrament offered up, and the blessing given and recollected I was in church, I could only say in very perplexity my own words, "How shall I name thee, Light of the wide west, or heinous error-seat?" and felt the force of the parable of the tares – who can separate the light from the darkness but the Creator Word who prophesied their union? And so I am forced to leave the matter, not at all seeing my way out of it. – How shall I name thee?'[28]

It was during Holy Week that Newman and Froude had their two conversations with Wiseman at the English College. They also attended Vespers on consecutive evenings in the Sistine Chapel, and heard the Miserere. All other services were shunned because, as Newman explained to Henry Jenkyns back at Oriel, they contained so much 'mummery' that it required a stomach to endure them, and they had not dared make the experiment. However, to his mother he wrote on Good Friday that he was more attached to the Catholic system than ever. Was he finding this at Rome? It was only what he thought of as Roman that he detested so much; he understood that the

Italian priesthood was corrupt which caused far-spreading scandals. Yet he had fallen in with a number of interesting Irish and English priests, and quite regretted that his limited stay hindered a more intimate acquaintance. In spite of the abundant 'mummery', he could not help noticing a deep substratum of true Christianity. The one ritual he had risked had affected him, and it seems likely that the experience at Sta Maria sopra Minerva had in some measure prompted the desire to be accepted on any terms to which his conscience might be twisted, when Froude and he called upon Wiseman for the second time. What is certain is that Wiseman's reply, that they should accept the doctrines of the Council of Trent, had shocked them profoundly, and put them off the idea of uniting with Rome completely, so that Newman could write the next day, 'As to Rome, a union with her on our part is impossible and ever will be.'[29]

On Easter Day he assisted in the English Chapel at both the morning and evening services, and dined later in sight of the dome of St Peter's which was illuminated. 'It is a splendid sight, – but so difficult and dangerous in execution that it is surprising they make it so much a matter of course. The men who are employed are let down by ropes outside the dome.'[30]

Newman had decided earlier to part company with the Froudes, who had arranged to leave for Marseilles on 10 April. His plan was to return to Naples and cross over to Sicily, 'a shadow of Eden', spend some time there, then sail directly from Palermo to Marseilles in a trader and return to England, arriving about the third week in May. He would not travel entirely alone, but would take a servant for company. So it was that on the evening after he had bidden the Froudes farewell he was seated happily in the Hotel Crocelle in Naples with a variety of dishes before him after the Italian fashion, delicate mincemeats of giblets and a large dish of green peas.

Now that Hurrell had departed Newman felt a foreboding 'with anticipations for the future too painful to mention'.[31] At Malta there had been a definite improvement in Froude's health, but the careless way which on several occasions he had allowed himself to get soaked through was alarming. Newman had warned him to wear more suitable clothing, advice which Froude had heeded, but more recently it had become impossible not to fear the worst. As a priest visiting the sick, Newman had seen this disease do its worst, and there was only one end. It was only a matter of time.

Time was not now on Newman's side either. He had intended to be back home in May: in fact, he did not return until 8 July. It is important to know why, for when he arrived back in Oxford those who saw him knew he had changed.

5

Lead Kindly Light

$$\boxed{1833\text{--}34}$$

Newman had intended to leave Naples on 16 April but he found the steamer was so crowded that there was not even standing room on deck. Besides the sirocco was blowing ceaselessly, making the seas very rough. Neither did he relish the prospect of being 'poured upon Sicily with the flood of Steam-passengers':[1] it would be difficult to find lodging and the prices would be bumped up for the crowd. So allowing the packet to leave without him, he managed to book a passage on a sailing ship, an English merchantman, the *Serepta* of Yarmouth, and waited for news of her embarkation.

The unexpected extra days in Naples, though enjoyable, made him apprehensive. Perhaps this next stage of his travels was only an act of wilfulness. The Froudes had attempted to dissuade him. On two nights recently there had been slight earth tremors. Was Vesuvius about to erupt? Newman looked out in expectation, but any moodiness was enveloped in mist. On the morning of Friday 19 news came suddenly that he and his servant were required on board. The choppy sea meant sea-sickness, but the wind dropped during the night, and during Saturday the other three passengers chattered away in French. Newman discovered his French was even worse than his Italian, but he conversed with the captain, a thorough Englishman.

From the sea Stromboli had looked harmless enough. Messina on the Sunday morning presented a problem as Newman tried in vain to find a Church of England service; neither was there a chapel, and passport business could not be sorted out until the next day. However, a satisfactory breakfast and dinner were taken at the Leon d'oro where he stayed the night.

The next day he felt almost ashamed of the figure he was cutting. 'I was chief of a cavalcade consisting of a servant, two mules, and several muleteers.'[2] He wore a straw hat and a flannel jacket and, apart from his black clerical neck-cloth, had succeeded, as he put it, in fully uncassocking himself. However, he had to admit to feeling terribly tired.[3]

Several days were spent sightseeing, though always on the move, journeying about twenty miles or so each day and spending the nights in cheap inns with doubtful linen, bothered by bed-bugs and fleas, 'the most inveterate enemies of slumber'.[4] Gennaro, his Neapolitan servant, sprinkled water under the bed in an attempt to keep the fleas at bay. St Paolo, Taormini, Nicolosi; the chestnuts on the slopes of Etna were not worth the fatiguing journey; then at Catania a visit to Froude's friend, Dr Gemellaro, who advised that the overland route between Catania and Syracuse was hazardous: it would be better to go by sea. Newman acquiesced, but contrary winds meant an uncomfortable night in the boat next to the only vulgar Italian he had met.

Newman already realised his Sicilian adventure was going to be one on which he could look back with pleasure rather than one to be enjoyed at the time, since in retrospect 'all bodily pain vanishes, and mental feelings alone live'.[5] He had seen the fount of Arethusa and rowed up the Anapus to gather the papyrus, and seen the temple of Minerva. Reading Thucydides in the boat, he had felt he knew the layout of the island pretty well, yet all the time he was feeling desperately tired, and had an uneasy feeling that he was sickening for something.

Because of the lack of wind it became impossible to return to Catania by sea, so the boat put back for Syracuse, and Newman landed and slept in a cove. He spent another restless and chilly night, which was to have a disastrous result. Rather than wait for the boat he travelled overland, a tedious trek of thirty-two miles, arriving at Catania very late at night. Mercifully he was able to rest all the next day, though he knew his sickness was getting worse. It was important to disguise his illness as best he could, for if it were noticed he might be denied lodging. Two days later on reaching Leonforte he was so ill he collapsed.

It says much for Newman's fortitude that even now he was determined to continue. For three days he remained at Leonforte, dosing himself with camomile, and spending most of the time in bed, but intermittently dressing and walking out a little way into the street. On Sunday, 5 May he was very weak; nevertheless the following morning he left the town as day was breaking. After seven miles he collapsed again and had to be taken into a wayside hut to rest; in the afternoon he managed to carry on as far as Castro Giovanni, where as soon as a suitable lodging was found he was put to bed and bled.

For eleven days Newman was seriously ill with what was almost certainly scarlet fever; for much of the time he was delirious, but with periods of clarity. Those who attended him thought it unlikely he would recover; the patient, however, felt certain he would: he knew God had work for him to do. In spite of this assurance, he gave Gennaro directions to convey news of his death to England if necessary. Gennaro nursed him like a child; he was, humanly speaking, the preserver of his life. Newman did not think an English servant could have done what he did. There had been a doctor too, with whom he conversed during his calmer moments in Latin: Newman's 'Patior sub subpressione urinae' would be answered with 'Cras dabo te sulphure', and so on.

It was not until 20 May that he was well enough to get up. For several days he remained at Castro Giovanni, taking chicken broth, gradually regaining strength enough for the rest of the journey. During this anxious time he was given to violent fits of weeping; when consoled, all he could say was that he was sure God had work for him to do in England. Not until Saturday, 25 May did he set off for Palermo by carriage, taking six days to get there. On arrival he was still too weak to get out of the carriage unaided and could only speak by drawling.

At Page's Hotel, a comfortable inn run by a motherly English woman married to an Italian, Newman waited for a passage back to England. He waited three weeks for a suitable vessel, writing a poem a day and walking with a stick about the city. He visited the churches; though he attended no services, these visits seemed to calm his impatience. Recalling this in later life he realised he had been in the presence of the Blessed Sacrament but knew nothing of it. For much of the time he sat in the shade on a seat in the public gardens; often the wind when it blew was like a furnace. He knew his friends in England would be worried, but there was no way of contacting them. Eventually, the Sicilian captain of the *Conte Ruggiero*, an orange boat bound for Marseilles, promised to attempt the journey in spite of the expected calms that he warned might draw out the passage from anything between twelve to twenty days, and six days delay was almost inevitable. Newman was fortunate: the boat was only becalmed in the Straits of Bonifacio for a week.

In the stillness of the water the clear sky was reflected by day, the moon and stars teased at night. Newman wrote verse after verse and longed for home; the very thought of it had reduced him to tears for the past two months. God was giving him a severe lesson in patience. There was work to do in England. In that week, without the distraction of land-locked things, he was able to think deeply, with some dread it was true, of the task ahead of him. England seemed spiritually lost. The success of the Liberal cause in France alarmed him; when he saw a French vessel he could not even bring himself to look at the tricolour. Liberalism in all its aspects was poised to destroy his Church. One could never leave her in the hands of men like Thomas Arnold, who wished, if the rumours were true, to 'broaden the base', to unite the Church of England with the Protestant Dissenter sects. Newman knew personally radical clergy who cared little for Christian dogma, who considered the Church to be merely the State in its religious aspect; yet he knew also that deliverance from such abuse was wrought, not by the many but by the few, and not by bodies but by persons. Something had to be done: 'Ye cannot halve the Gospel of God's grace.' He knew his own mission was about to begin.

It was during that week in that still boat that he composed the lines that express better than anything else he wrote his complete acceptance of suffering and his firm trust in Providence. There was work to do in England. He would let his Redeemer guide him from now on.

> Lead kindly light, amid the encircling gloom,
>   Lead Thou me on!
> The night is dark, and I am far from home –
>   Lead Thou me on!
> Keep Thou my feet; I do not ask to see
> The distant scene – one step enough for me.
>
> I was not ever thus, nor prayed that Thou
>   Shouldst lead me on.
> I loved to choose and see my path; but now
>   Lead Thou me on!
> I loved the garish day, and spite of fears,
> Pride ruled my will; remember not past years.
>
> So long Thy power hath blessed me, sure it still
>   Will lead me on,
> O'er moor and fen, o'er crag and torrent, till
>   The night is gone;
> And with the morn those angel faces smile
> Which I have loved long since and lost awhile.[6]

The *Conte Ruggiero* berthed at Marseilles. Newman set off on the two days' journey for Lyons. When he arrived on the evening of 30 June he found his ankles so swollen and inflamed that he could only hobble about. He might be forced to rest for some time. The next day he wrote home to his mother. 'So it is a simple trial of my patience. I am quite desolate. I am tempted to say, "Lord, heal me, for my bones are vexed." But really I am wonderfully calm. Thwarting awaits me at every step.'[7] However, he felt well enough to continue in the morning, and struggled on via Paris and Rouen, unable to sleep at night, till he embarked by steam-vessel from Dieppe at three o'clock in the morning of 8 July for Brighton. Taking the night mail for London, and visiting his bank early on the following day, he caught the coach for Oxford, reaching his mother's house in time for dinner to find his brother Frank had only just arrived home from Persia.

Newman's fears for the state of the Established Church were shared by many of his closest friends: Keble, obviously, and other Oxford men of whom Hurrell Froude and Isaac Williams were chief. But there were others: William Palmer of Worcester College, and some he knew less well like Hugh James Rose, the Rector of Hadleigh in Suffolk, described as a firm but cautious high-churchman, a Cambridge man, an authority on German Protestantism, and editor of the recently founded *British Magazine* to which Newman contributed. Some think Rose was the instigator of what became known as the Oxford Movement, but this was never Newman's view; for Newman the Movement began with the assize sermon preached by Keble in St Mary's on 14 July 1833.

While he was in Rome, Newman had written to Jemima, 'We find Keble is at length roused, and (if once up) he will prove a second Ambrose; and others too are moving.'[8] During his illness in Sicily he had begun to think of all his professed principles and felt they were mere intellectual deductions from one or two admitted truths. 'I compared myself with Keble and felt that I was merely developing his, not my own convictions.'[9]

Certainly Keble had been closer to events in the early months of 1833. What had 'roused' him was the way the newly assembled Reform Parliament had decided to deal with the difficulty of collecting Irish tithes. In fact, there was much sense in its action since, particularly in the south of Ireland, a predominantly Catholic population was having to pay tithes to keep up the almost empty churches of the Church of Ireland. However, it was not that the Government wished to abolish the Church cess (as the tax was called), which obliged the community to maintain the buildings; rather, it was that, in order to compensate for the loss of revenue, the Government had decided to suppress ten Irish bishoprics. The move was hotly opposed by Howley, the Archbishop of Canterbury, and by most on the Bench of Bishops, though Blomfield, the Bishop of London, supported the move. The bishops regarded the proposed bill as an act of spoliation; here was a Government composed of laymen, some of whom were not even believers, others dissenters and heretics, deciding for the Church against the express wish of its bishops. As Keble was to put it in verse, 'The ruffian band, / Come to reform where ne'er they came to pray.'[10]

A sermon preached in the University Church at the opening of the Oxford Assizes, while the Irish bill was still under discussion, was an opportunity not to be missed. Keble took his text from the First Book of Samuel where the people reject God's prophet and demand a king, and made a comparison with the present situation. Englishmen, Keble argued, had taken it for granted that the nation was part of Christ's Church, and bound, in all her legislation and policy, by the fundamental laws of that Church. But when a government and people so constituted 'throw off the restraints which in many respects such a principle would impose upon them, nay, disavow the principle itself, this was nothing less than direct disavowal of the sovereignty of God. If it be true anywhere that such enactments are forced on the legislature by public opinion, is apostasy too hard a word to describe the temper of such a nation?'[11]

It was time for action. Keble appealed to his congregation to face up to a dangerous situation. But how were Christians and Churchmen to face it?

Surely it will be no unworthy principle if any man is more circumspect in his behaviour, more watchful and fearful of himself, more earnest in his petitions for spiritual aid, from a dread of disparaging the holy name of the English Church in her hour of peril by his own personal fault and negligence. As to those who, either by station or temper, feel themselves more deeply interested, they cannot be too careful in reminding themselves that one chief danger in times of change and excitement arises from their tendency to engross the whole mind. Public concerns, ecclesiastical or civil, will prove indeed ruinous to those who permit them to occupy all their care and thought, neglecting or undervaluing ordinary duties, more especially those of a devotional kind. These cautions being duly observed, I do not see how any person can devote himself too entirely to the cause of the Apostolic Church in these realms. There may be, as far as he knows, but a very few to sympathise with him. He may have to wait long, and very likely pass out of this world, before he see any abatement of the triumph of disorder and irreligion. But, if he be consistent, he possesses to the utmost the personal consolations of a good Christian; and as a true Churchman, he has the encouragement which no other cause in the world can impart in the same degree: he is calmly, soberly, demonstrably sure, sooner or later, his will be the winning side, and that the victory will be complete, universal, eternal.[12]

The Church Temporalities (Ireland) Bill did not become law until 14 August. It had been stripped of the clause that might have allowed surplus money to provide stipends for Catholic priests. When the House of Commons heard that the clause was to be omitted Daniel O'Connell shouted out, 'I repudiate it on the part of the people of Ireland!'[13] It had been a betrayal: the Whigs had broken faith. 'The pith, substance, the marrow and essence of the bill is plucked out of it, and the husk, the rind, the void and valueless shell, the shrivelled and empty skin, is left behind.'[14]

Nevertheless, to the majority of the Tory bishops who had opposed the bill and to many like-minded clergy, it seemed clear that, if the Government could so tamper with the Church of Ireland, the Church of England would be the next victim. Already dissenters and radical Whigs were calling for disestablishment. Keble had called for action: the result was the Tractarian Movement.

The decision to issue what became known as 'Tracts for the Times' was taken at a small gathering at Rose's Rectory between 25 and 29 July. Neither Keble nor Newman was present, although they were well aware of what was toward and Froude travelled to Suffolk to represent them. There are several differing accounts of what was discussed, and it seems that Rose and Palmer found Froude's wild scheme for getting Parliament to repeal the Act of Praemunire far too radical. They would have benefited greatly from Newman's being there. 'I deeply regret that I could not have the pleasure of seeing you at Hadleigh,'[15] Rose wrote. The poor man was not in very good health and he was uncertain about his own future. One thing all were agreed upon was that it was no use relying on the bishops to start anything. 'If I were a Bishop,' wrote Newman, 'the first thing I would do would be to excommunicate Lord Grey and half a dozen more, whose names it is almost a shame and a pollution for a Christian to mention.'[16] He knew, however, that whatever the state of things it was hardly worse than in Arian times; but then there had been a likelihood of 'true-minded men becoming Bishops, which is now almost out of the question. If we had one Athanasius, or Basil, we could bear with twenty Eusebiuses – though Eusebius was not all the worst of the bad.'[17] He could not help adding that it was a pity Archbishop Howley did not have something of the boldness of the old Catholic prelates. 'No one can doubt he is a man of the highest principle, and would willingly die a Martyr; but, if he had but the little finger of Athanasius, he would do us all the good in the world. Things have come to a pretty pass, when one must not speak as a Christian Minister for fear of pulling down the house over our heads.'[18] Perhaps, if he held high station, Newman admitted, even he might suddenly become very cautious.

It was an urgent matter: the clergy must be roused to maintain the doctrine of the Apostolical Succession and defend the Liturgy from illegal alterations. This was the main purpose of the Tractarian Movement; in letter after letter Newman repeats the call. Soon, largely through Palmer's energy, there were representatives in many counties. By the end of August, Newman was announcing that small societies had been established in Oxfordshire, Devonshire, Gloucestershire, Berkshire, Suffolk and Kent. Rose's *British Magazine* would continue as a mouthpiece but tracts would also be issued. Newman set about writing the first himself; Keble drafted 'Suggestions for an Association of Friends of the Church' and Froude continued to talk of Praemunire.

It was not long before Bowden became enthusiastic as a result of a visit from Newman. 'I do not believe that, at this present time, one tenth of our church congregations know that an apostolical origin is even claimed by the Church,'[19] he wrote.

There was so much to be done.

Froude confessed to liking Rose, a man who had many good notions, but he was not an Apostolical and, as he was deliberating whether or not to accept the Divinity Professorship at Durham, Froude had fears for the future of the *British Magazine*. It would be far better in his view for the Oriel men to start their own. Newman was very much against the idea; it was bound to be a failure. 'We must pull with Rose, and bide our time,'[20] he told Froude. He agreed that Rose was not the best person to lead their group. 'We must use him without making him our head, but a head we must have.'[21] Keble was the obvious choice: 'We must puff Keble as our head.'[22] However, even Newman had had doubts as to whether Keble would 'go lengths' when the time came: 'I have never till the last month or two thought Keble would go lengths; but I now hope he will – I think he is unchained.'[23]

Keble's Assize sermon was published under the title *National Apostasy*, with a preface dated 22 July, calling upon Churchmen 'to consider what was their duty in the face of this usurpation by the State; for if they were to submit to such profane intrusion, they must at least record their full conviction that it was intrusion.'[24] As some measure towards 'puffing' Keble, combined with natural affection, Newman had decided to dedicate his book on the Arians to him; this came out at the beginning of November.

At the same time Newman was becoming increasingly anxious about Froude. It was a pity he would have to leave the country just when they were 'setting to', but it was essential he should be in a better climate during the winter months. In fact, Froude was to spend the best part of a year in Barbados, where he found the bishop's library particularly helpful. During that time he communicated with Newman fairly regularly and in turn received letters and parcels containing articles and pamphlets. Even from such a distance he remained involved.

By the Christmas of 1833, twenty anonymous tracts had been distributed of which a dozen had been written by Newman himself, and the rest by various hands: Keble, Froude, Bowden, and Pusey, but also Harrison of Christ Church, and Menzies of Trinity. Almost from the start Newman ran into trouble; he had hurled himself into the task with such energy that Palmer took alarm. His plan had been to found an Association, which would draw its membership from all like-minded clergy. Newman was certain that the Tracts could only strengthen the Association; he knew they gave offence to some, but they also did good. After all, Oxford was only doing what Rose was doing elsewhere with his magazine. But he had no desire to upset Palmer. Newman wrote to Palmer saying he would join his Association in spite of his dislike of it, but he would not cease to issue his Tracts, and he planned to make a missionary tour to the Midlands.

'Whenever you talk of the Tracts', Newman told Bowden, 'mind and persist they are not connected with the Association, but the production of "Residents of Oxford". I wish them called "the Oxford Tracts", but I cannot myself so-call them for modesty-sake. So I think that I shall soon advertise them as "Tracts for the Times by Residents of Oxford".'[25] It was arranged with Turrill, one of the publishers of the *British Magazine*, to act as agent, though the pamphlets were printed in Oxford by King who had premises in St Clement's.

On 15 December, in a letter to Froude, Newman related how they had been subject to a furious attack in the *Christian Observer*. 'Can we have more favourable signs? Men do not cry out till they are frightened.'[26] Even the British Museum had written asking for a set of Tracts!

Froude had demanded that the Movement should make a 'row in the world'. The tone of Tract Number 1, a four-leaved pamphlet entitled *Thoughts on the Ministerial Commission*, came up to his expectation. Newman wrote to his fellow clergy: 'I am but one of yourselves – a Presbyter; therefore I conceal my name, lest I should take too much on myself by speaking in my own person.'[27] But speak he must, for the times were evil. He exhorted his readers to treat their bishops as Luke and Timothy had treated St Paul; they should welcome, if necessary, the spoiling of their goods and martyrdom, and they should exalt their Holy fathers the bishops, 'as representatives of the Apostles and the Angels of the Churches';[28] and they should magnify their office.

Title followed title, but each tract either reiterated or endorsed the central theme of upholding the Apostolical Succession. Then, towards the end of December 1833, Pusey's first contribution, much longer than the earlier publications, brought a new authority to the cause. *Thoughts on the Benefits of the System of Fasting enjoined by the Church*, signed with the initials E.B.P., showed, as Newman put it, Pusey's disposition to make common cause with the Movement, but he did not openly become associated until 1835.

Of the early tracts, one issued in two parts during the summer of 1834, and written by Newman, seems very important not only to the Movement, but also to Newman's own development. *Via Media*, written in the classical manner, in the form of a dialogue between a clergyman and a layman, asserts that the glory of the Church of England is that it had taken a 'middle road' between the so-called Reformers of the sixteenth century and Romanism. But the antiquity of the Church had been forgotten, Newman argues, and the Articles of Religion could only be considered a rule of faith if the Church had begun at the Reformation. But the Church was Apostolic.

Clericus: I cannot consent, (I am sure the Reformers did not wish me,) to deprive myself of the Church's dowry, the doctrines which the Apostles spoke in Scripture and impressed upon the early Church. I receive the Church as a messenger from Christ, rich in treasures old and new, rich with the accumulated wealth of the ages.

Laicus: Accumulated?

Clericus: As you will yourself allow. Our Articles are one portion of that accumulation. Age after age, fresh battles have been fought with heresy, fresh monuments of truth set up. As I will not consent to be deprived of the records of the Reformation, so neither will I part with those of former times. I look upon our Articles as in one sense an addition to the Creeds; and at the same time the Romanists added their Tridentine articles. Theirs I consider unsound; ours as true.[29]

Laicus had complained that the new system being advocated suggested that the Church had an existence independent of the State; that the State could not interfere with the Church's internal concerns; that no one might engage in ministerial works except such people as are episcopally ordained; that the consecration of the Eucharist was especially entrusted to Bishops and Priests. 'Where do you find these doctrines in the formularies of the Church; that is, so prominently set forth, as to sanction you in urging them at all, or at least so strongly as you are used to urge them?'[30] Clericus replied that he was free to urge them even though they were not mentioned in the Articles.

Our Articles are not a body of divinity, but in great measure only protests against certain errors of a certain period of the Church. Now I will preach the whole counsel of God, whether set down in the Articles or not. I am bound to the Articles by subscription; but I am bound, more solemnly even than by subscription, by my baptism and by my ordination, to believe and maintain the whole Gospel of Christ. The grace given through those seasons comes through the Apostles, not through Luther or Calvin, Bucer or Cartwright.[31]

Nevertheless, one thing was certain, Clericus said, that no party would be more opposed to their doctrine, if it ever prospered and made noises, than the Roman Church. This had been proved before now. In the seventeenth century the theology of the divines of the English Church, which had been substantially the same as the Via Media, had experienced the full hostility of the Papacy. It was the way of the true Via Media that Rome had sought to block up just as fiercely as the Puritans had done. Laicus replied that he had much to reflect upon, but the subject seemed to involve such deep historical research that he hardly knew how to find a way through it.

On 29 January 1834 the Duke of Wellington had been elected Chancellor of Oxford University. 'Everyone is vexed and annoyed,' Newman told Bowden. The Duke had been elected by 'a minority of the University in a not over creditable way'.[32] Several members of the Oriel Common Room had nominated the Archbishop of Canterbury. 'We could command no Common Room for him – and Ogilvie, his Chaplain (at his desire I suppose) ratted from him to the Duke.'[33] Newman knew it had been a risk putting the Archbishop's name forward; perhaps it was improper to do so. In the afternoon he walked with two of his former pupils and in the evening dined in Hall with a small group which included Gladstone, who had already begun his Parliamentary career and was to prove a keen supporter of the Movement.

About a week later in the Library of Lambeth Palace, the Archbishop of Canterbury was presented with a Declaration signed by 7,000 clergy. The Declaration in Newman's and Froude's view should have been a protest against 'extra-ecclesiastical interference'; it was scandalous that Parliament had the power to appoint bishops. They had each produced drafts for consideration, but there were some like Palmer who doubted the wisdom of offering what amounted to menaces to the Government. In the event, this view prevailed and the Declaration gave a tacit agreement to any necessary reforms, 'should anything from the lapse of years or altered circumstances require renewal or correction'.[34]

Newman at this time was quite certain Archbishop Howley represented the authority of the Church. He was also a saintly man, but there were unreliable bishops like Whateley and Blomfield, who seemed ripe for anything, and if Arnold were offered a diocese ... The result of the matter was that the Tory element felt more assured that the Church's establishment could not be eroded away. 'The fox and the monkey', so it was said, 'had too long usurped the dominion of the forest. The lion is at length aroused.'[35]

For those who dissented from the Established Church, the business of the Declaration might have caused some amusement, but their own situation under the law was in urgent need of reform, particularly as regards the question of marriage. Apart from the ceremonies of Quakers and Jews, which had earlier gained parliamentary approval, all marriage ceremonies were illegal unless they were solemnised in the parish church. So it was that Unitarians, Baptists, Methodists and Roman Catholics were compelled to go through a Church of England ceremony before their marriages could be registered.

During the summer of 1834, Newman was surprised to find himself in trouble with the Bishop of Oxford over his refusal to officiate at a wedding in St Mary's. The bride, Miss Jubber, the daughter of a pastry-cook, was a Baptist who had never been baptised. The *Weekly Dispatch* reported the incident with relish. 'The Vicar of St Mary the Virgin in his hyper-anxiety to signalize his zeal against dissent and in favour of "orthodoxy" refused on Tuesday to marry a young couple of very respectable connexions solely because the blooming to-be-Bride had not been christened, and was in the reverend bigot's phraseology an "outcast". The matrimonial knot was however tied directly afterwards by the more tolerant and less pharisaical minister of a neighbouring parish-church, and the happy pair were very properly relieved from the cruel disappointment which threatened them.'[36]

Newman felt himself as one man against a whole multitude; there seemed no one to encourage him. He told his mother of so many black or inverted faces; unless from his youth up he had been schooled to fall back on himself he would have been quite out of heart. It was to school, in a sense, he went for comfort, for he sat twenty minutes with Mrs Small, the old dame school mistress at Littlemore, by way of consolation.

However there was encouragement too; both Keble and Pusey approved of his action. 'I trust it will do good,' wrote the latter, 'through evil report and good report.'[37] Keble spoke of 'a distinct and conscientious protest against one of our crying grievances'.[38] In his letter to the bishop Newman explained that he knew the family concerned and there had been talk of the daughter being baptised, though this had come to nothing. 'I felt I could not on my own responsibility bestow the especial privilege of Christian matrimony on parties who had not taken on themselves even the public profession of Christianity.' Had he had time to consult the bishop he would have done so, but he had not known the names of the persons to be married until the morning of the proposed wedding. 'It seemed as if inconsistency in me to profess that unbaptized persons are "children of wrath" and outcast from God's covenanted mercies in Christ, yet to treat them as Christians; moreover that to do so was throwing suspicion on the sincerity of my own professed belief.'[39]

No such scruple appears to have worried the incumbent of St Michael's who performed the ceremony. The Archdeacon wrote, 'It certainly is the Bishop's wish that parties should be married if they offer themselves under circumstances similar to those of Miss Jubber's case. Probably the Bishop will write to you on the subject. Meanwhile I can assure you that such is his wish.'[40]

Newman had never thought his action would become so public; that it was still plaguing him two months later was a sign of his growing importance. The Tracts had evidently begun to do their work. What he had done, he assured Rose, he had done in good conscience, believing he could not have done otherwise. He had looked at the Rubric of the Book of Common Prayer where it was forbidden to bury unbaptised infants, and burial was not, like matrimony, a divine ordinance. Later he would acknowledge matrimony as a Sacrament. 'How could I more forcibly attest to every dissenter who heard it that my notion was not a theory but a practical principle? Men will not believe one is in earnest – they do not feel words – deeds startle them.'[41]

It was not until the Marriage and Registration Acts became law in 1836 that the argument was resolved. Ironically, it had been while he was fussed by the Jubber marriage that Newman heard that Henry Wilberforce had married.

Rumours of Wilberforce's engagement had been in the air for many weeks, but Newman refused to believe a marriage was imminent. Surely he would have been among the first to know? When it was thought Isaac Williams was going to give up the curacy of St Mary's through illness, Newman had offered the post to Henry. Had he been upset the plan had fallen through? On 27 May a letter from Henry revealed that his sister-in-law was thinking of becoming a Papist; her husband, Henry's brother William, had laughed at the possibility, in the same way as Henry had so often laughed when people told him that Newman would one day turn Papist. The letter had shown great warmth.

> I have loved you like a brother; and my saddened feelings have been often
> in thinking that, when in the events of life I am separated from you, you
> will perhaps disapprove or misunderstand my conduct, and will cease to feel
> towards me, as you have done; or that our minds will grow asunder by the
> natural progress of change, which goes on in this changing world; and
> therefore every such mark of continued kind feelings warms my heart. How
> wonderful will it be hereafter, if we attain to a state where souls can hold
> intercourse immediately, and where space makes no division between them.[42]

Wilberforce continued to say he was afraid he might be untrue to himself one day, that Newman might break off the friendship, and the letter ended with an explanation that he could not accept Newman's offer of rooms at Oxford as he had to attend George Ryder's wedding. 'The time of my own marriage is not yet fixed; it must in some degree depend upon my getting a curacy.'[43]

The fact was that Wilberforce and Ryder were about to become brothers-in-law and each knew how much both Newman and Froude valued celibacy as the ideal. By marrying, the young men felt they were letting their mentors down, but they were very much in love. Theirs is a remarkable and romantic story. Dr John Sargent, the Rector and Squire of Lavington, in Sussex, who had tutored the Wilberforces, had four very beautiful daughters, known as the 'sylph-like Sargents', and each married clergymen. Emily married Samuel Wilberforce, later the Bishop of Oxford; Caroline married Henry Manning, the future Cardinal, and Sophia and Mary married Ryder and Wilberforce respectively. Dr Sargent had died in 1833 and Manning, who had been his curate, succeeded him as rector.

On 14 June Newman wrote to Froude:

> H.W. engaged to marry Miss S last December – was afraid to tell me and left Oxford without – spread abroad I had cut Ryder for marrying. He now wishes to go into orders, but cannot get a title, because he wants one with a house and £100 a year. Precious nonsense and foolery – it makes one half beside oneself. Yet he has not ratted, and will not, (so be it!) Marriage is a sin which it is sinful to repent of.

When on 11 July Ryder and his bride passed through Oxford, Newman wrote: 'he seems proud of showing her off; which I suppose is proper.'[44]

There seems little doubt that Newman felt wounded; he had hoped that Henry Wilberforce in Froude's absence would become a fellow pilgrim in the great work at hand. What hurt him most was that Henry had let Harriett know of his intimate plans.

6

The Movement

$\boxed{1834\text{--}38}$

When Newman visited his mother and sisters at Rose Bank he was often very tired, and his family felt that he was not as concerned for them as he used to be. 'I wish you would a little more show in your manner towards us the affection and tenderness which I know you feel in your heart. How much happier we should all be! Oh, how I wish you would open your eyes to your mistakes in this respect,'[1] complained Harriett. Newman found he had little to say to Frank; in fact between 1833 and 1855 the two would only meet twice. 'I got into disgrace because I did not accept the shibboleth that Christ is Jehovah,'[2] Frank said mockingly. There had been most worry about Charles; while Newman had been abroad, Charles had raised credit and squandered away the £1,000 which he was to receive on his mother's death, and had behaved in a deeply disturbed manner. In April 1834 Newman received a letter from a stranger which spoke of his brother's madness. 'I would do anything in my power to place him under the care which the present deplorable situation demands,'[3] the writer had said. They succeeded in getting Charles into St Bartholomew's Hospital. However, after a month or two he had recovered sufficiently to be asking his brother for a reference for an Usher's place at a school, employment he had tried before. Over the next few years he was constantly writing begging letters to both of his brothers.

Mrs Newman found it more and more difficult to sympathise with her eldest son's religious development. She was certain he should marry and never came to terms with his decision to be celibate. Newman, for his part, grew to wish he had not brought his family to Oxford.

Meanwhile Froude remained in Barbados. His letters arrived periodically, having been written, like Newman's to him, over a period of weeks. It was obvious that his health was deteriorating rapidly. By the autumn he was telling Newman he could barely sleep for half an hour at night; he spoke of having 'fits of blue devils'. He had decided against eating meat. 'My dinner is toast and a basin of very weak chicken broth, breakfast is my chief meal and consists of a vast joram of milk and arrowroot.'[4] He had never liked drinking milk at the best of times, but now it was necessary. He found a little cinnamon added made it enjoyable. He had been advised not to take any exercise, since it increased his cough, but discovered that on the rare occasions he had done so his health had improved. Here was a dilemma: he thought that he might borrow one of the bishop's horses instead of walking. He told Newman how tired he was of the climate; during the summer months particularly he had found it far too hot, as well as in the 'hurricane months'. Nigger land, he said, was a poor substitute for the *limen Apostolorum*.

Newman wrote from London where he was staying with Bowden, whom he described as *Apostolicum princeps*. The reason for the visit was concern for his own health; the effects of his Sicilian illness had not left him entirely. He had had a field of pain opened to him which had thrown a new light upon the whole subject of martyrdom; yet, as he told Froude, he was very well in spirits. The worst was won and over, and he trusted he would be set right altogether.

The early Tracts had now been collected together and published in one volume, and a second would soon be necessary, as month by month new Tracts appeared. At the same time the first volume of Newman's sermons had proved so popular that the publisher was calling for more. The second volume of *Parochial Sermons* came out towards the end of March 1835. Newman wrote to Froude that Manning of Merton had quite come round to the Tractarian position and was preaching in all the 'synagogues'. He begged Froude to return to them as soon as he safely could; perhaps in the following winter he could go again to Rome. But when in May the sick young man did appear in Oxford, his friends were horrified by his wasted appearance. If only he could put on some weight. When Newman learnt that Froude had refused to try ass's milk he saw it as a 'remnant of that old self-will' which he had sometimes seen in his friend. By hook or by crook he should try to gain flesh.

Froude spent only a few days at Oxford, then retired home to Dartington. In August, Newman was addressing him as his 'most Catholic-hearted brother', and telling him that the Tracts were defunct, or at least *in extremis*. Pusey had produced a pamphlet of some ninety pages on Baptism which was to be printed at his own risk. Newman was not sorry the series seemed to be coming to an end; he was tired of being editor; but, in fact, there were several more tracts to come, including the notorious Tract 90, which brought the series to an end in 1841.

Much of the summer was taken up by the vexed question of Dr Hampden.

Renn Dickson Hampden had been a Fellow of Oriel since 1814 and was well known to Newman, Keble and Froude. In 1833 he had been appointed Principal of St Mary Hall where he introduced many reforms and spent some £4,000 of his own money on the buildings. No one could doubt Hampden's sincerity, but he was to become the centre of a fierce theological controversy which marked an important development in the progress of the Oxford Movement. He had first drawn notice by suggesting that the time-honoured custom obliging all matriculating undergraduates to subscribe to the Thirty-Nine Articles of Religion should be abandoned, so that Dissenters and non-believers could enter the University. The suggestion was not a new one, but Hampden's position in the University made his advocation of it a serious matter. Eventually it was brought to the vote and soundly defeated in Convocation. The matter might have rested there had not the Prime Minister, Lord Melbourne, with the Archbishop of Canterbury's approval, appointed Hampden Regius Professor of Divinity in February 1836. Immediately there was uproar at the appointment. Newman was quick to remind the University of the wildly unorthodox views Hampden had revealed during the course of the Bampton Lectures he had delivered in 1832. Two days after news of the appointment reached Oxford, Newman produced his *Elucidations of Dr Hampden's Theological Statements.*

As one might expect, Newman's chief objection to Hampden's position was his denial of Apostolical tradition. 'He deprives us of the barest dream of enjoying an Apostolical voice in illustration and confirmation of an Apostolical writing, he assures us that the very idea of Tradition is a mistake, that there is no such thing as a succession of preaching and hearing.'[5] In fact, Hampden's position, as expressed in the lectures, had been what one now recognises as the extreme Protestant position, namely that the only Christian authority is the authority of Scripture. 'There might be interpretations and inferences from Scripture, by the hundred or the thousand, but no one certain and authoritative one; none that warranted an organised Church, much more a Catholic and Apostolic Church, founded on the assumption of this interpretation being the one true faith, the one truth of the Bible.'[6] However, as Dean Church explained, it was only Hampden's muddled-headedness that had led him to a position that virtually denied the creeds and all dogma. Nonetheless it did show the unfitness of such a man to be the official guide and teacher of the clergy. It was not surprising therefore that, at the beginning of May, a 'Statute' against Hampden was carried in Convocation. The Tractarians had won another battle, but it was not the end of Hampden, a man who 'stood before you like a milestone and brayed like a jackass'.[7] In 1847 he was offered the see of Hereford and amid much protest was elected, the dean and one canon voting against him.

While the business of Hampden was at its height intense sorrow came swiftly, though it had been for so long expected. Newman had not seen Hurrell Froude since he had spent the best part of a month at Dartington in the autumn of 1835; then he had found his friend still full of thoughts and plans, but physically very weak. It was astonishing that he had survived; perhaps he had been merely kept alive by the prayers of his friends, 'as the Israelites by Moses's uplifted hands'.[8] While in Devon Newman had managed to see as many Apostolical friends as possible, and on one happy occasion after a Confirmation at Totnes the Froudes had entertained the Bishop. Also the two friends had been able to discuss the future of the Movement. It was becoming necessary to begin an assault on Roman Catholicism, for if the situation were left as it was, and definite lines were not drawn between themselves and Popery, inquiring minds might turn Papist. It was important to show how their ideas differed from those of the Papists and to give their own views of Romanism; besides, it would be 'a very effectual though unsuspicious way of dealing a back-handed blow at ultra-protestantism'.[9]

October 10 was the last full day the two men were to spend together; it was also the day when Keble was married at his brother's parish church at Bisley to his sister-in-law, Charlotte Clarke, a girl of 'sweetness and cultured intellect, a strength to him, thoroughly able to enter into all his hopes for the Church, and to help him in his work'.[10] Sadly she would seldom enjoy very good health.

The next day, as Newman set off for Exeter after taking what was to be his 'last sight of dear Hurrell',[11] he must have felt more lonely than ever. During the following months the Archdeacon kept him closely informed from the Parsonage, and in a letter written on 18 February he made it clear that Hurrell was gradually losing ground. The least exertion brought with it a greater difficulty of breathing, so the patient was no longer allowed to get out of bed. All hope of recovery was now gone, but there was little pain. 'His thoughts continually turn to Oxford, to yourself, and to Mr Keble',[12] his father had written. Newman replied that although he had so long expected the event, yet he was not at all prepared for it. He offered to come down immediately. 'I put myself entirely in your hands, if you and Hurrell wish me to come down to him.'[13] In the same post he wrote his last letter to his dearest friend. 'I will only say that you are ever in my thoughts and prayers, and (by God's blessing) ever shall be – may I ever be in yours – Though you are at distance, I feel you are now with me in Oxford.'[14] Newman's anxiety was shared: Isaac Williams added a short note to the letter promising his prayers. 'It often occurs to me as a matter of great comfort,' he wrote, 'that the Church affords us no Prayers for length of life– but the contrary.'[15]

On 23 February Hurrell seemed a little better, but the doctor held out no hope of any change having taken place that should raise the family's expectation beyond that of a short respite. Nevertheless, the Archdeacon thought no good could come of a visit from Newman, but 'Should he, contrary to all reasonable grounds, get a little about again – do tell Mr Williams, his paying us a short visit will give us great pleasure indeed.'[16] The letter conveyed Hurrell's thanks, adding: 'He is sorry he has given you any trouble about those stupid accounts.'[17] Unwittingly the Archdeacon rubbed salt into the wound, but what did that matter now? On the evening of 28 February, a Sunday, the grieving father took up his pen again to say that his son's life had come to an end.

> After a more than usually restless night he spoke of himself as being quite
> comfortable this morning, and appeared to hear the service of the day and
> a sermon read to him, with so much attention that I did not think the sad
> event so near as it has been. About two o'clock as I was recommending him
> to take some egg and wine, I observed a sudden difficulty in his breathing
> and some weak efforts to free his throat from accumulated mucus. He
> attempted to speak, and then after a few slight struggles his sufferings were
> at an end.[18]

The Archdeacon went on to invite Newman to take anything he wished from Hurrell's room at College as a token of remembrance. Newman chose Froude's breviary. A few days later in a letter to Bowden he revealed something of his feeling of grief.

> He had been so very dear to me, that it is an effort to me to reflect on my
> own thoughts about him. I can never have a greater loss, looking on for the
> whole of life – for he was to me, and he was likely to be ever, in the same
> degree of continual familiarity which I enjoyed with yourself in our
> Undergraduate days; so much so that I was from time to time confusing him
> with you and calling him by his right name and recollecting what belonged
> to him, what to you, by an act of memory.[19]

If only Bowden had known him, Newman continued, it would have given such pleasure. It was so very mysterious that anyone so remarkably and variously gifted, and with talents so fitted to the times, should be removed.

> I never on the whole fell in with so gifted a person – in variety and perfection
> of gifts I think he far exceeded even Keble – for myself, I cannot describe
> what I owe to him as regards the intellectual principles of religion and morals.
> It is useless to go on to speak of him – yet it has pleased God to take him,
> in mercy to him, but by a very heavy visitation to all who were intimate
> with him. Yet every thing was so bright and beautiful about him, that to
> think of him must always be a comfort. The sad feeling I have is, that one

cannot retain in one's memory all one wishes to keep there and that as year passes after year, the image of him will be fainter and fainter.[20]

Keble for his part told the Archdeacon he felt sure it was not wrong to 'cherish the thought and hope of invisible communion'. 'Of the loss to the Church I will say nothing – indeed I do not like to use the word loss any how with regard to his separation from us; and who knows as dear Mr Newman says what good he may in some unknown manner be still an instrument of to us all.'[21]

Newman felt certain that the longer he lived the more he would miss his friend, 'the most angelic mind of any person I ever fell in with – the most unearthly, the most gifted',[22] he told another friend, Maria Giberne. It was, he thought, a loss such as he could never feel again; but, although he did not know it, 1836 was to become a year of sorrows. In May his mother fell ill. Mrs Newman had not been well enough to attend Jemima's wedding to John Mozley on 28 April, and the excitement of it all was too much for her. On 4 May Harriett wrote to her brother chidingly, 'Every one knows she is ill, and no one wonders at that ... Our plans were not entirely made up – you would have heard, had you been able to give more time.'[23] It was the same old reproach.

The fact was that although Newman knew his mother's mind had begun to stray, 'she was not herself even before the end',[24] he had not realised she was in any danger. Apparently a letter from Harriett alerting him had gone astray 'through the stupidity of a servant'. When he saw his mother he was extremely shocked and immediately sent for a second opinion, but the second doctor confirmed that her condition was hopeless. He did all he could to remain near her, and on the day before her death he went straight up to Iffley after church and spent the rest of the day in the house, only returning to Oxford in the evening to take a service and deliver a lecture in Adam de Brome's Chapel of St Mary's, but he returned to Rose Hill that same night. The following day Mrs Newman sank into unconsciousness and died in the early evening. She was sixty-three years old. 'Every thing is strange in this world – every thing mysterious,' Newman wrote to his Aunt Elizabeth: 'Nothing but sure faith can bring us through.'[25] He had never thought when his mother had laid the foundation stone of his new church at Littlemore that she would not live long enough to see the building completed.

Neither of his brothers attended the funeral in St Mary's which was conducted by Williams, but his sisters and several members of the Mozley family were there together with Dr and Mrs Pusey, Copeland, Rogers, and many others. Mrs Newman was buried in a vault within the chancel rails. After the service Newman remained kneeling at the altar deep in prayer until

Williams tapped him on the shoulder as the mourners were leaving the church. Since his mother's death those about him had seen how dreadfully dejected he looked; this was natural enough. But when the party arrived back at the house the sun was shining brightly and it was noticed how much more lively he looked. As one present reported: 'As if he thought that grief had reigned long enough, he seemed by a sort of resolute effort to throw it from him, and resume his usual manner.'[26] In his diary for that day he simply wrote *Requiescat in pace* and a short list of those present.

Coming so soon after Froude's death, it was such a bitter affliction that, as he told Bowden, unless he and Harriett knew Christ was coming he did not know how they should bear it. 'I trust it will make us look out more simply for His coming – and literally to wait for it.'[27] What made it worse was the fact that he had not known his mother was in danger until the day before she died.

The new church at Littlemore was consecrated on 22 September and dedicated to St Mary and St Nicholas, the patron saints of the pre-Reformation Benedictine convent for whose ruins, which remained close by, Newman had a great affection. On the morning of the consecration he preached to a packed church in the presence of the bishop amid a profusion of bright flowers. Afterwards he helped to distribute buns to all the children, two of whom had been baptised after the service. It was, as he informed Keble, a happy and pleasant occasion coming just fourteen months after his dear mother had laid the first stone. Among those present he was pleased to welcome Henry Wilberforce and his wife.

A few days later he travelled to Derby to attend Harriett's wedding to Tom Mozley. Since their mother's death he had worried about his sister's future; she was thirty-three and her younger sister had reached the altar before her. Alone at Rose Bank she had become deeply depressed; then in July Mozley had proposed to her; Newman set aside £30 for her preparatory expenses, and offered her all their mother's plate, but he could not help feeling the marriage was a little too hasty, coming only three months after the engagement. He wished he had been consulted; in fact, Harriett had left it to Jemima to tell him.

Marriage meant that Mozley would have to resign his Fellowship, but Newman did all he could to find him a suitable parish; this was Cholderton, in Wiltshire, in the Salisbury diocese. Nevertheless, he felt upset that yet another of the 'bachelor party' had succumbed. 'Everyone when he marries is a lost man – a clear good for nothing – I should not be surprised to be told Mozley would not write another letter all his life,'[28] he wrote to another Oriel Fellow, John Christie.

'The controversy with the Romanists has overtaken us like a summer's cloud,'

Newman wrote in Tract Number 71. 'We find ourselves in various parts of the country preparing for it, yet, when we look back, we cannot trace the steps by which we arrived at our present position. We do not recollect what our feelings were this time last year on the subject – what was the state of our apprehensions and anticipations.'[29] It seemed that he and his party were ignorant of why they were not Roman Catholics, while on the other hand the Roman Catholics themselves were said to be spreading and strengthening on all sides of them 'vaunting of their success real or apparent, and taunting us with our inability to argue with them'.[30]

Roman Catholic 'success', such as it was at this time, was very largely owing to the energy of Nicholas Wiseman, who had arrived in England from Rome in 1835. During the autumn Wiseman was offered the temporary post of priest in charge of the chapel of the Sardinian Embassy in Lincoln's Inn Fields while the resident chaplain was away visiting Italy. Wiseman used the opportunity to deliver a course of lectures in English intended to instruct non-Catholics in the tenets of the Faith; these were held on Sunday afternoons during Advent. As one eye-witness noted:

> He had come to England with a very considerable reputation for learning and ability; and this took many to the Sardinian Chapel. The lectures more than sustained his reputation, and produced an immense sensation. I date from their delivery the beginning of a serious revival of Catholicism in England.[31]

The lectures became so popular that the chapel was packed to overflowing and their success prompted Dr Bramston, the Vicar Apostolic of the London District, to invite Wiseman to give a further series during Lent. This time the venue would be the Church of St Mary at Moorfields, the largest Catholic church in London.

It was in one of these lectures that Wiseman cited Newman's book on the Arians to prove the point that it was the practice of the Church at that time to instruct Catechumens in the mysteries of the Gospel by oral instruction and not by Scripture. This reference to Newman was introduced with 'vast pomp and preparation, and circumstance', as one of Newman's friends was quick to relate. Certainly Wiseman had been watching the progress of the Oxford Movement with the keenest interest, and ever since Newman and Froude had visited him in Rome his mind had been intent on forging some link with such members of the Church of England. In the same lecture he had proclaimed, 'This same Mr Newman proves all I want; and he is a witness to the truth to whom no member of the Establishment can object.'[32] No doubt there was a note of satisfaction in his voice as he called upon 'that learned divine of the Established Church' in support of his argument, quoting fairly lengthy passages from the book.

Wiseman had wished to explain to his audience, so Newman's friend James Tyler related,

> the necessity and the existence of an infallible Church, which was the guardian and teacher of the truth, and to demonstrate the fallacy of the modern popular doctrine of the duty and right of private judgment, the preposterous practice of putting the Bible into the hands of the laity, and making them the judges of the doctrines of the Church; that this infallible Church must be in Communion with the see of Rome.[33]

Newman must have read Tyler's letter with some alarm; he tended to agree that such a Church had once existed, but that since the Council of Trent she had swerved seriously from the true path. Yet there was no doubt Wiseman was a force to be reckoned with, and in April Newman learnt that the latter had begun the *Dublin Review*, a magazine with himself as editor, but under the auspices also of Daniel O'Connell. The fact that such a trouble-maker as O'Connell was in some way involved brought from Newman the wry comment: 'Really, if one wished a plain practical direction as to one's behaviour towards Romanism this surely would seem a sufficient one.'[34] However, Newman's attitude to Wiseman remained dignified. In an article in the *British Critic* he acknowledged that Romanism had great truths in it which had been almost forgotten, but the people likely to be persuaded by Wiseman were Dissenters and irregulars, not members of the Church of England. If the lectures were to have any effect on Anglicans it would be only to awaken them to the Catholic doctrine which lay dormant in their own Church, something which he and his friends had been attempting to do themselves. However, there were many who did not share this view and saw Wiseman as a considerable danger. In a later issue of the *British Critic* Dr Turton, the Professor of Divinity at Cambridge, viciously attacked Wiseman's lecture on the Eucharist. He accused him of subtlety, dexterity, and of being a controversialist totally lacking in wisdom, though he showed plausibility.

Wiseman himself knew that he had begun something important, and that he had adopted the wisest form of approach, as he was to tell the audience of his last lecture.

> I have but scattered a little seed, and it is God alone who can give the increase. It is not on those effects, for which I am grateful for your indulgence, and on which till my dying hour I must dwell with delight, – it is not on the patience and kindness with which you have so often listened to me under trying circumstances, in such numbers, and at such an hour, that I presume to vest my hopes and augury of some good effect. No, it is on the confidence which the interest exhibited gives me that you have abstracted from me individually and fixed your thoughts and attention upon the cause which I

represent. Had I come before you as a champion, armed to fight against the antagonists of our faith, I might have been anxious to appear personally strong and well appointed; but the course which I have chosen needed no such prowess; a burning lamp will shine as brightly in the hands of a child, as if uplifted by a giant's arm. I have endeavoured simply to hold before you the light of Catholic truth; and to him that kindled it be all the glory![35]

The success of the lectures prompted a bowdlerised version of them from some of Wiseman's adversaries. Realising that this might frustrate all his efforts he quickly prepared an authorised edition in two volumes, 'as the only effectual means to prevent injury to myself or to my cause'.[36] It was not long before Newman's review in the *British Critic* of Wiseman's *Lectures on the Catholic Church* was itself being reviewed in the *Dublin Review*.

All the controversy only served to make Newman better and better known outside the University, but his weekly lectures in Adam de Brome's Chapel and his sermons from the pulpit of St Mary's were making a deep impression, particularly upon the younger generation of undergraduates. One of these, Francis Doyle, who later became Professor of Poetry, recalled the effect which Newman had had on him.

That great man's extraordinary influence drew all those within his sphere like a magnet, to attach themselves to him and his doctrines. Whenever I was at Oxford, I used to go regularly, on Sunday afternoons, to listen to his sermons at St Mary's, and I have never heard such preaching since. I do not know whether it is a mere fancy of mine, or whether those who knew him better will accept and endorse my belief, that one element of his wonderful power showed itself after this fashion. He always began as if he had determined to set forth his idea of truth in the plainest and simplest language – language as men say, 'intelligible to the meanest understanding'. But his ardent zeal and fine poetical imagination were thus to be controlled. As I hung upon his words, it seemed to me as if I could trace behind his will, and pressing, so to speak, against it, a rush of thoughts, of feelings, which he kept struggling to hold back, but in the end they were generally too strong for him, and poured themselves out in a torrent of eloquence all the more impetuous from having been so long repressed. The effect of these outbursts was irresistible, and carried his hearers beyond themselves at once. Even when his efforts of self-restraint were more successful, those very efforts gave a life and colour to his style which riveted the attention of all within the reach of his voice ... His manner may have been self-suppressed, constrained it was not. His bearing was simply quiet and calm, that calmness, intense feeling was, I think, obvious to those who had instinct of sympathy with him.[37]

While he preached Newman never used his hands, but he moved his head to emphasise a point. Another who heard him described how his sermon would begin in a calm musical voice, the key slightly rising as it went on; 'by and by the preacher warmed with his subject, and it seemed as if his very soul and body glowed with suppressed emotion.'[38] Even those out of sympathy with Newman's doctrine paid tribute to the remarkable effect of his preaching.

> Who could resist the charm of that spiritual apparition, gliding in the dim afternoon light through the aisles of St. Mary's, rising into the pulpit, and then, in the most entrancing of voices, breaking the silence with words and thoughts which were a religious music, – subtle, sweet, and mournful? Happy the man, who in that susceptible season of youth hears such voices! They are a possession to him for ever.[39]

So wrote Matthew Arnold whose father had called the Tractarians the 'Oxford Malignants'.

It was Dean Church's view that without Newman's sermons the Oxford Movement might never have happened; it would certainly not have been what it was. Richard Church himself was among those who came under Newman's influence as an undergraduate, and attended the weekly soirées that had begun in February 1837. Others who came on the scene at about this time were Frederick Faber and William George Ward, the latter having been persuaded somewhat against his will to hear Newman preach but who afterwards never looked back. Soon it was being said that Dr Pusey and Newman 'ruled' Oxford. This was not a view shared by those in authority.

Pusey gave the Movement a position and a name. Newman was to attribute his vast influence to his deep religious seriousness. Not only was he a Canon of Christ Church Cathedral, but he was also the Regius Professor of Hebrew; he had illustrious family connections and 'easy relations with the University authorities'. Just when Newman was becoming disheartened by all the misunderstandings and the charges of Romanism that the Tracts had aroused, so that he considered bringing the whole project to an end, it had been Pusey who had saved the situation by offering a substantial theological treatise on Baptism which was published as three Tracts. Pusey had given his moral support almost since the beginning, and he had allowed his initials to be added to his Tract on Fasting, but now he was out in open support. 'He was able to give a name, a form, and a personality, to what was without him a sort of mob,' Newman recalled, 'and when various parties had to meet together in order to resist the liberal acts of the Government, we of the Movement took our place by right among them.'[40] Pusey had seen that there should be 'more sobriety, more gravity, more careful pains, more sense of responsibility in the Tracts, but more than this: with Newman's support he prepared translations of the early Church Fathers and their 'Library of the Fathers' would eventually extend to some fifty volumes.

Another important aspect of Pusey's life was that, unlike Newman, he had a wife and family. Pusey was of a passionate nature and he had met Maria Barker first soon after he had left Eton; he was eighteen years old and she a year younger. There was an immediate attraction, but neither family approved of the match, and it was not until Maria's father died that an engagement became possible. Marrying in 1828 the couple were to have four children, a son and three daughters, though one daughter, Katherine, only lived for a few months. Newman was to become a great favourite with the children, and there is a charming description of one of his visits given by John Fuller Russell, a visitor from Cambridge in the autumn of 1837. He saw Newman as a 'dark, middle-aged, middle-sized man, with lanky black hair and large spectacles, thin, gentlemanly, and very insinuating'.[41] The spectacles, however, were a source of amusement.

> Presently, after dinner, Dr Pusey's children ran into the room. One climbed Newman's knee and hugged him. Newman put his spectacles on him, and next on his sister, and great was the merriment of the Puseyan progeny ... He told them a story of an old woman who had a broomstick which would go to the well, draw water, and do many other things for her; how the old woman got tired of the broomstick, and wishing to destroy it broke it in twain, and how, to the old woman's great chagrin and disappointment, two live broomsticks grew from the broken parts of the old one.[42]

Sadly, such happiness was short-lived, for it soon became obvious that Maria Pusey was consumptive. Her health rallied a little after a long visit to the Channel Islands. Newman had recommended the Maltese climate, remembering how Froude's state had improved while they had been there, but over the next two years she gradually faded away and, like Froude, suffered a slow, lingering death which did not come until May 1839.

Meanwhile, with the publication of Froude's papers, it seemed to the Movement as if Hurrell Froude had risen from the dead.

7

The Church of the Fathers

1838–42

The two volumes of Froude's *Remains* were published on 24 February 1838, the result of intensive hard work on Keble and Newman's part to put their friend's papers into some sort of order. Archdeacon Froude had been most cooperative and had sent all that he could find at the parsonage. In the previous October, Newman had travelled to Hursley to spend time with Keble to discuss the forthcoming publication.

'What a marvel it is! but I really do think that a fresh instrument of influence is being opened to us in these Papers. They do certainly portray a saint,'[1] Newman wrote to Bowden. All persons of 'unhacknied feelings' and youthful minds must be taken in by them, he added, but others might think them romantic, scrupulous, or over refined. Yet, although he knew he might receive criticism from all quarters, he felt it was important to present 'a picture of a mind; and that being gained as the scope, the details may be left to take their chance'.[2] Froude's was a mind 'only breaking out into more original and beautiful discoveries, from that very repression which at first sight seemed likely to be the utter prohibition to exercise his special powers'.[3] It had always been Froude's ambition to be 'a humdrum', Newman noted, and by relinquishing the prospect of originality he had become more original.

The first volume consisted of Froude's journal, memoranda and letters, many of which were addressed to Keble who chose to transcribe them himself. Newman lightly edited the journal which covered the years 1827–28. He found it more interesting than anything else, except perhaps the letters to Keble. It seemed as though Providence was putting things into their hands for something special. A further batch of papers from the Archdeacon, he said, had quite made his head whirl.

The second volume comprised sermons and essays, and two further volumes to include Froude's extensive study of St Thomas à Becket were already under discussion. When Rivington, the publisher, saw the material he was so excited that he increased the print run from 750 to 1,000 copies. However, the immediate effect of the *Remains* on the Movement's reputation was harsher than Newman had feared, and it seemed he might have made a gross error in not editing more judiciously. Surely it was enlightening to see a young man in the process of development at that interesting period of life, from eighteen to twenty-eight or thirty when his opinions are forming? Here was Froude's mind: his curious change from Tory to Apostolical; the interesting growth of that mind; his overcoming indolence; his remarkable struggle against the lassitude of disease; his working to the last. All these things were certainly true, but the problem was largely the rough directness of Froude's style, for unlike Newman he had not been one to weigh his words. He had always said exactly what he felt like saying and wrote very much in the manner in which he spoke, but that manner, without the impish smile and the charming, infectious laugh known so well to his friends, only served to shock many of his readers. 'Its predominant character is extraordinary impudence,'[4] Arnold wrote to Hawkins, both of whom, of course, had known Froude well. What infuriated Arnold most was Froude's irreverent attitude to the Protestant Reformers. If Luther could be reviled as a bold bad man, so could St Paul be reviled. How zealously would some of the Oxford men have joined in the stoning of Stephen, he said bitterly.

It was not long before references to the *Remains* were appearing in the magazines. Newman, now editor of the *British Critic*, spoke of expecting a 'volley from the whole Conservative Press'. 'I can fancy the Old Duke sending down to ask the Heads of Houses whether we cannot be silenced.'[5] James Mozley received a newspaper article which he passed on to Newman, which revealed how some of Froude's phrases had been quoted during a debate in the House of Lords.

The Debate was rendered remarkable for bringing before the notice of the country, through Lord Morpeth, a sect of damnable and detestable heretics of late sprung up in Oxford: a sect which evidently affects Popery, and merits the heartiest condemnation of all true Christians. We have paid a good deal of attention to these gentry, and by the grace of God we shall show them up, and demonstrate that they are a people to be abhorred of all faithful men. We do not hesitate to say they are criminally heterodox.[6]

Even some who had supported the Movement felt uneasy. 'I shall ever regret that the pruning knife was not more extensively used in the preparation of those extraordinary papers,'[7] wrote Edward Churton. He told Newman that a plain good cause had been encumbered. 'You must perceive that since the publication of Froude's *Remains*, your friends are perplexed, and some who were neuters have declared against you.'[8] Churton added that he had not been able to find anyone to defend the publication except Dr Pusey.

It was certainly true that Newman had published many intimate thoughts that Froude had never meant to become public; the details of his attempts at asceticism, for instance, where he described the temptation of smelling food after a day's fast, but he would have approved whole-heartedly of the world relishing his scourging of the Reformers. As Christopher Dawson has said, 'His ironic self-depreciation could have found no better monument than this posthumous exposure which discomfited his opponents at the same time that it humiliated himself. It saved the Movement from becoming prematurely respectable, while at the same time giving it a fresh impulse towards the Catholic ideal.'[9]

Among those who enthused at the *Remains* was Ward who told Pusey the book had delighted him more than any other book he had read. 'This is what I have been looking for. Here is a man who knows what he means and says it. This is the man for me! He speaks out.'[10] This from one who had never set eyes upon Froude in his life.

What Newman called 'Romanism' remained the chief problem. One of the results of the publication of Froude's *Remains*, with its clear attack on the English Protestant Reformers, was that some clergy felt the noble work done by men like Ridley, Latimer and Cranmer had been mocked and their influence was in danger of being undermined. In Oxford, where these three had suffered their deaths, it was thought important to make some memorial, so with the full support of the University subscriptions were sought towards the erection of a monument. The appeal was successful, and the result, the Martyrs' Memorial, may still be seen today at the end of St Giles' Street, near the church dedicated to St Mary Magdalene, which of all the Oxford churches, with its Anglo-Catholic ritual, is probably the best monument to the Oxford Movement.

That the plan to erect a monument to the sixteenth-century Reformation divines was intended to embarrass Newman and his friends seems certain, for if they failed to support the idea they could be justly accused of failing to uphold the foundations of the Church of which they were ordained ministers. The mind behind it all was that of Charles Golightly, a former pupil of Newman's, who for almost a year, between 1835 and 1836, had been his curate at Littlemore until he was dismissed. Golightly had become a jealous opponent of the Movement, being highly suspicious of its tendency towards Rome. 'I have the sole charge of the Alarm-bell,'[11] he would later boast, by which time he had become a thorn in Newman's flesh.

Newman had naturally opposed the plan from the start, and its resounding success was a blow, particularly when he learnt that many he had looked upon as his supporters seemed to favour it, and he was horrified to be told that 'in the interest of harmony' even Pusey had made a donation.

Meanwhile Newman's published sermons and lectures were being read and discussed in many a parsonage and college common room. They were criticised in ecclesiastical magazines, and in the pulpit his ideas praised or blamed according to the theological inclination of the preacher. Earlier in the year the Lady Margaret Professor of Divinity, Canon Godfrey Faussett, had denounced the Tractarians from Newman's own pulpit in St Mary's. The Tracts were leading to Popery, Faussett argued, and Rome was Antichrist. 'Old Faussett has been firing off at us,' Newman informed Jemima. 'He is like an old piece of ordnance, which can do nothing but fire – or like an old macaw with one speech ... He can do nothing but fire.'[12] Newman anticipated that Faussett would publish his sermon and set to immediately to give his reply. The 'goose' knew literally nothing at all on the subject, but he would be answered anyway. It was not long before Newman was feeling a sense of satisfaction that his reply had sold more copies than Faussett's sermon.

Of course, with the benefit of hindsight we may see now that the 'goose' or 'macaw' was justified in his fears, but he had failed to understand the ground of Newman's argument for the middle way. All Faussett saw was a 'singular and instinctive coincidence' between Newman's and Dr Wiseman's lines of thought. At the time Newman did not see this so clearly, since his faith in the soundness of the Via Media remained firm. In one of his lectures in Adam de Brome's Chapel he had said, 'We Anglo-Catholics do not profess a different religion from that of Rome, we profess their Faith all but their corruptions.'[13] The Anglo-Catholics were, therefore, the only true Catholics, faithful to the teaching of the Apostles and the early Fathers, free from all corruptions.

No one was reading Newman more assiduously than Wiseman himself. In the *Dublin Review* he published long articles on the Anglican claims, and in October 1838 he concluded an article with the words: 'We covet their brotherhood in the faith, and their participation in our security of belief and their being bound to us in cords of love, through religious unity.'[14]

Wiseman's courteous manner brought him much respect, but the central question remained: which of the two 'Catholic' churches in England was the real one, the Church of England or the Church which acknowledged the Pope? In 1839 Wiseman provided the answer by comparing the position of the Church of England with that of the Donatist Schism in the fourth and fifth centuries.

The Donatists, so named after one of their leaders, Donatus, flourished for a while in North Africa. Their main tenet at odds with orthodox Catholic teaching was that the validity of a sacrament depended on the moral disposition of the priest who administered it. This doctrine had rather a bizarre origin: during the persecution of the Church by Diocletian, Bishop Mansurius of Carthage was accused of the sin of *traditio*, that is, the surrendering of sacred books, which was seen as being tantamount to denying the faith. The fact that the wise bishop had replaced the treasured books with others of no value, and had allowed the despoilers to take heretical books instead was of no consequence to a zealot like Donatus. The result was that any sacrament administered by the bishop was considered invalid, and matters came to a head when Mansurius died and his archdeacon, Caecilian, was consecrated in his stead. Seventy Numidian bishops protested on the grounds that Caecilian's ordination was invalid and appointed their own candidate. Eventually in AD 313 a priest, also named Donatus, became Bishop of Carthage and the sect's influence spread throughout the region. The false teaching was condemned by Pope Melchiades at the Council of Arles and again at the Council of Milan, but, as was seen in the case of the Arians, condemnation only served to make the sect more popular. An Athanasius was needed!

St Augustine, the young new Bishop of Hippo, took upon himself the task of sorting the matter out. In the year AD 411 he confronted 279 Donatist bishops in conference at Carthage, and showed how their claim to be the true Church did not stand up to serious scrutiny. Augustine appealed to the universal Church in words which Wiseman was to seize upon, words which Newman admitted gave him a stomach-ache. *Quapropter securus judicat orbis terrarum, bonos non esse qui se dividunt ab orbe terrarum quacumque parte orbis terrarum.* (The entire world judges with security that they are not good, who separate themselves from the entire world in whatever part of the world.)

Newman did not see Wiseman's article until it was pointed out to him by Robert Williams, a friend who was not even a Tractarian. On reading it he did not see its relevance to begin with, although he saw immediately the similarity between the Donatists' position and that of the Monophysite sect of the fifth century which he had recently been studying. The Monophysites had denied that Christ had a divine and a human nature, yet they claimed like the Donatists that their position was the true one; they were the Catholic Church. Newman had felt most unhappy as he read into their history. As he would describe in a well-known passage of the *Apologia*:

> My stronghold was Antiquity; now here, in the middle of the fifth century,
> I found, as it seemed to me, Christendom of the sixteenth and the nineteenth
> centuries reflected. I saw my face in that mirror, and I was a Monophysite.
> The Church of the Via Media was in the position of the Oriental communion,
> Rome was where she now is; and the Protestants were Eutychians.[15]

It was difficult to explain how the Eutychians or Monophysites were heretics, if the Protestants and Anglicans were not also. At the time Newman had found it only difficult, but perhaps it was not impossible. Then Wiseman had quoted St Augustine, and it was those words *Securus judicat orbis terrarum*, which haunted him. As to the Donatists themselves Newman knew enough about them to discount them as a wild bunch of fanatics, but he could not discount St Augustine's argument: this must be the test of all those sects which set themselves up without the consent of the historic Catholic Church, thus any National Church was necessarily in schism from the Universal Church.

Williams had repeated the words over and over again and, when he had gone, they kept ringing in Newman's ears.

> *Securus judicat orbis terrarum*; they were words which went beyond the occasion of the Donatists; they applied to that of the Monophysites. They gave a cogency to the Article which had escaped me at first. They decided ecclesiastical questions on a simpler rule than that of Antiquity; nay, St Augustine was one of the prime oracles of Antiquity; here then, Antiquity was deciding against itself. What a light was hereby thrown upon every controversy in the Church! . . . not that, in the Arian hurricane, Sees more than can be numbered did not bend before its fury, and fall off from St Athanasius; not that the crowd of Oriental bishops did not need to be sustained during the contest by the voice and the eye of St Leo; but that the deliberate judgment, in which the whole Church at length rests and acquiesces, is an infallible prescription and a final sentence against such portions of it as protest and secede.
>
> Who can account for the impressions which are made on him? For a mere sentence, the words of St Augustine, struck me with a power which I never had felt from any words before. To take a familiar instance, they were like the 'Turn again Whittington', of the chime; or, to take a more serious one, they were like the *Tolle, lege – tolle, lege*, of the child, which converted St Augustine himself. *Securus judicat orbis terrarum*. By these great words of the ancient Father, interpreting and summing up the long and varied course of ecclesiastical history, the theory of the Via Media was absolutely pulverized.[16]

For a while Newman tried to suppress the rising tide of doubt that now threatened to drown him. It was the 'first real hit from Romanism'. The Movement had sprung a leak, as he wrote to Frederick Rogers. 'Sharp fellows like Ward, Stanley and Co would "not let one go to sleep on it".'[17] Not long after this he confided in Henry Wilberforce that, though he prayed that it might never happen, in the end he might find it his duty to join the Roman Catholic Church. Perhaps there was still a way out.

Since 1837 Newman's curate at Littlemore had been John Rouse Bloxam, a man some six years younger than his vicar, and a Fellow of Magdalen College. Bloxam was extremely efficient in all aspects of his duty and Newman found he could rely on him; not only was he active in the parish, taking a particular interest in the building of the small school next to the churchyard, but he also keenly supported the Movement, bringing to it his considerable liturgical and historical knowledge. It gives some idea of how lacking in ritual the Church of England was before the Oxford Movement to learn that Bloxam was one of the first clergymen to wear a stole at the altar.

At his own expense Bloxam improved the little church in various ways, adding five stained-glass windows and a lectern; he would have installed two antique chairs besides had Newman allowed them. Like Newman he grew to love the small hamlet and he spent as much time there as possible, lodging with a Mr and Mrs Barnes near the George Inn. He might well have remained the curate there had not an unfortunate incident occurred, which again illustrates how touchy and on their guard everyone had become. As an antiquarian Bloxam was interested in pre-Reformation, not to say Catholic, ritual and had become an admirer of the work of the architect Pugin; to this end he decided to see for himself the Catholic chapel at the Earl of Shrewsbury's mansion, Alton Towers, in Staffordshire. As a guest of the chaplain, Dr Rock, Bloxam had attended Mass in a 'Romish Chapel' and was seen, so it was rumoured, to bow his head at the Elevation of the Host. Newman, who had been aware of the Staffordshire visit, was informed that such an event might have occurred in a letter from William Dodsworth, the Vicar of Christ Church, Regent's Park, an Evangelical who had lately adopted Tractarian views. Newman was somewhat alarmed by the infor-mation, but on hearing Bloxam's account of the matter he was relieved, and in answering Dodsworth he was able to quote verbatim:

> I went into the Gallery of the Chapel every day morning and evening and
> said there our Morning and Evening Service for the day according to our
> Book of Common Prayer. After Morning Service I used to stay some time
> on my knees, during which the family came in and had Service in which
> I took no part. This Service, on the Friday, and the Friday only, was Low
> Mass; in which I took no part either, but remained just as on other days
> without changing my posture.[18]

Newman added that had he bothered to ask Bloxam any further details, no doubt, he would have replied, 'I had no intention whatever of bowing down to the Host'. Nevertheless, he revealed he had informed the Bishop of the matter, and continued to give what he saw as some explanation. 'I suppose the case is simply this, that we have raised desires, of which our Church does not supply the objects, and that they have not the patience, or humility, or discretion to keep from seeking those objects where they are supplied.'[19]

It had been essential to let the Bishop know in case he learnt of 'Bloxam's Escapade' from anyone else. 'I brought it before your Lordship simply because I did not like anything to happen connected with St Mary's of a certain character at the present time, without your being put at once in possession of the facts.'[20] In the event his Lordship took the line that it was a matter for the Vicar to sort out for himself. 'If from any apprehension of Mr Bloxam really having a propensity towards Romanism, or from the great indiscretion he appears to have shown at Alton Towers, you think he has acted in a manner unbecoming a Minister of our Protestant Church, and therefore as one whom you could not with comfort to yourself, employ as your Curate, the proposal of separation should come from yourself, and it would only be in the event of your Curate's refusal to resign his Curacy that the Bishop's aid or interference would be necessary.'[21]

The Bishop added that he was off to Canterbury on the following day. On 5 January 1840 Newman informed him that Bloxam was not in very good health and the occurrence had greatly upset him. 'I think it will end, much against my wish, in his retiring from the charge of Littlemore.'[22] And so it did, but such is the irony of the time that of the three it was Bloxam who remained a true and faithful member of his own Church and Dodsworth and Newman who did not.

On the same day that he had informed the Bishop of Bloxam's impending resignation Newman gave an account of the incident to his old friend Bowden in which he confesses that he had been frightened by it. Perhaps Bloxam in good faith had done no more than desire a consecrated place in which to pray when there was no other near. Even so it was very indiscreet of him. Fortunately the matter did not seem to be generally known in Oxford. What was certain was that no time could be lost in asserting the Catholicity of the English Church and stopping up the leak in the boat which Wiseman had made in comparing it with that of the Donatists.

What Newman came to call his last arrow shot against Rome, the essay entitled 'Catholicity of the Anglican Church,' appeared in the January issue of the *British Critic*. Here he revealed a deep understanding of both the Anglican and Roman positions and argued for each in turn.

The Anglican view of the Universal Church had always been that its separate portions need not be united together for their essential completeness, except by the tie of descent from one original. The Apostolical Succession was necessary in order for a branch of the Church to claim descent, but that being secured, each branch was bound to conform to the country and form an alliance with the institutions in which it found itself, quite irrespective

79

of all the rest. Did this mean a National Church under the supremacy of the state or monarch? Certainly, it did mean that. Although Ordination was solely the bishop's prerogative, everything else came from the king. 'The whole jurisdiction is his; his are all the spiritual courts; his the right of excommunication; his the control of revenues; his the organisation of dioceses; his the appointment of bishops.'[23] Such was the extreme view upon which Cranmer had acted, but such absorption of a branch of the Church into a nation was nothing else but a formal state of schism, if the Church was essentially one and one only, an organised body in every age and country.

Once again Newman found himself presented with the same old problem. If the Church was one, was the Roman Church outside it, or was the Anglican Church outside it, for if they were both inside, how came it that they were not in communion? Of course, the Anglican Church as proclaimed and explained by the Tractarians, the true Catholic Church, would soon be recognised, Newman asserted, had she only that one note of the Church upon her – sanctity. As much as Roman Catholics denounced her at present as schismatical, they could not resist her once she showed her holiness.

> In vain would a few controversialists taunt us in that case with the disorders
> of the sixteenth century, or attempt to prove our alienation from the
> commonwealth of Israel. The hearts of their own people would be with us;
> we should have an argument more intelligible than any which the schools
> could furnish, could we appeal to this living evidence of truth, in our bishops,
> in our chapters, our clergy, our divines, our laity, causing men to glorify our
> Father which is in heaven. We should not be unwilling to place the matter
> on this issue. We are almost content to say to Romanists, Account us not
> yet as a branch of the Catholic Church, though we be a branch, till we are
> like a branch, so that when we do become like a branch, then you consent
> to acknowledge us. Unless our system really has a power in it, making us
> neglectful of wealth, neglectful of station, neglectful of ease, munificent,
> austere, reverent, childlike, unless it is able to bring our passions into order,
> to make us pure, to make us meek, to rule our intellect, to give government
> of speech, to inspire firmness, to destroy self, we do not deserve to be
> acknowledged as a Church, and we submit to be ill-treated.[24]

The matter was much the same with the Romanists.

> Till we see in them as a Church more straightforwardness, truth, and openness,
> more of severe obedience to God's least commandments, more scrupulousness
> about means, less of a political, scheming, grasping spirit, less of intrigue, less
> that looks hollow and superficial, less accommodation to the tastes of the
> vulgar, less subservience to the vices of the rich, less humouring of men's
> morbid and wayward imaginations, less indulgence of their low carnal

superstitions, less intimacy with the revolutionary spirit of the day, we will keep aloof from them as we do.[25]

The Roman Church was wily.

We see it attempting to gain converts among us, by unreal representations of its doctrines, plausible statements, bold assertions, appeals to the weaknesses of human nature, to our fancies, our eccentricities, our fears, our frivolities, our false philosophies. We see its agents smiling and nodding and ducking to attract attention, as gipsies make up to truant boys, holding out tales for the nursery, and pretty pictures, and gold gingerbread, and physic concealed in jam, and sugar-plums for good children.[26]

It was passages like that which were to cause Newman such embarrassment later, as much as he must have enjoyed writing them at the time. There was something hollow about it all, as if the real point had been missed. As he admitted, he was always asking himself what the Fathers would have done. What arguments would they have put forward? No doubt they would have agreed about sanctity.

What would those whose works were about my room, whose names were ever meeting my eyes, whose authority was ever influencing my judgment, what would these men have said, how would they have acted in my position? I had made a good case on paper, but what judgment would be passed on it by Athanasius, Basil, Gregory, Hilary, and Ambrose? The more I considered the matter, the more I thought that these Fathers, if they examined the antagonist pleas, would give it against me.[27]

In his essay Newman had cited St Cyril's test that a man asked in the street to direct the way to the 'Catholic' place of worship would never dream of pointing to any other than the Catholic church in communion with Rome, no matter how many other sects might claim the 'Catholic' title. In like manner Newman feared already in his heart that should St Athanasius or St Ambrose come suddenly to life, it could not be doubted what communion they would mistake for their own. 'All surely will agree that these Fathers, with whatever differences of opinion, whatever protests, if we will, would find themselves more at home with such men as St Bernard, or St Ignatius Loyola, or with a lonely priest in his lodgings, or the holy sisterhood of Charity, or the unlettered crowd before the altar, than with the rulers or members of any other religious community.'[28]

Those early Fathers, should they travel northwards to England, to reach a 'fair city, seated among groves, green meadows, and calm streams', if they were to find themselves beside the Isis or the Cherwell or walk the streets and lanes of Oxford, Newman feared it would not be towards St Mary's

81

those holy brothers would be drawn. No, they would 'turn from many a high aisle and solemn cloister which they found there, and ask the way to some small chapel, where Mass was said, in the populous alley or the forlorn suburb'.[29]

The English liked 'manliness, openness, consistency, truth', and Newman knew they would never accept these things from Rome while Rome remained what she was. 'Rome will never gain on us till she learns these virtues, and uses them,'[30] he wrote. It was not impossible that Rome might reform herself, and should that happen 'then it would be our Church's duty at once to join in communion with the Continental Churches, whatever politicians at home may say to it, and whatever steps the civil power may take in consequence'. It was not enough, either, to wait for Rome to reform: an Anglican was bound to pray for it, and it was most touching news to be told that Christians on the Continent were praying together for the spiritual well-being of England.

> We are the debtors thereby. May the prayer return abundantly into our own bosom, and while they care for our souls may their own be prospered! May they gain light while they aim at unity, and grow in faith while they manifest their love! We too have our duties to them; not in reviling, not of slandering, not of hating, though political interests require it; but the duty of loving brethren still more abundantly in spirit, whose faces, for our sins and their sins, we are allowed to see in the flesh.[31]

In the following month Newman brought out his *The Church of the Fathers*, which, in spite of its sombre title, is among the most enjoyable of his writings. The energetic accounts of the lives and conflicts of those who over the years had become his heroes: St Basil, St Gregory, St Antony, whose life Athanasius had written, and St Augustine had originally been in the form of letters appearing in the correspondence column of Hugh Rose's *British Magazine*. Rose, who had become Principal of King's College, London and Domestic Chaplain to the Archbishop of Canterbury, had died in Florence two years previously after a tragic illness. Newman felt the loss, although Rose had never entered fully into the Movement; neither was he in deep sympathy with the line Newman had taken. Yet Newman was to pay him this tribute:

> To mention Mr Hugh Rose's name is to kindle in the minds of those who knew him a host of pleasant and affectionate remembrances. He was the man above all others fitted by his cast of mind and literary powers to make a stand, if a stand could be made, against the calamity of the times. He was gifted with a high and large mind, and a true sensibility of what was great and beautiful; he wrote with warmth and energy; and he had a cool head

and cautious judgment. He spent his strength and shortened his life, *Pro Ecclesia Dei*, as he understood that sovereign idea.[32]

It was with 'warmth and energy' that Newman approached the lives of the Fathers. In his account of the early life of St Antony, the first monk, he argued that it would be a mistake to suppose that we needed to quit our temporal calling and go into retirement, in order to serve God more acceptably. Christianity is a religion for this world, for the busy and the influential, for the rich and powerful, as well as for the poor; but he felt that it was praiseworthy that a few should take up this calling, and it is undeniable that for some it was a duty. The mind of true Christianity was expansive enough to admit such a vocation of abandonment; but Newman saw that the Protestant philosophy forbade it; in the England of the day St Antony 'would have been exposed to a serious temptation of becoming a fanatic'.[33] Protestantism forbade all the higher and noble impulses of the mind, and forced men to eat, drink and be merry, whether they would or no.

> If the primitive Christians are to be trusted as witnesses of the genius of the Gospel system, certainly it is that elastic and comprehensive character which removes the more powerful temptations to extravagance, by giving, as far as possible, a sort of indulgence to the feelings and motives which lead to it, correcting them the while, purifying them, and reining them in, ere they get excessive. Thus, whereas our reason naturally loves to expatiate at will to and fro through all subjects known and unknown, Catholicism does not oppress us with an irrational bigotry, prescribing to us the very minutest details of thought, so that a man can never have an opinion of his own; on the contrary, its creed is ever what it was, and never moves out of the ground which it originally occupied, and it is cautious and precise in its decisions, and distinguishes between things necessary and things pious to believe, between wilfulness and ignorance. At the same time, it asserts the supremacy of faith, the guilt of unbelief, and the divine mission of the Church; so that reason is brought round again and subdued to the obedience of Christ, at the very time when it seems to be launching forth without chart upon the ocean of speculation. And it pursues the same course in matters of conduct. It opposes the intolerance of what are called 'sensible Protestants'. It is shocked at the tyranny of those who will not let a man do anything out of the way without stamping him with the name of fanatic. It deals softly with the ardent and impetuous, saying, in effect – 'My child, you may do as many great things as you will; but I have already made a list for you to select from. You are too docile to pursue ends merely because they are of your own choosing; you seek them because they are great. You wish to live above the common course of a Christian; – I can teach you to do this without arrogance.'

Meanwhile the sensible Protestant divine keeps to his point, hammering away on his own ideas, urging every one to be as every one else, and moulding all minds upon his small model; and when he has made his ground good to his own admiration, he finds that half his flock have after all turned Wesleyans or Independents, by way of searching for something divine and transcendental.[34]

With what satisfaction Newman noted that the life of St Antony, written by his friend, the great Athanasius, had been handed down to us. Although some scholars had doubted its authenticity, he could not conceive that any question could be raised with justice about its substantial integrity. It was true, he admitted, that Antony must be accounted an enthusiastic, according to the English view of things, but he had been longing for some higher rule of life than any which the ordinary forms of society admitted. Had Antony lived in nineteenth-century England he would have found the lines of behaviour too rigidly drawn to include any character of mind that was much out of the way, any rule that was not 'gentlemanlike', 'comfortable', 'established', and hearing nothing of the Catholic Church, he might possibly have broken what he could not bend.

The question is not, whether such impatience is not open to the charge of wilfulness and self-conceit; but whether, on the contrary, such special resignation to worldly comforts as we see around us, is not often the characteristic of nothing else than selfishness and sloth;— whether there are not minds with ardent feelings, keen imaginations, and undisciplined tempers, who are under a strong irritation prompting them to run wild;— whether it is not our duty (so to speak) to play with such, carefully letting out line enough lest they snap it,— and whether the Protestant Establishment is as indulgent and as wise as might be desired in its treatment of such persons, inasmuch as it provides no occupation for them, does not understand how to turn them to account, lets them run to waste, tempts them to dissent, loses them, is weakened by the loss, and then denounces them.[35]

Newman saw in the conflict and the calm of the first founder of the monastic system a possible pattern for himself. With the resignation of Bloxam and his vacating the Barnes household, during the Lent of 1840 Newman decided to move into his room and, apart from the necessary attendance at St Mary's on Sundays, he remained at Littlemore, subjecting himself to a rigorous regime of fasting and penance. He slept on the floor, and his particular care in reciting the breviary slowly and reverently took him several hours of the day. This austere period of forty days turned out to be one of the happiest of his life. After he had been there for only a week he wrote to Bloxam, 'I am so drawn to the place ... it will be an effort to go back to St Mary's

... If it were not for those poor undergraduates who are, after all, not my charge and the Sunday Communion, I should be sorely tempted to pitch my tent here.'[36] During the day he would visit the school and instruct the children, and lead them in singing with an old violin he had 'rummaged out'. His attempts to introduce the children to Gregorian chant made them smile, though he realised it was probably him and not the music they were smiling at, though one imagines they might have smiled more at the school mistress who had taken to the bottle. 'She does drink badly,'[37] Newman informed James Mozley. Each morning and afternoon he said prayers in the little church and on Sundays, besides his visit to his larger church, he catechised the children there.

After Easter Newman returned to Oriel, but he had laid plans for a dramatic change in his life. On 28 May he informed Jemima:

> We have bought nine or ten acres of ground at Littlemore, the field between the Chapel and the Barnes's, and, so be it, in due time, shall erect a monastic house upon it. This may lead ultimately to my resigning my fellowship; but these are visions as yet. The children are improving their singing; we hope to be able to chant the whole service with them.[38]

The secret was out, but only to a few friends. It seems Bloxam, whose father had just died, had been influential in persuading the farmer to part with the land. Although no longer Newman's curate, a position now held by William Copeland, he had remained close to him. During Lent he recalled how, after seeing to his father's funeral, he had hurried out to Littlemore to visit the vicar, now living in his old room. 'As I passed the window,' he remembered, 'I saw him kneeling in prayer.'[39]

Newman had seen St Antony as 'calm and composed, manly, intrepid, magnanimous, full of affectionate loyalty to the Church and to the Truth'.[40] If he were an enthusiast there was nothing unstable or undutiful about his enthusiasm which was of a subdued and Christian form. The state of Newman's own mind, however, was far from 'calm and composed'. As he continued to reason out the true position of the Anglican Church he was determined to be unswayed by imagination. It would be a matter of reason alone, whatever the emotional appeal might be, yet he knew that his main argument was now reduced to the positive and special charges he could bring against Rome. He no longer had a positive Anglican theory. As he put it simply: 'I was very nearly a pure Protestant.'[41]

From now on, as his doubt increased, he fought the harder to suppress it. He told Jemima of his serious apprehensions 'lest any religious body is strong enough to withstand the league of evil but the Roman Church'.[42] It was certainly wonderful, he said, how good principles had shot up in the

Church of England; as yet he was not clear that they were not tending to Rome. He was very averse to speaking against doctrines, which might possibly turn out to be true, though he had no reason yet for thinking they were; but he had for two years now recognised in himself a growing dislike of speaking against the Church of Rome or her formal doctrines. One thing was certain, many of the younger members of the Movement were fast veering that way.

The Anglican formularies remained the chief stumbling-block. By them all Anglicans seemed bound to Protestantism. Was it possible that the Thirty-nine Articles might be given a Catholic interpretation? At the time Newman had hopes they might and during the autumn he endeavoured to argue the case. The result appeared anonymously in February 1841 as *Remarks on Certain Passages in the Thirty-nine Articles*, the famous Tract 90.

The Thirty-nine Articles, a transformation of Cranmer's original Forty-two, had been framed in Elizabeth i's reign by Convocation in 1553 and ratified by Parliament in 1571; they have remained unchanged ever since. Whether the intention of the bishops had been to assert an agreement between the Church of England and the Catholic Church seems doubtful in view of the fact that, to begin with, only those who had been ordained by Catholic rites were obliged under penalty of deprivation to set their names to the Articles, though, later, acceptance of them became a condition of every ordination. It is certain, however, that the Articles asserted the power and independence of the English State in its relation to the Church as one of the forms of national life, and they underlined the Church of England's attitude towards Rome and the other Protestant bodies.

Newman's intention in Tract 90 was to remove all obstacles that lay in the way of recognising that Anglican teaching was Apostolic and Catholic in character. His first principle was 'Our Church teaches the Primitive Ancient Faith', and, therefore, 'It is the duty which we owe both to the Catholic Church, and to our own, to take our reformed confessions in the most Catholic sense they will admit.'[43] It did not matter, he argued, what the framers of the Articles had intended, their particular belief was not necessary to a true interpretation of them; what mattered was a Catholic interpretation as far as the wording would admit or any ambiguity required.

> Their framers constructed them in such a way as best to comprehend those who did not go as far in Protestantism as themselves. Anglo-Catholics are but the successors and representatives of those moderate reformers; and their case has been directly anticipated in the wording of the Articles. It follows that they are not perverting, they are using them for an express purpose for which among others their authors framed them.[44]

As the Articles had been framed before the Council of Trent Newman was able, though not for the first time, to draw a distinction between the word 'Romish' as used in the Articles and 'Tridentine'. The Council had clearly defined its doctrine, but the framers of the Articles, Newman argued, had used the term 'Romish' in a vaguer and more indeterminate sense. It was not necessary perhaps, as Wiseman had insisted, to swallow the Council of Trent as a whole.

Throughout his life Newman continued to defend the main argument of Tract 90; the Articles were 'patient but not ambitious of a Catholic interpretation'. However, he later realised he had misinformed his readers over Article 31 which spoke of Masses for the dead as 'blasphemous fables and dangerous deceits'. Newman had quibbled over the words 'Mass' and 'Masses', arguing that the sacrifice of the Mass itself was not meant by the phrase 'The sacrifice of Masses'.

> It is conceived that the Article before us neither speaks against the Mass itself, nor against its being an offering for the quick and the dead for the remission of sin; but against its being viewed, on the one hand, as independent of or distinct from the Sacrifice on the Cross, which is a blasphemy, and, on the other, its being directed to the emolument of those to whom it pertains to celebrate it, which is imposture in addition.[45]

So he had written in 1841, but in 1883, seven years before his death, he admitted that 'What the 31st Article repudiates is undeniably the central and most sacred doctrine of the Catholic Religion; and so its wording has ever been read since it was drawn up.'[46]

The Tract had ended with words which seemed doubtful to most people even at the time.

> The Protestant confession was drawn up with the purpose of including Catholics; and Catholics now will not be excluded. What was an economy in the Reformers is a protection to us. What would have been a perplexity to us then, is a perplexity to Protestants now. We could not then have found fault with their words; they cannot now repudiate our meaning.[47]

How wrong he was! Protestants were perplexed in the extreme, and some were outraged. 'Do you know I am getting into a scrape about Tract Ninety?'[48] he informed Bowden. 'People are so angry they will attempt to do anything. I have just heard that the Board of Heads of Houses is most fierce with the Tract, and Tracts generally, and means to do something.'[49]

Even to his sympathisers he seemed to have gone too far. Although the Tract had appeared anonymously, its style was recognised immediately. Golightly was quick to arouse opposition. As Richard Church informed Frederick Rogers, Golightly had ordered so many copies of the Tract, which he was describing as the greatest 'curiosity', that the bookseller, Parker, could hardly supply him. Golightly's diligence and activity were unwearied and he sent copies to all the bishops. 'In the course of a week he had got the agitation into a satisfactory state, and his efforts were redoubled.'[50] Through his efforts four Senior Tutors charged the editor of the Tract with 'suggesting and opening a way, by which men might, at least in the case of Roman views, violate their solemn engagements to the University'.[51]

On 12 March Newman told Jemima he feared he was 'clean dished'. The Heads of Houses were at that very moment concocting a manifesto against him, but he did not fear for his cause; he and his friends had had too great a run of luck. It was necessary, he felt, then to explain his intention more fully and, as was the custom in controversy, he wrote a letter to an impartial observer. Richard Jelf was a Fellow of Oriel and a Canon of Christ Church, and in his *Letter to Dr Jelf* Newman claimed he had been misunderstood; but he admitted that, although in principle he had no doubt he was right, he might have advocated truth in a wrong way. He was anxious particularly to emphasise that the Articles did contain a condemnation of the authoritative teaching of the Church of Rome on the doctrines of Purgatory, of Pardons, of the Worship and Adoration of Images and Relics, of Invocation of Saints, and of the Mass.

> As to the present authoritative teaching of the Church of Rome, to judge by what we see of it in public, I think it goes very far indeed to substitute another Gospel for the true one. Instead of setting before the soul the Holy Trinity, heaven and hell; it does seem to me, as a popular system, to preach the Blessed Virgin and the Saints and Purgatory. If there ever was a system which required reformation, it is that of Rome at this day, or in other words (as I should call it) Romanism or Popery.[52]

Surely such words were enough to satisfy his critics? They were, but the timing of his letter was too late to prevent the Hebdomadal Board by a majority of nineteen to two from censuring the Tract. The Board found that the Tract aimed at reconciling its readers with the very errors the Articles were designed to counteract and copies of the censure were displayed prominently in all the Colleges. Church was to describe the Board's action as 'an ungenerous and stupid blunder, such as men make, when they think or are told that "something must be done", and do not know what'. Certainly, it has been generally accepted that had Newman's letter to Jelf been awaited the censure would have been unnecessary.

It was not long before Bishop Bagot became involved. 'I cannot refrain from expressing my anxious wish that for the peace of the Church discussions upon the articles should not be continued in the publication of the "Tracts for the Times",' he wrote. 'You will not, I am sure, mistake the spirit and feeling with which this wish is expressed, but will consider it as the wish of one who has a sincere personal regard for yourself.'[53] The Bishop's attitude appeared to show great generosity, for he neither endorsed the University censure nor did he support the Four Tutors, but he decided to discuss the matter with Pusey, summoning him to Cuddesdon 'for a little private conversation on this painful position of things'. He proposed that the Tracts should be discontinued, Tract 90 should not be reprinted, and Newman should make it known publicly that this was done in deference to the Bishop's wish. When Newman was informed he realised the second proposal amounted to the suppression of the Tract; this put him in a difficult position, but if the Bishop wished it he would do it. 'It seems to me that I shall be observing my duty to the Bishop by suppressing the Tract, and my duty to my principles by resigning my living,' he told his friend Dr Walter Hook, the Vicar of Leeds.

In the event the Bishop did not insist on suppression, but instructed that Newman should write a letter stating that Tract 90 had been 'objectionable, and may tend to disturb the peace and tranquillity of the Church'. He was also to suggest that the 'Tracts for the Times' should be discontinued. The letter was sent on 31 March. Two days later the Bishop acknowledged:

> I cannot let our late communications terminate without a few last words to express my entire satisfaction, and gratification with your letters received yesterday morning, both printed and written.
>
> It is a comfort to me too (now that calm has, as I hope, succeeded the threatened storm) to feel assured, that though I have perhaps caused pain to one in whom I feel much interest, and for whom I have a great regard, you will never regret having written that letter to me. It is one calculated to soften and to silence opponents, as also to attach and to regulate friends, whilst the tone and temper of mind with which it is written must please and gratify all who read it.[54]

By his obedience to his Bishop Newman gave up his place in the Movement, but he knew he could not give up his duties towards the many and various minds who had more or less been brought into it by him. He was entering that period of 'tedious decline, with seasons of rallying and seasons of falling back', in his relationship with his Church, a period he would later look upon as his Anglican 'death-bed'.

PART II

The Old Religion

8

Nicholas Wiseman

1840–43

In the autumn of 1840 Nicholas Wiseman, now a Bishop, had become President of St Mary's, Oscott. This college, situated close to the old road, the Icknield Way, a little north of Birmingham, had been opened as a school and seminary in 1794, but it had long existed as a Catholic mission since Father Andrew Bromwich, a priest trained at the English College in Lisbon, had come to work there in 1678. Knowing its long history and its ideal position more or less equidistant between the south and north, Wiseman was determined that Oscott should become the centre of the Catholic movement in England, for he had no doubt that it would not be long before his vision of a new era would come to fulfilment.

> Among the providential agencies that seemed justly timed, and even necessary for the hoped-for influx of converts appeared to me the erection of this noble College in the very heart of England. Often in my darkest days and hours, feeling as if alone in my hopes, have I walked in front of it, and casting my eyes towards it, exclaimed to myself, 'No, it was not to educate a few boys that this was erected, but to be the rallying point of the yet silent but vast movement towards the Catholic Church, which has commenced and must prosper.' I felt as assured of this as if the word of prophecy had spoken it.[1]

Wiseman knew Oscott well, having preached a retreat there during his visit to England in 1839. This was just a year after the College had moved into its fine new buildings designed by Pugin, so that Wiseman's arrival at Pugin Lodge where he vested for the procession on the morning of 9 September 1840 was the beginning of one of the most magnificent Catholic ceremonies held in England since the Reformation. The new President, wear-

93

ing the Odescalchi cape donated by the Earl of Shrewsbury, and a jewelled mitre, processed up the drive and along the terraces in front of the college, while the choir sang *Ecce Sacerdos Magnus*. As he entered the chapel to the chanting of the *Te Deum* it seemed as though the whole splendour of Rome had once again returned in England. But was England ready? Not in the least; neither were Wiseman's fellow Catholics particularly impressed.

When Oscott had opened as a seminary in 1794 it was only recently that Catholics in England were able to worship legally in public after some two hundred years restriction. The Second Catholic Relief Act of 1791 meant that the Mass could be celebrated openly, though only in specially licensed buildings, without the possible fear of reprisal or punishment under the various Penal Laws against Catholic life and practice passed by Parliament gradually since Elizabethan times. How strongly those laws were enforced had always varied from region to region, and during the eighteenth century they had been barely enforced anywhere, although the last man to be sentenced to perpetual imprisonment 'for exercising the functions of a Popish priest' was John Baptist Maloney, brought to trial at the Surrey Summer Assizes in Croydon as recently as 1767. In fact, Maloney was released after four years and his sentence commuted to banishment, but the case had led to much anti-Catholic feeling, especially in the south, and some Mass centres which had survived for many years without trouble were closed down.

In order that the position of Catholics in England at the beginning of the nineteenth-century religious revival should be properly understood a very brief account of their immediate past may be helpful.

Although Catholics have little to thank James ɪɪ for, it was on 11 January 1688, at his request, that Pope Innocent xɪ divided England into four Vicariates, each with its own titular bishop. These bishops were not formally known as such, being referred to as Vicars Apostolic; neither did they take their titles from English place-names, but were raised to sees *in partibus infidelium*, places no longer dioceses in lands long overrun by the Muslims. For instance, Bishop Giffard, the first Vicar Apostolic of the Midland District, was the Bishop of Madaura, and Wiseman himself was to become Bishop of Melipotamus. The arrangement had been set up only just in time, for with the flight of James ɪɪ the Catholics were to suffer a bitter retribution, and together with the Unitarians they were excluded from the Toleration Act. Two of the newly-appointed Vicars Apostolic were imprisoned in the Tower. This was the beginning of what came to be known as the 'the era of bloodless martyrdom'.

Early in William and Mary's reign an Act was passed 'for amoving papists and reputed papists from the cities of London and Westminster, and ten miles distance from the same'. In spite of this restriction the Mass continued to be said secretly in both those 'cities' and openly in several foreign Embassy Chapels, the Sardinians having built their Chapel especially large to accommodate a swelled congregation. Under an Act of 1690 no Catholic was admitted into either the legal or the medical professions, which meant that Dr Betts, who had been physician to both Charles II and James II, was expelled from the College of Physicians. In 1700 another Act 'for further preventing the growth of Popery', allowed the next Protestant heir in a family to inherit any Catholic estate, and offered £100 to anyone willing to inform on a priest. It had been under this Act that Fr Maloney was convicted. Because of the bounty-hunters greedy for their £100, in 1706 Bishop Gifford, who had moved to the London District, was forced to move his lodgings fourteen times to avoid arrest.

When Elizabeth I came to the throne it has been estimated that some two-thirds of the population were Catholics, or at least Catholic sympathisers, but by the beginning of the eighteenth century, owing to the 'success' of the Penal Laws, the number had dwindled to very few. In 1717, two years after the First Jacobite Rebellion, the number was estimated at 70,000, with some 500 priests, all trained abroad, active in the country. The number was always higher in the north, and in some few areas, like Ribblesdale, in Lancashire, the population had remained almost exclusively Catholic, as though the Reformation had never happened.

The fact that many important families and local gentry had stood firm throughout the penal times was to give strength and inspiration to the less hardy. Large houses, often conveniently situated in remote areas, where a priest could be reasonably safe from arrest, were, during the eighteenth century, able to keep Catholic life alive. It was to such centres as these that the Vicars Apostolic would tour the country to confirm and exhort their dwindling flocks, and it was from these families and their retainers that young men went overseas to train for the priesthood at the English Colleges in Rome, Lisbon, Madrid, Seville, Valladolid, and especially at Douai, the college founded by William Allen, which had trained hundreds of priests, some 160 of whom had sacrificed their lives to serve the 'Old Religion'. Such men did not hold with the Established Church's claim to continuity. The Mass was quite clearly condemned, but England had been Catholic for over a thousand years and would one day be Catholic again. With St Edmund Campion those martyred priests would have said to their fellow countrymen who brought them to the scaffold as traitors, in what lies our treachery? In condemning us, you are condemning your own ancestors.

The Jacobite Rebellions aroused much anti-Catholic feeling, though Catholics were not alone in supporting the Stuart cause. In 1715 the Catholic Lord Derwentwater and several others were executed, and the estates of any gentleman thought to have played an active part were confiscated. This resulted in an Act of 1722 which required all Catholic landowners to pay a double land tax, causing some families who had struggled nobly for years to conform to the Established Church, bringing about the closure of their chapel and forcing the priest to move elsewhere. However, although Prince Charles Edward had much support from Scottish Catholics in 1745, few of note joined him in England, and Bishop Challoner, the coadjutor of the London District, actively discouraged support. Inevitably the bishops came under suspicion, and in 1747 Dr York, coadjutor of the Western District, was 'compelled to fly from house to house and from city to city'.[2]

Although they were liable to contempt and barred from all offices of state, many Catholics achieved fame of one sort or another, men like the poet, Alexander Pope, and the Benedictine, Bishop Walmesley, of the Western District, who was a noted mathematician and a Fellow of the Royal Society. It is recorded of Walmesley that he had voluntarily given up his mathematical studies because a theorem had once distracted him while offering the Mass.

No Vicar Apostolic achieved more than Richard Challoner, who worked as a bishop in the London District from 1741 until his death forty years later. At first he was coadjutor with right to succession to Bishop Petre, who through weak health was living in semi-retirement. Challoner succeeded in 1758 at the age of sixty-eight. Not only was he energetic pastorally, travelling round his vast district in very difficult circumstances, but also his simple, straightforward writing became a great source of encouragement. Challoner knew that his people needed instruction and strengthening, but also that they needed to resist the constant barrage of Protestant propaganda directed against them, so that such formidable titles as *The Unerring Teaching Authority of the Catholic Church in Matters of Faith* and *The Catholic Christian Instructed* became as important as his devotional *The Garden of the Soul*, a guide to the spiritual life 'meant not to supersede but to supplement other prayer books'. Besides such works as these, and there were many, with the help of a collaborator, the Carmelite friar, Fr Francis Blyth, Challoner revised the Douai Bible and added notes. This was published in 1750 and, although some alterations were made later to his version of the New Testament, the Old Testament remained as he left it and is used by many Catholics still. His other important book *Memoirs of the Missionary Priests* related the heroic suffering of the many post-Reformation martyrs who had died for their faith, particularly in Elizabethan times.

Incidents in Challoner's life give a vivid insight into the secrecy necessary at certain times to avoid arrest: he preached and confirmed in locked rooms, in taverns and cock-pits, where a steady watch could be kept for informers. At the Ship in Little Turnstile, in Lincoln's Inn Fields, the congregation would sit with ale-mugs at their elbows, so that a celebration of Mass might swiftly be seen as a rowdy night at the tavern.

When Challoner had succeeded Bishop Petre as Vicar Apostolic his own health was failing, so he took as his coadjutor the brother of the Earl of Shrewsbury, Bishop James Talbot, but he continued to work himself, living through even more difficult times. During the campaign of terror that imprisoned Father Maloney, Bishop Talbot was also arrested, though he was quickly released, and Challoner too was subjected to constant questioning about his priests and where they were working. It saddened him that the chief informer, William Payne, had tricked him by pretending he wished to be received into the Church and beginning a course of instruction. Such meanness impressed few people, however, and even those entrusted to enforce the law were sympathetic. The Lord Mayor issued a warning against Payne's treachery, and eventually the Lord Chief Justice, Lord Mansfield, was able to get round the law by insisting that a priest's ordination must be proved before a case could be brought to trial.

In 1778 a respite came through the passing of the First Catholic Relief Act, which swept away some but by no means all of the penal restrictions. This measure was not the result of charity so much as the need to recruit more troops for the American and French wars. But now Catholics were free to inherit or purchase land and priests were free from prosecution provided, within six months of the Act, a Catholic had sworn an oath of allegiance to George III. Challoner issued an instruction to his clergy to offer prayers for the King and Queen, but soon he was exclaiming: 'Alas! How soon may all this be turned against us', for almost exactly two years later the Gordon Riots broke out, and the bawling of 'No Popery' was heard in the London streets. These riots were incited by the Protestant Association under the leadership of its recently elected President, Lord George Gordon. Lord George's part in the business had a distinct irony about it since his family came from a staunchly Catholic part of Scotland; his father, the Duke of Gordon, had been brought up a Catholic, and his aunt, the Duchess of Perth, had been the mainstay of Scottish Catholicism. As Bishop Matthew expressed it in his *Catholicism in England*, 'while the Londoners supporting the Association had the most ingenuous hatred of Popery, a religion of which they had the slightest knowledge, Lord Gordon had a fanatical distaste for the familiar.' It was widely realised even at the time that Gordon was a mindless fanatic; Walpole called him a 'mad dog', a debauchee 'with more knavery than mission,' but he was able to stir up the crowd and several Embassy Chapels were destroyed; anywhere, in fact, associated with the dreaded papists was burnt and pillaged. Challoner took refuge in a friend's house in Finchley, but the whole experience was so distressing that during the following months, although he gave to his faithful what comfort he could, his health gave way completely and he died early in the January of 1781. As one of his priests said of him:

Examples of virtue have at all times a much greater influence on our practice than the strongest reasoning, though unfortunately they are so much harder to be met with in these depraved days. When I say that Bishop Challoner was a model of Christian virtue, every breast glows with the conviction of the truth ... when on every occasion I represent Bishop Challoner as a saint, I say no more of him now after his death, than all who knew him have said of him during his life.[3]

When Wiseman came to consider the life and achievement of his most humble predecessor in 1842 he wrote:

Of the truly venerable, learned and saintly Dr Challoner, it would be both unjust and ungrateful were any English Catholic to speak in terms other than of profound admiration and sincere respect. He has alone furnished us with a library of religious works, the privation of which would create a void, not easily to be filled up by many other men's writings. The catechism from which we learnt the first rudiments of our faith, that by which we early became acquainted with sacred history, or versed in controversial discussion, the prayer book with which we have been most familiar, the meditations which have afforded daily instructions to us in families and in communities, many of our most solid and most clear works of controversy, the charming records of our fathers in the faith, the missionary priests, the martyrology of our ancient Church and many other works, we owe to this really great and good man; and we know not what we should have done, or what we should have been without him. He supplied, in fact, almost the entire range of necessary or useful religious literature for his fellow-countrymen; and that at a time when such a supply must have been truly as a boon from heaven. Yes, and at a time when such works were not published without some personal risk and danger.[4]

Newman too would soon be speaking of 'the pious prelate, to whom the English Church is so much indebted'.

The two Relief Acts had made it easier for Catholics to enter into public life, although still no Catholic peer might take his seat in the House of Lords, neither might any Catholic read for a degree at Oxford or Cambridge, but under the Act of 1791 the Bar was thrown open to Catholic lawyers. However, throughout the penal times there had been Catholic lawyers actively involved in giving advice and protection, as far as they were able, though not officially recognised; some, like James Booth, John Maire and Matthew Duane, rose to the highest eminence as conveyancers.

One distressing result of the First Relief Act had been a growing rift between the Catholic gentry and the bishops. Not unnaturally the leaders of the laity, who had more than anyone during the difficult times helped to keep the

Faith alive by their support of the priests and their missions, wished to enter fully into the affairs of the country, and they saw the bishops as potential frustrators of their aspirations. It did not apply to all by any means, but there was certainly a growing feeling of distrust; the bishops were, to some minds, thought to be taking too strict a view of the position of Catholics. 'There was undoubtedly a feeling that the accepted attitude of dependence on the Holy See was incompatible with the national aspirations and duties of an Englishman; and it was even questioned whether the Penal Laws themselves had not been, at least to some extent, due to the unreasonable attitude assumed by the Catholics of former days.'[5]

The Vicars Apostolic, for their part, felt that now they could work completely openly. They should take full control of the affairs of the Church in England, and their anxiety over the way things seemed to be developing was not without cause. Fortunately, they would find a champion in the person of John Milner, a priest of the mission in Winchester from 1779 till 1803, who himself would become Vicar Apostolic of the Midland District, remaining there until his death in 1826.

It was at the chambers of the Catholic lawyer Mr William Sheldon in Gray's Inn Square that what was called the Catholic Committee came into being; this was a group of leading laymen anxious to 'manage the public affairs of the Catholics in the kingdom'. One measure they felt important was the replacement of the Vicars Apostolic by a hierarchy of bishops, something wished for, it was argued, by the majority of the clergy. There was no doubt that the members of the Committee were more suited to negotiate with the government than the bishops might have been, and it was largely owing to them, in the wake of a rapid move towards toleration in Ireland, that the Second Relief Act was passed. Gradually Catholics were less seen as foreign and subversive, and among the Catholic gentry themselves there developed more strongly a spirit which had over the years come to be known as Cisalpine, a word suggesting the lands north of the Alps, looking away from the city, as opposed to the Ultramontane attitude, which looked 'beyond the mountains', directly towards Rome. Simply, those who fostered a Cisalpine spirit were quite prepared to accept the dogmatic teaching of the Holy See, but scorned all other papal interference likely to come through the Vicars Apostolic who were answerable for their every action to Propaganda, the name given formerly to what since the Second Vatican Council has become the Congregation for the Evangelisation of Peoples. The Cisalpine spirit was in many ways similar to the Gallican spirit which had prevailed for so long in France. Ironically, it was events in France that would come to the bishops' rescue.

The French Revolution affected England in many ways, but for the Catholics, it was to change their situation radically. Firstly, all the religious houses, schools and seminaries which had operated in France for almost two hundred years were forced to move back home and, secondly, the conditions became so difficult for many of the French clergy, those that had supported the *ancien régime* and now refused to take the Civic Oath, that in 1792 literally thousands of them sought refuge in England. It is true that most of them returned to France as soon as possible, but for a while there were almost a thousand refugee priests living out their time in the King's House at Winchester alone. By 1797 it was estimated that some twelve thousand French were still living in the country, of which number six thousand were laity, including women and children.

The arrival of the French emigrés meant that immediate plans were implemented to raise funds for their relief. This great act of charity first instigated by the Marquis of Buckingham and John Wilmot, the Member of Parliament for Tiverton, also involved men like Pitt and Burke and Wilberforce. In very few weeks £33,775 had been raised, sufficient money to meet the exiles' immediate needs. The University of Oxford had donated £480.

The French were exceedingly grateful, and their leader, the Bishop of St Pol de Léon, issued a pastoral letter expressing his deep feeling of gratitude which Milner translated into English. The Bishop also gave careful instructions as to how his priests should behave while in England, in which he repeated his thanks.

> The first feeling with which every French priest was filled on his arrival in
> this hospitable land must doubtless have been an outburst of thankfulness
> to the God who has delivered him from all the dangers which have overtaken
> his unfortunate country. Every one will certainly have hastened to return their
> thanks to the God of goodness, especially by celebrating the holy sacrifice
> of the Mass for that intention. It was indeed a small thing for this merciful
> God to rescue us from the most horrible persecution which impiety has ever
> raised against the priesthood. The asylum to which he has led us offers to
> each nothing but tender and generous hearts. In the midst of this nation,
> once the rival of our own, who amongst us has not found friends and brethren,
> who hastened to recompense him for all he has suffered![6]

The patience with which the majority of these priests accepted their situation, their piety, and above all their cheerfulness were noticed by all who came in contact with them. Although the nineteen French bishops came from noble Royalist families, most of the priests came from among the poorer classes, 'the most lowly and humble human beings, not only the friends, but the companions of the poor, who broke their bread with them, and who shared with unfeigned sympathy in all their abjection and want'. However, they all saw their exile as an opportunity to pray earnestly, not only for their own country, but also for the country that had given them refuge, as their Bishop exhorted the priests at Winchester.

> Let us specially beg of God that He will ever preserve England from those principles of ungodliness, license and anarchy which have brought on France the scourges now afflicting her. These suffrages and frequent prayers have become to us a real duty; for gratitude is such to all men.[7]

When the news reached England that Louis xvi had been executed, a solemn Requiem was sung in the new Catholic chapel in Winchester at which so many people attended that there was not even standing room. Milner had preached himself, and had published his sermon. There had been great curiosity in the town and all the approaches to the chapel were impassable because of the crowd, a crowd that would learn in a few days that France and England were at war.

Milner held a similar service in the following year after the death of Marie Antoinette, as he recorded.

> We had a service for the French Queen last Saturday, helped by the regimental band, and attended by the Marquis and all the officers, most of the clergy, and the principal people of the city and the neighbourhood. The Cenotaph was graced with the bust as large as life in chiaroscuro of the deceased, from the elegant pen of Lady Buckingham.[8]

Such an open display of Catholic worship was something new in England, as were many of the religious exercises which the French took for granted. At the King's House in the city the Blessed Sacrament was exposed throughout the day, and every priest at some time each day would offer his own Mass. One of the problems with so many clergy was finding enough altars for their need. Milner took inspiration from such fervour, finding the French 'highly edifying and worthy of imitation in many respects'. As David Matthew has said: 'Throughout the country the French priests awakened sentiments of respectful compassion. They bore their sufferings with a dignity in keeping with their respectful character and it was understood that they encouraged their flock in their moral duty by lofty considerations. On the other hand the very generosity of the sentiments which animated their hosts prevented the English from contemplating the possibility that these priests had a religious message for England.'[9]

Yet the influence of all this on the native Catholic population was very great, as was the other effect of the Revolution, the closing down of the English Colleges abroad. In the autumn of 1793 the students and professors at Douai were all sent to prison.

Although the Relief Act of 1791 had expressly forbidden the foundation of religious houses, it was felt that the circumstances were so unusual that provided colleges and convents were established quietly the English might slowly become accustomed to them. In fact, there were already schools in existence, schools like Old Hall Green, at Ware in Hertfordshire, and Crook Hall near Durham. It was relatively easy for Dr Douglass, the Vicar Apostolic of the London District, to develop a school like Old Hall Green into a larger establishment. So it was that St Edmund's College came to be the new Douai in the south, and Crook Hall, later to move to Ushaw, became the Douai in the north.

As the war dragged on it began to dawn on many of those who had spent much of their lives teaching in the colleges abroad that their future now lay in England; besides they could see that the attitude towards Catholics had changed. While this attitude was by no means enthusiastic, it was certainly tolerant. During the following few years the Jesuits, 'the Gentlemen of Liège', as they were discreetly named, settled at Stonyhurst, a mansion given to them by Thomas Weld of Lulworth. The Benedictines came to Acton Burnell, in Shropshire, the home of one of their former pupils. Eventually, in 1803, a group of these moved to Ampleforth, in Yorkshire, while others remained in Shropshire until their move to Downside, near Bath, in 1814.

Among those who had fled home from France was Dr John Bew, the President of St Gregory's Seminary in Paris. In 1794, Dr Bew was appointed the first President of Oscott, and therefore Wiseman's predecessor, though it would be another eight years before Wiseman was born.

Nicholas Patrick Stephen Wiseman had been born in Spain on 3 August 1802, so he was a year younger than Newman. His grandfather, James Wiseman, an Irishman from Waterford, had established the firm of Wiseman Brothers trading between Ireland and Spain. Largely to evade the rigours of the Penal Laws, his son, also named James, had settled in Seville in 1771. James Wiseman married twice, and Nicholas was the younger son of his second wife, Xaviera Strange, a well-connected girl, whose family lived at Aylwardstown Castle in County Kilkenny. Sadly, James Wiseman died in 1805, after collapsing at the table during a birthday party. For two years his widow remained in Spain, before taking her three children to London and subsequently home to Ireland.

'I arrived in this neighbourhood at Aylwardstown without being able to form a sentence, or perhaps being able to speak ten words in the language in which I now address you,'[10] Wiseman told a Waterford congregation in 1858. His early memories of life in Seville remained vivid and, although he had only been three at the time, he used to recall in later life 'seeing the prize crews brought ashore at Cadiz after the battle of Trafalgar'.[11]

After the boys had spent two years at a boarding school in Waterford,

Mrs Wiseman moved to England and took a house in Durham, so that Nicholas and his elder brother, James, might attend St Cuthbert's College at Ushaw, which was just organising itself after the move from Crook Hall. The first winter in the new, but still unfinished buildings – some walls were unplastered, and windows unglazed and boarded up – was made worse by an outbreak of typhus, which took off five of the fifty students. One of the first sights the young Wisemans might have seen on their arrival were the five small graves all in a row, the only graves in the newly-consecrated college cemetery.

Wiseman was seldom happy at Ushaw. 'I was always considered stupid and dull by my companions,' he recalled, claiming that he made hardly any friends, and never got any notice or favour from superiors. 'But I knew that I was reading a great deal more than others without saying a word about it, both in study time and out of it, and I made myself happy enough. I am sure I never said a witty or clever thing all the time I was at the college, but I used to think a great deal.'[12] Wiseman must have meant that he was considered stupid out of class, for in class he was usually top. Also the claim that his superiors ignored him is unfair, since the Vice-President, John Lingard, the historian, noticed the young boy's ability immediately, and gave him much encouragement, 'specific acts of thoughtful and delicate kindness, which showed a tender heart'. In spite of the difference of age, and though he left the college fairly soon after Wiseman's arrival, Lingard did not forget his former pupil. Wiseman did not see him for fifteen years, but as he later put it: 'There grew up an understanding first, and by degrees a correspondence and an intimacy between us, which continued to the close of his life.'[13] In fact, Lingard died in 1850, a very important year in Wiseman's life.

Wiseman studied at Ushaw from 1810 until 1818, when he was chosen with five other boys to go to the newly-opened English College in Rome. Wiseman never forgot the unusually hair-raising journey from Liverpool to Leghorn by sea, when he witnessed a man falling overboard and drowning off Cape St Vincent, a dog raving about the deck for lack of fresh water, a fire on board, and the time when 'All the passengers were nearly lost in a sudden squall in Ramsey Bay, into which they had been driven by stress of weather, and where they of course landed'.[14] The remaining part of the journey by land was scarcely more inviting; the wayside posts were adorned by the bodies of bandits recently caught and hanged on the spot.

When he arrived at the College Wiseman felt at home immediately.

The house belonged to no one else; it was English ground, a part of the fatherland, a restored inheritance. And though all was neat and trim, dazzling in its whiteness, relieved here and there by tinted architectural members, one could not but feel that we had been transported to the scene of better men and greater things than were likely to arise in the new era that day opened.

The Rector, Dr Gradwell, had prepared as well as possible for the arrival of these, the first students in twenty years, since the College had been forced to close down in 1798. Pillaged by the French, the place had been uninhabited except for the old Italian porter. Next door the Church of the Holy Trinity was largely a ruin when Wiseman first saw it. On that day, 18 December, he had gazed around the roofless building, noticing how the painted walls marked the frames of the altar-pieces. He had stared at the scattered memorials of the past, at the shattered and defaced tombs, some once richly effigied, of an Archbishop of York, or a Prior of Worcester. Among the 'sadder wreckage of the recent storm' he saw bones and skulls from coffins dragged up from the vaults by the French who had taken the lead to convert it to munitions. He had stood where 'many an English pilgrim, gentle or simple, had knelt, leaning on his trusty staff cut in Needwood or the New Forest ... where many and many a student, like those now gathered here, had sobbed his farewell to the happy spring days and the quiet home of youth, before starting on his weary journey to the perils of evil days in his native land'.[15]

On Christmas Eve, Wiseman was among the few privileged students to be presented to Pope Pius VII. As Dr Gradwell recorded in his journal: 'The Holy Father received them standing, shook hands with each, and welcomed them to Rome. He praised the English clergy for their good and peaceful conduct, and their fidelity to the Holy See. He exhorted the youth to learning and piety, and said: "I hope you will do honour both to Rome and to your own country."'[16]

This first meeting with a Pope was, of course, the first of many during Wiseman's life, but it made a lasting impression on him.

Whatever we had read of his gentleness, condescension, and sweetness of his speech, his manner, and his expression, was fully justified, realized, and made personal. It was not from what we had heard, but from what we had seen and experienced, that we must needs now revere and love him. The friendly and almost national grasp of the hand – after the due homage had been willingly paid – between the Head of the Catholic Church, venerable by his very age, and a youth who had nothing even of promise; the first exhortation on entering a course of ecclesiastical study – its very inaugural discourse, from him who was believed to be the fountain of spiritual wisdom on earth – these surely formed a double tie, not to be broken, but rather strengthened by every subsequent experience.[17]

Wiseman was no youth 'who had nothing even of promise'; for the next six years he devoted his time to hard and regular study, gaining distinction in the natural sciences as well as in dogmatic and scholastic theology. In July 1824, at the age of twenty-two, he took his degree of Doctor of Divinity, after sustaining a successful public disputation before a celebrated audience, some of whom were there to try to catch him out.

> I remember well in the particular instance before my eye that a monk, clothed in white, glided in and sat down in the inner circle; but though a special messenger was despatched to him by the professors, he shook his head and declined becoming an assailant. He had been sent to listen and report. It was Fr Cappellari, who, in less than six years, was Pope Gregory xvi.[18]

Wiseman was ordained to the priesthood eight months later on 19 March 1825, and in the following year he became Vice-Rector of the College. Although he would never be renowned for his organising ability, he carried out his duties in this respect reliably enough, but, more to the point, his reputation as a scholar of distinction was growing rapidly. No one recognised this more than Pope Leo xii, who had been elected to the papacy on the death of Pius vii in 1823. After the remarkable success of Wiseman's *Horae Syriacae*, a short work in which he among other things argued for the literal meaning of the text *Hoc est enim corpus meum*, the Pope sought to honour him, and in 1827 appointed him Professor of Hebrew and Syro-Chaldaic at the Roman University, a fitting reward for the many hours Wiseman had spent in the Vatican Library poring over Syriac manuscripts under the helpful eye of Cardinal Mai. Soon he was in communication with all the Orientalists of the day.

Wiseman's command of foreign languages was something that amazed Newman, for not only was he fluent in Spanish, Italian, French, German and Portuguese, often preaching in these languages without notes, but he had also mastered Hebrew and Chaldee, Syriac, Arabic, Persian and Sanscrit. It was not surprising that he was sought out by the many scholars who visited the City, or that he himself should have gained a European outlook as he followed the developments in Germany and France. In 1831 Wiseman became intimate with Lamennais, Lacordaire and Montalembert while they were in Rome. 'To these missionaries of a wider and braver Catholicism', wrote Monckton Milnes, 'Dr Wiseman proffered a generous hospitality, which was thankfully received.'[19] With Lamennais he had discussed the situation of the Catholics in England; prejudice had to be overcome and public opinion won over, Lamennais suggested, and he encouraged Wiseman to begin to 'find the men by which the work would be performed'. This was what he and his friends were doing in France.

One such man arrived at the College in 1830; this was the Hon. George Spencer, a recent convert from Anglicanism. Wiseman had never met anyone whose mind and heart so unreservedly exhibited themselves in every action. 'He is candour and openness itself . . . I have no doubt that Divine Providence has brought him to the truth, not only for his own sake, but for the salvation of others, so that in his conversion "many shall rejoice".'[20] Spencer's candour even prompted him to tell Wiseman bluntly that he should apply his mind to something more practical than Syrian manuscripts.

Spencer's conversion caused something of a sensation. As a privileged, rich young man, and as the son of a peer, he had gone through his career at Cambridge and entered London society as carefree as most until, on a visit to Paris in 1820, he had his first religious experience during a performance of *Don Giovanni*. While he watched the end of the opera at the point where the libidinous don is dragged by devils down to the flames of hell, George Spencer became terrified by his own state. It was what he called a 'holy warning'. 'I knew that God, who knew what was in me, must look on me as one in the same class with such as Don Giovanni,'[21] he recalled. Forsaking what other delights Paris might have to offer, on his return home he sought ordination in the Church or England from the Bishop of Peterborough, and became in time the Rector of Great Brington after his father had persuaded the previous incumbent to retire on a pension and agreed to pay off his debts.

At the time Spencer's theological position was very vague, though he worked assiduously in his parish among the poor. So devoted, in fact, was he to this task that his family began to fear for his health and dreaded that such zeal might lead to his entering a monastery. His family's fears were well-founded, for it was not long before through the influence of another well-connected young man, Ambrose Phillipps, Spencer came to seek conversion to Catholicism.

Phillipps had shocked his parents by becoming a Catholic while still at school at the age of fifteen. A French emigré priest had been taken on to the staff of the school at Edgbaston and, although the old man was totally innocent of seeking to convert his pupils, young Ambrose Phillipps had been so impressed by his holiness that he decided to seek instruction from the Catholic priest in Loughborough during the holidays, an act which on being discovered led to his headmaster demanding that he leave the school immediately.

The Phillipps family were evidently less successful than the Gibbons had been when their son Edward, the future historian, had made a similar move at about the same age in 1753. Mr Gibbon swiftly sent Edward off to Lausanne to have all vestiges of Catholicism eradicated and replaced by sound Protestant doctrine, with the result that he spent the rest of his life in a bitter state of religious confusion, wondering why the Catholic clergy had never attempted by letter or message to rescue him from the hands of heretics.

Ambrose Phillipps, on the other hand, remained impenitent in spite of his parents' constant hope that he might 'come to his senses'. However, on his coming of age in 1830 his father made over part of the estate to him in the form of Grace Dieu Manor, and gave him a generous annual income, which led to the beginning of Phillipps's many building ventures. These included not only the Tudor manor house he built for himself and his wife at Grace Dieu, but also, with Lord Shrewsbury's and Pugin's help, the Trappist monastery of Mount St Bernard, in Charnwood Forest.

Early in 1830 Phillipps had invited George Spencer over to his father's house, Garendon Park, Loughborough, to discuss theology, and during the course of a few days so prevailed upon him that the latter decided to seek out Father Caestryck, a Dominican priest working in Leicester. The result was that Spencer resigned his Anglican living and went over to Rome.

Seven years later when Bishop Walsh, the Vicar Apostolic of the Midland District, consecrated the temporary chapel used by the Trappist monks at Mount St Bernard, it was Father George Spencer, the priest in charge of the Catholic mission at West Bromwich, who delivered the homily.

When Spencer returned to England after his ordination, Bishop Walsh had sent him to Walsall to assist Mr Martyn, the first priest since the Reformation to have been trained entirely in England and one of the ablest in the District. Martyn gave Spencer charge of a more closely populated part of the parish at West Bromwich, with the task of overseeing the building of the new chapel, a wise move in view of the fact that Spencer was able to donate £2,000 out of his own pocket towards the cost of construction. Contrary to what might be expected, Lord Spencer had welcomed his son home to Althorp warmly and had made generous provision for him financially. He had even invited Wiseman to stay.

Spencer's energy at the mission knew no bounds and within three years he had founded several schools in the area. He was also instrumental in opening a chapel at Dudley, where he received many into the Church. At the end of 1833 Bishop Walsh confirmed seventy converts. No doubt Spencer's social position added to his popularity, but he remained throughout modest and was often the victim of violence, as one of his first parishioners recalled:

> I remember one morning when he was going his accustomed rounds to visit
> the poor and sick, he had to pass a boys' school at Hill Top. They used
> to hoot after him low names, but, seeing he did not take any notice, they
> came into the road and threw mud and stones at him: he took no notice.
> Then they took hold of his coat and ripped it up the back. He did not mind,
> but went on all day as usual through Oldbury, Tipton Dudley, and Hill Top,
> visiting his poor people. He used to leave home every morning, and fill his
> pockets with wine and food for the poor sick, and return home at about six
> in the evening, though he might have walked twenty miles in the heat of
> summer. One winter's day he gave all his clothes away to the poor, except
> those that were on him. He used to say two Masses on Sunday at West
> Bromwich and preach. I never saw him use a conveyance of any kind in
> his visits through the parish.[22]

107

Had Bishop Walsh allowed it Spencer would have spread his activities further afield. He offered to make a begging tour round Ireland to raise funds for a larger church at Dudley, but the Bishop advised that such begging were better done nearer home. Spencer had kept in close touch with the Passionists, particularly with Dominic Barberi whom he had known in Rome. What England needed were zealous evangelists; he knew that God was able to change the face of a whole country in a day if only the right men could be found. It was not easy to imagine how this might be actually done; he saw worldly mindedness in every direction 'and the unbelieving proud spirit which Protestantism has engendered'.

'Whether the Passionists will find a settlement here depends on God's will alone,'[23] he told Father Dominic, though there must be hope since Bishop Walsh was anxious to see all sorts of religious orders established within the bounds of his jurisdiction. In fact, Wiseman himself was largely instrumental in seeing the Passionists installed in 1841 at Aston Hall, near Lord Shrewsbury's home, and it was there six years later that Spencer would join them.

Like Wiseman Spencer knew his life's work was to labour for the conversion of England. In 1838 he travelled across to France in the company of Ambrose Phillipps to ask the Archbishop of Paris to encourage his priests to pray specially for this intention. The Archbishop was enthusiastic and arranged that prayers for the conversion of England should be said each Thursday throughout the diocese. The General of the Lazarists and the Provincial of the Jesuits agreed similarly. 'It appeared to me,' Spencer wrote, 'that there was reason to say that all France would soon be united in prayer, and I trust other countries of Europe will follow their example.'[24] Besides visiting bishops personally Spencer wrote to others outlining his plan. He received enthusiastic answers from the Irish archbishops whose heroic prayers he considered might have more force than 'all the Continent put together'. On Ash Wednesday 1839 he received an answer from Wiseman in Rome.

> In our conference this time last year, I spoke very strongly to the students
> upon the wants of England, and the necessity of a new system of many things.
> One of the points on which I insisted was the want of systematic prayer for
> the conversion of England, and, at the same time, of reparation for her
> defection. I observed that it is the only country which has persisted in and
> renewed, in every generation, formal acts of apostasy, exacting from every
> sovereign, in the name of the nation, and from all that aspired to office or
> dignity, specific declarations of their holding Catholic truths to be superstitious
> and idolatrous. This, therefore, assumes the form of a national sin of
> blasphemy and heresy – not habitual, but actual; it is a bar to the Divine
> blessing, an obstacle of a positive nature to God's grace.[25]

Wiseman went on to advocate contrary acts to remove the effects of this 'blasphemous repetition of national apostasy'. The two main points on which this had fastened were Transubstantiation and veneration of the Blessed Virgin. 'These are the points towards which the reparation, and for it, the devotion of Catholics should be directed in England.'[26] The two contrary acts therefore would be to bring back devotion to the Blessed Sacrament and devotion to the Blessed Virgin, 'chiefly through the propagation of the Rosary'.

Within weeks of his receiving Wiseman's encouraging letter the Bishop of the Midland District, Dr Walsh, asked Spencer to leave West Bromwich and take up the post of Spiritual Director at Oscott. Once he had settled at the College he decided to make a direct approach to the Tractarian leaders in an attempt to persuade them to join in the prayers for the conversion of England, and to this end he visited Oxford early in the following year. Hoping to speak with Newman he had thought it more prudent to approach William Palmer first. Palmer's attempt to bring the two to the dinner table failed, Newman wishing to have 'no familiar or social intercourse with him'. However, Newman agreed to meet Spencer, but the meeting could hardly be called a success. 'I wish these R.C. priests had not so smooth a manner, it puts me out,' Newman complained to Bowden. 'He was very mild, very gentlemanlike, not a controversialist, and came to insist only on one point, that we would get Anglo-catholics to pray for R.C.s. He said he was sure that if we felt the desirableness of unity, and if we prayed for each other, where there was a will there would be a way.'[27] Newman had mistrusted Spencer's intention at the time, 'the voice was Jacob's voice, but the hands were the hands of Esau'. Spencer had not come as an individual R.C. priest, but on a religious purpose, he said when he heard how Spencer had been puzzled at his refusal to dine with him. When he came to recall his behaviour years later Newman felt remorse, for he admitted to having been glad in his heart to see that 'zealous and most charitable man', and yet he had felt compelled to be rude to him.

Spencer must have left Oxford feeling that his visit had been a failure, for he could not have known that soon after his departure Newman did draw up prayers for his intention. To add to his difficulties, he learnt that Dr Baines, the Vicar Apostolic of the Western District, had recently issued a pastoral letter in which he held out no hopes for the conversion of England, and prohibited public prayers being made to that end. Although this dismal information caused Spencer great distress, the uncharitable tone of Dr Baines's letter served to give new strength to his cause. It was nevertheless with a great sense of relief that he heard that Wiseman was to be Dr Walsh's coadjutor and would be taking up residence at Oscott.

9

Tract 90

1843–44

Father Spencer had not been the only link between the English Catholics and the Tractarians, since Pugin had also made contact with some of the younger members of the Movement, men like Oakeley, Faber, Ward, Dalgairns and Bloxam, the latter having become a close friend. In their view a corporate reunion with Rome was the preferable course. In spite of Pugin's own conversion he did not at this time press individual action upon others. However, although reunion was constantly talked about, the form this might take remained undefined. Then came the catastrophe of Tract 90.

While Newman had been at work on his Tract, Pugin had continued to receive letters from Oxford which encouraged him to report to Wiseman that the English mind was fast becoming sympathetic to Catholic ideals. What was necessary in his view was to keep the Roman question out of sight in favour of developing the monastic system, encouraging devotion to Our Lady and the Saints, in short, practising the Faith openly with all its ritual in churches designed for the purpose.

Such information only served to spur Wiseman on. In the spring of 1841, seeing the furore that Tract 90 was creating, he decided to address a letter to Newman personally rather than commit his thoughts to the pages of the *Dublin Review*. Wiseman argued that there was no real discrepancy between the decrees of the Council of Trent and the authoritative teaching of the Catholic Church as the Tract had asserted. Newman had attempted to show that the Thirty-nine Articles had not been directed against the Tridentine decrees and he had spoken of 'the Roman schools as sanctioning superstitions which were at variance with Trent'. Here Wiseman was able to speak with authority.

'Bear with me if I speak too prominently in my own name,' he wrote.

I have some right to come forward as a witness in this matter. I have resided for two-and-twenty years in Rome, intimately connected with its theological education. For five years I attended the Roman schools in the Roman College, where all the clergy of the city were obliged to be educated. I went through the entire theological course and publicly maintained it in a Thesis. Since then I have always been engaged in teaching theology in our national College, and for some years have held the office of professor in the Roman University. I ought, therefore, to be tolerably well acquainted with the doctrines of the Roman schools.[1]

He went on to demonstrate that Newman had grossly misjudged the true balance between doctrine and sentiment by setting out a brief analysis of the theological course. Yes, Catholics did place a certain emphasis on devotion to Our Lady and the Saints. There was a deep feeling for Our Lady in sorrow, and for Our Lady in joy, but how was this blasphemous? 'Is not this the sin of Heli,' he wrote, 'who, witnessing the deep feeling of Anna's prayer, pronounced her drunk? And has not many a poor Italian been equally unjustly judged when on similar evidence he is pronounced an idolater?'[2] Nevertheless, in the Mass and in all the critical parts of Catholic devotion trust in Our Lord and meditation on His example were all-important.

The last part of the letter must have upset Newman, for Wiseman continued, revealing how carefully he had read not only the Tract but also the *Remains*:

You will remember that your late amiable friend, Mr Froude, in one of his unhappy moments of hasty censure, pronounced us, not Catholics, but 'wretched Tridentines'. This expression was quoted, with apparent approbation, by his editors, in their preface. It seems hard that now we should be deprived of even this 'wretched' title, and sunk by you a step lower in the scale of degradation. Still more it seems unaccountable that you should now court that title, and assert (as your Tract does) that while we have abandoned the doctrines of Trent, you, and those who take the Articles in your sense, interpret them in accordance with those doctrines. I say this in a spirit, not of reproach, but rather of charitable warning. That which you once considered a heavy imputation, you seem now to consider comparatively a light blame: for you would now be glad to see us in stricter conformity (according to your views) with the decrees of that Council. You then blamed us for adhesion to them; you now blame us for departure from them. Why not suspect your judgments, if you find that they vary? If there ever was a time when you did not see many of our doctrines as you now view them; when you utterly rejected all comprecation with, as much as prayers to, saints; all honour, without reserve, to images and relics; when you did not practise prayers for the departed, nor turned from the congregation in your service; when you did not consider bodily mortification necessary, or the Breviary so beautiful; when, in fine, you were more remote from us in practice and feeling than your writings now show you to be, why not suspect that a further approximation may yet remain; that further discoveries of truth, in what to-day seems erroneous, may be reserved for to-morrow, and that you may be laying up for yourself the pain and regret of having beforehand branded with opprobrious and afflicting names that which you will discover to be good and holy.[3]

The point had been made; it was irrefutable, and Newman knew it. Choosing not to reply himself he left it to Palmer, who began his pamphlet by denying that Wiseman could claim episcopal orders.

Wiseman took Newman's own silence as a good omen. He continued to be certain that it was only a matter of time before Newman must come to acknowledge the truth of his position. As far as the other Vicars-Apostolic were concerned, and for a year now their number had been increased to eight instead of the original four, Wiseman's attitude seemed far too optimistic. Dr Griffiths, the Bishop of the London District, warned him against unwise impetuosity. The Tractarians, in his view, were far from coming over to Rome in a body; there was no precedent for such a happening: 'scarcely shall we find in history a body of schismatics returning with sincerity to the obedience of the faith,'[4] he wrote. A similar warning came from Wiseman's early mentor, John Lingard, reminding him how disillusionment had so often been the reward of English Catholics during the Reformation. In fact, apart from the staunch support of a few men like Spencer, Pugin and Phillipps, Wiseman was seen by the majority of old Catholics as being completely out of touch with the time. Surely, he should be able to see that Newman was fighting a rearguard action in an attempt to prevent the submission of 'great and good men who, tired of the Church of England as it is, had almost fully determined to join the ancient religion of their forefathers'. 'The embrace of Mr Newman is the kiss that will betray us,' wrote one Catholic priest.

The Holy Week of 1841 was to see a surprising development. Good Friday fell on 9 April. 'We have had several young men come here to make their Easter, or join the Retreat, or enjoy our functions, which has given me much comfort,' Wiseman wrote. 'Mr C. Hemans, son of the poet, a charming young man, with all her feeling and inspiration, came here on Thursday, a Protestant, and leaves us this evening a Catholic. He is not the only straggler towards Rome that has come my way; I have several most singular and interesting correspondences, with persons I have never seen, but who are most anxious to become Catholics. I believe Mr Newman is right; a fire has been kindled – not by them, but by God, who can use the chaff and straw of His barn floor for this purpose (by which St Augustine understands those separated from the Church) as well as burning brands from His altar – and this fire no man can extinguish.'[5]

On the day before, Maundy Thursday, while Wiseman had been busy at Oscott, his friend and co-editor of the *Dublin Review*, Charles Russell, a young priest at St Patrick's College, Maynooth, felt a sudden impulse to sit down and write a lengthy letter to Newman. Russell had recently been reading Tract 90 and, after celebrating the public service of the day with its emphasis on the Blessed Sacrament, he had been even more deeply distressed by Newman's misconception of the Catholic doctrine of Transubstantiation. In his explanation of Article 28 Newman had argued that what was opposed was 'the shocking doctrine that the "body of Christ" is not given, taken and eaten, after a heavenly and spiritual manner, but is carnally pressed with the teeth, that it is a body and substance'. Russell answered as follows:

> Your whole exposition of this Article proceeds on the supposition that our conception of 'Transubstantiation' is of the most gross and repulsive nature, that we think of the adorable Body of Our Lord in the Eucharist as of an earthly and fleshly thing; of the eating and drinking as animal and corporeal actions, a carnal eating – it is painful to write it in this sense – 'tearing with the teeth', of the Blessed Body – a natural and bloody drinking of the adorable Blood.
>
> That you should explain the Article of your Church in the most Catholic sense of which the words or the circumstances render them susceptible; far from complaining, I rejoice and am sincerely thankful. But I equally lament that this explanation of your own belief should involve the imputation upon us of doctrines as odious and repulsive, as they are opposed to our true creed. It is to this I beg to call your attention in the spirit of most respectful, but, I must add, of most earnest remonstrance. Far from entering in any way into our belief of the Eucharist, the gross imaginations ascribed to us are rejected with horror by every Catholic.[6]

Newman replied to the effect that he did not accuse Catholics of holding Transubstantiation in such a shocking sense, but that some had held such a doctrine in the past and that it was towards that idea the Article had been originally framed. He went on to add: 'O that you would reform your worship, that you would disown the extreme honours paid to St Mary and the Saints, your traditionary view of Indulgences, and the veneration paid in foreign countries to Images. And as to your own country, O that, abandoning your connection with a political party, you would, as a body, "lead quiet and peaceable lives in all godliness and honesty". It would do your religious interests as much good in our eyes, as it would tend to rid your religious system of those peculiarities which distinguish it from primitive Christianity.'[7]

It was the beginning of one of the most important correspondences in Newman's life and, after Russell's several visits to Oxford, a friendship developed which led Newman to admit that Russell had had more to do with his conversion than anyone else. For one thing he felt in no way threatened by him as he had by Wiseman. Wiseman in spite of his tact seemed patronising, whereas Russell, a man much younger, eleven years, in fact, wrote in a quieter tone. Nevertheless, unknown to Newman, Wiseman was always behind the scenes, since Russell informed him of the corrrespondence and even sent him Newman's letters.

Wiseman had assured Russell that what appeared on the surface was nothing to what was working in the deep. The Catholic Movement in the Church of England was not merely in its outward forms and phrases adopted by the Tractarians, as some imagined, but in their hearts and desires. They were every day becoming more and more disgusted with Anglicanism, its barrenness, its shallowness, and its 'stammering' teaching. Their advance was so steady, regular and unanimous, that one of two things must follow: either they would bring or push on their Church with them, or they would leave her behind.

> The first is their great object; the second may be their gain. If their Church repels them and attempts to damp their effort, they will abandon her, for their hearts have allowed Catholicism to take too deep a root in them for it to be plucked up by the *telum imbelle sine ictu* of Anglo-episcopal authority.[8]

Many at Oxford were as yet terribly in the dark as to their individual duty, Wiseman continued; but if he were to be consulted by any one of them he would advise them to leave their father's house and kindred and come into the land which God's grace shows him, 'by at once yielding to his convictions and securing his own salvation'. However, it seemed that they had not been so far enlightened by faith and grace as to feel that it was a risk to their own salvation to remain united to the Anglican Church, though they considered it a duty of their Church to bring itself into communion with the Catholic Church.

> All we can do is to push them forward in their view so much as to make them diffuse it in every direction, and to invite them towards us rather than to repulse them, as some seem inclined to do. I should like to see them become Catholics at once, and one by one; but, if they will not do that, I should be sorry to check them in their present course.[9]

Wiseman went on to say that he had no doubt that Newman was acting in the greatest sincerity, and that his whole efforts were directed to a reunion; not a distant, theoretical union, but a practical one. This might happen as soon as it could be openly agitated without causing too great alarm. It could not be very far away now, Wiseman thought. Soon he was reaffirming his hope. 'I see no insurmountable difficulties in Oxford against the return to Unity. The passions of men and the gross prejudices of the mass of the people are real adversaries,'[10] he told Russell. He thought the Oxford men were more likely to remove prejudice than his own people, whereas perhaps Catholics were better equipped to cope with the passions of men. Certainly, it was high time the Holy See was informed of the dramatic situation now prevailing. He would approach the Pope through his old friend Cardinal Mai, and obtain instructions with a view to a possibly immediate reconciliation of Newman and his friends to Rome. A few days later he received a most distressing letter from Newman himself which, as he told Phillipps, 'has thrown me on my back and painfully dispirited me.' It was not long before he was referring to Newman as 'a timid man'.

The cause of pain was Newman's suggestion that Wiseman had attempted to vindicate the invocations of the Blessed Virgin used by the Church. It augured a bad omen, Newman said, that these were not given up. Wiseman had not even mentioned the Blessed Virgin in his letter. 'Now really, if Newman's expectation was that the Church, or that we, should give up our tender and confident devotion towards the Holy Mother of God, or that the least of her pastors would join (on his private judgment) with Mr Palmer in condemning expressions sanctioned and approved by her Pontiffs, how high indeed must his demands of condescension be before we can hope for reunion!'[11] he complained to Phillipps.

Wiseman might have taken this as a hopeful sign, but never having been in the position himself he did not see that Newman was now betraying one of the well-known symptoms of conversion: worrying himself over the Church's devotion to Mary, its constancy, its intensity, instead of dismissing it as an inessential part of Catholic 'mummery'. The problem would not go away, yet there remained the doubt that devotion to Mary to some degree must draw devotion away from her son. Russell had assured Newman this was not the case. 'If you knew us well, our doctrine on the Blessed Virgin and the Saints, if you knew the correctness of the views entertained by our very rudest people on the value of Indulgences and the use of Sacred Images, your fears of our "traditionary system" would disappear – you would feel that our worship needed no "reform" ... Where can the true spirit of our devotions be traced so surely as in the devotions themselves?'[12] Russell implored Newman to see for himself. Examine Catholic devotion carefully, he said, see how the Rosary, which was considered the most offensive of all Marian devotions, was but a series of meditations on the Incarnation, Passion, and Glory of our Redeemer.

> If I had no other security that these tender and consoling devotions, far from defrauding the worship of God, on the contrary elevate it, and give it that stability which our weak and frail hearts require, I should find it in the fact that the holiest servants of God – those like St Bernard, or, in later times,

Francis Xavier, or Vincent of Paul, whose souls burnt on earth almost with a seraph's fervour, whose piety towards God was of the sublimest as well as tenderest character – were also, in the same proportion, the most devoted clients of the Mother of God, and the humblest suitors of her intercession.[13]

At the time Newman remained unconvinced, but slowly he began to feel the force of another consideration: as he explained, 'The idea of the Blessed Virgin was as it were magnified in the Church of Rome, as time went on, – but so were all the Christian ideas; as that of the Blessed Eucharist. The whole scene of pale, faint, distant Apostolic Christianity is seen in Rome, as through a telescope or magnifier. The harmony of the whole, however, is of course what it was. It is unfair then to take one Roman idea, that of the Blessed Virgin, out of what may be called its context.'[14] Perhaps Apostolical doctrines had not been changed or corrupted; rather, they may have developed along logical lines without losing anything of their original force. This was not a new idea, for Newman had touched on it in his book on the Arians, neither had he ever lost sight of it in his speculations, but soon it became the central issue.

What Newman described to his sister Harriett as the 'serious mess' Tract 90 had got him into did not diminish. The Protestant reaction continued: Bishop Sumner of Chester, who had been the first to condemn the Movement and had spoken of the undermining of our Protestant Church by men who dwelt inside it, all clearly the work of Satan, was after 1841 joined by a buzz of episcopal condemnations. Men of ardent feelings and warm imaginations were being prepared for a return to the Roman mass-book, a matter of the deepest concern. 'Already are the foundations of apostasy laid; if we once admit another Gospel, Antichrist is at the door.'[15]

Newman consoled himself with the thought that bishops had no authority outside their own dioceses. 'A bishop's word,' he said, 'is to be obeyed, not as to doctrine, but as part of discipline.'[16] In acknowledgment of this he had complied with his own bishop's wish that he would issue no more tracts. Nevertheless, the charges brought by some of the bishops meant that truth was silenced in some dioceses. It was not impossible that the Church of England would lapse into heresy, even if she had not already done so. The great and anxious experiment that was going on, whether the Church of England was Catholic or no, might not be resolved in his lifetime, but, as Newman told his friend James Hope, 'I must be plain in saying that, if it does issue in Protestantism, I shall think it my duty, if alive, to leave it.'[17]

As if to sway the balance against him the news came that the Anglican Church intended to establish a bishopric in Jerusalem in alliance with the new State Church of Prussia for such 'stray Protestants as might be living in Palestine'. The plan was that each church should nominate a bishop alterna-

John Henry Newman by Sir William Ross, c. 1845

The Newman Family after a drawing by Maria Giberne, c. 1830. From left to right: Francis, Mrs Newman, Harriett, John Henry, Jemima.

John Bowden

Henry Wilberforce

John Keble

Edward Pusey

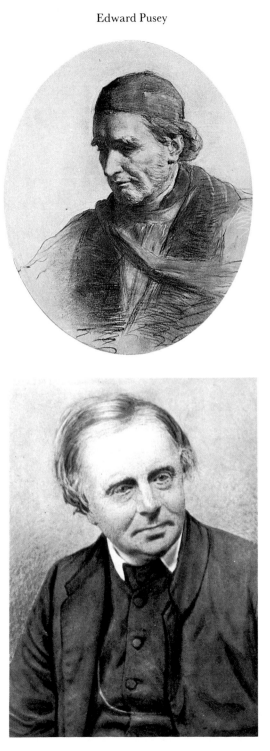

Frederick Faber

Ambrose St. John

THE NEWMAN-OOTH COLLEGE &c.

AT LITTLEMORE NEAR OXFORD.

The Newman-ooth College: a contemporary skit on Littlemore and Oscott at the expense of Maynooth College in Ireland.

Dominic Barberi

George Spencer

John Henry Newman

Nicholas Wiseman

William Ullathorne

Henry Manning

Luigi Gentili

St Mary's College, Oscott

The Oratory, King William Street, London

John Henry Newman by William Roden, 1874

tely, but all nominees would be inevitably consecrated by English bishops since the Prussian Church was non-episcopal. The arrangement was accepted without demur by most in England, but to Newman the idea was horrific. 'Have you heard of this deplorable Jerusalem matter? I do dread our Bishops will convert men to Rome, Dr Wiseman sitting still,' he told one friend; and to another he wrote, 'It seems that we are in the way to fraternise with Protestants of all sorts – Monophysites, half-converted Jews and Druses. If such event should take place, I shall not be able to keep a single man from Rome. They will all be trooping off sooner or later.'[18]

The whole matter quite unnerved him. Supposing the bishops declared that the Church of England was not part of the Catholic Church? It seemed quite likely; the Prussians did not even have bishops. Did they take an orthodox view of the Sacraments? Why must the successors of Augustine and Anselm become superintendents of a mixed multitude of Protestants and, what was more likely, men of no Profession whatever? What was there to hinder a congregation of Rationalists putting themselves under the jurisdiction of an Anglican bishop? What has a bishop to do with the matter at all? Why not send a consul instead? There were Wesleyan Methodists in Syria. Was a bishop being sent to them!

'It was one of the blows which broke me,' Newman later admitted, and it was one of the 'Three Defeats' listed by Dean Church in the chain of events which destroyed Newman's belief in the English Church. It had been a national issue, whereas the other two had been restricted to Oxford itself: the defeat of Isaac Williams in his attempt, with Newman's backing, to succeed Keble as Professor of Poetry in the January of 1842 was seen as a major setback for the Tractarians, and, more importantly, in the following year the proceedings taken against Dr Pusey for preaching heresy. In one of his sermons Pusey had proclaimed what amounted to an acceptance of the doctrine of the Real Presence in the Holy Eucharist, and thus was teaching doctrine contrary to that of the Church of England. The result was that the Vice-Chancellor suspended him from preaching within the University for two years.

Newman's sermons also had long been under scrutiny, and the Heads of some Colleges were discouraging undergraduates from attending St Mary's by altering the times of dinner. Newman felt inclined to leave off preaching altogether. He spent more and more time at Littlemore and early in 1842 he vacated his rooms at Oriel for good. As he informed Jemima, 'My books are all in motion – part gone; the rest in a day or two. It makes me very downcast; it is such a nuisance taking steps.'[19] The vast library he had been collecting since he was a boy, the 'glorious folios of the Fathers' given to him by his pupils when he had ceased to be tutor, and the 'huge fellows' Pusey had bought for him in Germany with the 'St Athanasius' that had once belonged to Bossuet, were all to find their way to Littlemore and give him some friendly warmth of comfort during the coming time of turmoil.

The college at Littlemore should not be confused with the monastery Newman had thought of founding there in 1840 when he had spent the weeks of Lent at Mrs Barnes's cottage. The college was improvised out of a row of old stables, which had once stalled the horses for the Oxford to Cambridge coach run by a Mr Costar. 'John's new rooms are in a place neither you or I know,' Harriett told Jemima, 'It looked like a wall. Now it has a dozen windows – one storey. Inside it is very pretty and neat – just my fancy. I do not wonder at John's present enthusiasm.'[20]

The library was housed in an old converted barn. 'There have been more unpromising establishments to start with,'[21] wrote John Dobree Dalgairns, a recent graduate of Exeter College. He cherished a vision of one day being there himself. Newman's library, he said, 'beats most monkeries to sticks'.

'No monastery is in the process of erection,' Newman assured the Bishop, who had got wind of the scheme. 'There is no chapel, no refectory, hardly a dining-room or parlour, the cloisters are my shed, connecting the cottages.'[22.] The place was, Newman explained, a parsonage-house; the newspaper description of an Anglo-Catholic monastery which had been related to his Lordship was totally false. However, the name stuck, and all contemporary Oxford would know it as 'The Monastery', and a satirical print elevated it higher, to 'The Newman-ooth College'.

In his justification to the Bishop, Newman argued that Littlemore had as many parishioners as St Mary's; it was expedient for him to reside in the village until the trouble over Tract 90 died down. 'With a view to personal improvement, I was led more seriously to a design which has long been on my mind. For many years, at least thirteen, I have wished to give myself a life of greater regularity than I have hitherto led,'[23] he wrote.

Of course, Newman knew full well that he had always hoped that others would join him, but in his letter to the Bishop he was careful to emphasise that the place was primarily a parsonage. He took up residence for the first time on 19 April 1842. 'I am literally solus,' he wrote to Bowden, 'without servants or anything else but I suppose we shall accumulate in time.'[24] He did not have very long to wait; after two days only he was joined by Dalgairns, only twenty-four years old, a native of Guernsey, and therefore fluent in French. Dalgairns already had strong leanings towards Catholicism. At once the two began to live a kind of community life centred on prayer and work. Each day they recited the Divine Office together from the Roman Breviary, and took meals at regular times. It was not long before the six sets of rooms were filled, though Newman complained that men tended to come and go. However, by 13 June he was describing himself to Jemima as a 'family man'.

He would not be able to visit her at Derby that summer because he could not leave 'home'.

Another young man who arrived at the college in the summer was William Lockhart, whose family had requested Newman to keep a close eye on him for fear he might go over to Rome. Lockhart was two years younger than Dalgairns; he promised faithfully that he would remain under Newman's care for three years. He was deeply aware of personal sin, and he desired to make his confession regularly, something he had found difficult to arrange in the Church of England. He had read Bishop Milner's *The End of Controversy* and in this 'Papist book' he learnt that the Sacrament of Penance was indeed mentioned in the Anglican rite of Ordination. When Archdeacon Manning came to Oxford to preach the University Sermon Lockhart had sought him out and made his confession to him in Merton College Chapel. Manning had advised the young penitent to contact Newman. Once he was installed at the college he made his confession every week, but Newman himself was soon in grave doubt as to whether he had the power to give absolution. 'Why will you ask me? Ask Pusey,'[25] he had replied to the young man in a 'tone of deep distress' in the spring of 1843.

It was in the May of that year also that Newman felt impelled to confide his deepest thoughts to Keble. 'To whom is it natural for me to go but to you whom I have tried to follow so long and on so many occasions? to whom would Hurrell go, or wish me to go but to you?' he wrote. On 4 May he had expressed his fear that as far as he could realize his own convictions, he considered the Roman Catholic Communion the Church of the Apostles.

> I am very far more sure that England is in schism, than that the Roman additions to the Primitive Creed may not be developments, arising out of keen and vivid realizing of the Divine Depositum of faith.
>
> All this is shocking to say, that I do not know whether to wish that I am exaggerating to you my feelings or not.[26]

What was so dreadful was the trust he was betraying. People assumed, and exacted, certain things of him. With what sort of sincerity could he obey his Bishop? How could he possibly remain Vicar of St Mary's, or, indeed, of any parish? Keble tried to smooth over the situation. Certainly he should not resign his living if any element of doubt remained. For the rest of the month letters passed to and fro between them, till by the end Keble admitted that the situation did seem to involve such constant peril of sin that on the whole his leaning was towards Newman's retiring as quietly as he could.

Newman did not resign his living until September. The final decision was precipitated towards the end of August by young William Lockhart's leaving

Littlemore. 'I have just had a letter from Lockhart, one of my inmates, who has been away for three weeks, saying that he is on the point of joining the Church of Rome and is in retreat under Dr Gentili of Loughborough,'[27] Newman informed Keble. Lockhart had promised to remain at the college and take no action for three years; on that understanding alone Newman had accepted him. During his time at Littlemore he had improved so much that people had remarked upon it.

> We all think he had no intention at all of any move in religion when he
> left. He went to Dr Gentili at Loughborough, on his way to Lincolnshire
> (I believe). And he was fascinated almost at once. Dr Gentili did not make
> any overtures whatever to him; and only admitted him, when (as he thought)
> his duty obliged him.[28]

It seemed Lockhart had not told the famous Italian missionary priest of his promise to Newman; somehow he had quite put it aside. The call had been so strong that he felt he dare not disobey it, and he was now determined on joining the novitiate of the Order of Charity, of which Dr Gentili was the superior in England. Newman could not help feeling the Order had gained its greatest prize. Nevertheless, the effect of Lockhart's conversion on himself was profound. As he told Hope, the Movement was going so fast the wheels were catching fire. Unless something very extraordinary happened, he expected to resign St Mary's in the course of a few weeks.

In his letter of resignation, written on 7 September, Newman told Dr Bagot he knew he would be causing him much pain, but said how much love and devotion he had always felt towards him. 'I have ever wished to please you ... I have honestly tried to bear in mind that I was in a place of high trust in the Church, and have laboured hard to uphold and strengthen her, and to retain her members. I am not relaxing my zeal till it has been disowned by her rulers. I have not retired from her service till I have lost or forfeited her confidence.'[29]

There would be much explaining to do. During October Newman corresponded with Manning, who admitted no surprise at the resignation, but became alarmed when Newman told him that it was with no disappointment, irritation or impatience at the way he had been treated that he had resigned his living, but because he thought the Church of Rome the Catholic Church, 'and ours not part of the Catholic Church, because not in communion with Rome, and I felt I could not honestly be a teacher in it any longer'.[30]

Manning was not the only one to be shocked at the disclosure; he had forwarded the letter to Gladstone who replied that his reaction had been, 'I stagger to and fro, like a drunken man, and am at my wits' end'.[31] If Newman's letters to Manning were divulged he would be a disgraced man, and the cause which he had advocated would be hopelessly discredited.

Manning felt he would have to act himself. He wrote to Pusey that he was reduced to the painful, saddening, sickening necessity of saying what 'he' felt about Rome. This he did in no uncertain terms in his sermon preached on 5 November. He intended to journey on up to Littlemore the following day to confront Newman. When he arrived at the college Newman refused to see him. However, by the end of December Manning was asking that 'we be guided and kept from and against ourselves'.[32] Newman replied that it was no pleasure for him to differ from friends, no comfort to be estranged from them, no satisfaction or boast to have said things which he must say.

> If my misgivings are from above, I shall be carried on in spite of my resistance. I cannot regret in time to come having struggled to remain where I found myself placed. And believe me, the circumstance of such men as yourself being content to remain is the strongest argument in favour of my own remaining. It is my constant prayer, that if others are right I may be drawn back – that nothing may part us.[33]

Again Manning sent Newman's letter to Gladstone who answered that Newman might be warned of the 'immense consequences that may hang upon his movements'. The event that now seemed possible would be a calamity for the Church. Could not Manning discreetly use his influence over the bishops to be moderate in their charges? Somehow Newman must be saved for the Church: 'Cords of silk should one by one be thrown over him to bind him to the Church. Every manifestation of sympathy and confidence in him, as a man, must have some small effect.'[34]

Newman had preached his last Anglican sermon in St Mary and St Nicholas's, Littlemore, on the morning of 25 September. The occasion was the anniversary of the little church's consecration and so many attended that extra chairs were placed outside. Close friends were there, not only the young men now in residence at the college, but also Pusey, who administered the Sacrament, Henry Wilberforce, Bloxam and Copeland, the latter having handed Newman's resignation in to the Archdeacon. Flowers had been placed round the memorial plaque to Mrs Newman, who had died so soon after the first ceremony at the church in 1836.

The sermon, known as 'The Parting of Friends', was Newman's 604th. It began with a reminder of Our Lord's parting from the Twelve Disciples at a feast before his Passion. 'He calls his friends around Him, though He was as Job among the ashes; he bids them stay by Him, and see Him suffer.' It was autumn, Newman said, the harvest was passed and the vintage was gathered. Now the corn and wine would be offered up as a propitiation. 'If we have had the rain in its season, and the sun shining in its strength, and the fertile ground, it is of Thee. We give back to Thee what came from

Thee.' In the same way each soul must be offered back alone. Newman went on to draw many instances of separation and departure from the Old Testament and the life of St Paul. What were all these but 'memorials and tokens of the Son of Man, when His work and His labour was coming to an end?' Yet Scripture was a refuge in any trouble; 'only let us be on our guard against seeming to use it further than is fitting, or doing more than sheltering ourselves under its shadow. Let us use it according to our measure.'[35]

Newman ended with words that only very few in the congregation might have understood. After exhorting them to eat their bread with joy, and drink their wine with a merry heart, for God now accepted their works, he continued:

> And, O my brethren, O kind and affectionate hearts, O loving friends, should
> you know any one whose lot it has been, by writing or by word of mouth,
> in some degree to help you thus to act; if he has ever told you what you
> knew about yourselves, or what you did not know; has read to you your wants
> or feelings, and comforted you by the very reading; has made you feel that
> there was a higher life than this daily one, and a brighter world than that
> you see; or encouraged you, or sobered you, or opened a way to the inquiring,
> or soothed the perplexed; if what he has said or done has ever made you
> take an interest in him, and feel well inclined towards him; remember such
> a one in time to come, though you hear him not, and pray for him, that
> in all things he may know God's will, and at all times he may be ready to
> fulfil it.[36]

Leaving the pulpit, it was noticed by some how Newman took off his Oxford hood and hung it over a rail, a sign that he no longer considered himself a preacher in the Church of England.

From that day until the October of 1845 the college became Newman's chief concern; though he could not have helped hearing news from Oxford he seldom visited it and only dined at Oriel a few times. C.P. Eden soon succeeded him at St Mary's, but Copeland remained as curate, still living at Mrs Barnes's and frequently attending prayers at the college; he would always be thought of as a friend, in spite of his increasing hostility towards the Catholic Church.

The college routine was rigorous, beginning at 5 in the morning and ending at 10.15 at night. The Office was recited through the day in a small oratory, a dark room lined with red curtains and lit by candelabra even during the day, since the one small window was also curtained off. Most of the four and a half hours of worship took place there, except that the community visited Littlemore Church every day for Morning Prayer at 10 o'clock, and Evening Prayer at 3p.m. Only two meals were taken: breakfast and supper, but there were four periods of study, making nine hours' study in all. Each day there were three periods of recreation. During Advent and Lent the community rose half an hour earlier than usual.

An important new addition to the community was Ambrose St John, a young clergyman aged twenty-eight, who had been Henry Wilberforce's curate at Walmer for two years. When Wilberforce had moved to East Farleigh, he had offered St John the chance to move with him, but decided not to press him too hard 'lest he should increase his perplexities'. The fact was that St John had found himself in much the same situation as Newman, with whom he was only slightly acquainted, being not quite ready to submit to the Catholic Church, but certain he could not remain a minister in the Church of England. In June he had sought out Newman at Littlemore and spent some hours in discussion. Soon after this St John wrote asking if he might spend more time at the college, perhaps three months or so, perhaps longer. Newman was quite prepared to let him come, but insisted that he must make up his own mind and not expect advice. So it was that St John arrived on 7 August as planned, but his possible three months' rest in Newman's company in the hope that order and tranquillity might 'reconcile him to things as they are' was destined to last for thirty-two years.

St John was born in 1815. His grandfather had been Dean of Worcester and brother of the 11th Lord St John of Bletsoe. Ambrose attended Westminster School before going up to Christ Church in 1834, from where he graduated four years later and was elected to a Studentship. After his ordination he joined Wilberforce at Walmer in 1841. When he arrived at Littlemore he was given the room vacated by Lockhart.

Only Hurrell Froude, perhaps, was ever closer to Newman's heart than Ambrose St John. At first Newman thought it was a common affection for Wilberforce that bound them together. 'That is the reason perhaps I love St John so much, because he comes from you and from your teaching,'[37] he wrote to Wilberforce in 1846. However, it was more than this. Newman found in St John someone with whom he could share every thought, every trial. God had given him St John just at the time when he seemed to be taking everyone else away He became the link between his old and his new life, and the two were seldom apart from that time forward, and not only in life, for, on Newman's insistence, the two now lie buried in the same grave.

10

An Incomprehensible Blessing

$$\boxed{1844\text{--}45}$$

During 1844 Newman and his small group of young men lived an ascetic life, fasting, working and praying: in Lent their efforts were more rigorous. At work they were busy with two main projects: the preparation of the *Lives of the English Saints*, and Newman's own translation of the works of St Athanasius. The idea of bringing out a complete hagiography for England had been suggested first to Newman's mind by the successful publication in 1841 of Bowden's *Life of Pope Gregory VII*. Two years later Bowden was invited to become involved in the new venture. 'Is there any one which you would like to take? Some are appropriated, but I hardly know which are in your way, since you are a Continentalist.'[1] St Boniface was suggested, and accepted. Richard Church had agreed to tackle Anselm and Lanfranc. The whole enterprise was a mammoth task, but even with the best will in the world impossible to complete. St Osberga would have to be omitted, because it was not easy to learn anything about her, and the Cornish saints were too numerous to be attempted. Among the men of note, not Saints, King Edward ii must be included, 'from piety towards the founder of Oriel College'. One cannot help wondering how aware these hagiographers were of that desperate king's particular weakness, or if, indeed, they had read their Marlowe.

The 'Lives' were intended to be historical and devotional, but not controversial; there was no need to bring in doctrinal questions. As to miracles, they should be treated as matters of faith – credible according to their evidence. The London publisher, James Toovey, had agreed to the project, thinking it would be useful 'as employing the minds of men who were in danger of running wild ... and keeping them from seeking sympathy in Rome as she is'.

The first in the expected series was Dalgairns's *Life of Stephen Harding*, the twelfth-century Abbot of Cîteaux and co-founder of the Cistercian Order. No doubt the Order's recent arrival in Leicestershire acted as a spur to the choice. The effect of this first effort, however, was such that the whole series, as planned, was brought to an abrupt halt. Newman had anticipated that some passages might cause a stir; had not Pusey warned against the project? In the event the reaction was worse than even Newman had feared. He knew Dalgairns had written in a style 'inconsistent with the profession of a beneficed clergyman' but his work was considered 'inconsistent even with its being given to the world by an Anglican publisher'. Newman retired immediately from the editorship, and in January 1844 it was announced that the other 'Lives' would be published 'by their respective authors on their own responsibility', so that during the following months various other volumes appeared accordingly.

Sadly, Bowden was not able to progress very far with his life of St Boniface. By the summer it was obvious his own life was fading fast. 'It is difficult to believe he is so ill,'[2] Newman told Keble after staying a night at Roehampton, but it seems Bowden had been able to move about with a crutch and dine downstairs, and when seated he had laughed at Newman's serious expression. 'It is your face – it reminds me of old times,'[3] he had said. It was hoped that he might be fit to visit Littlemore in August and read in the library for the St Boniface, though the prospect of his being well enough seemed bleak, and Elizabeth Bowden was evidently preparing for the worst, knowing on top of it all that the lease on the Roehampton house would soon run out.

On 3 July Newman informed Keble he had spoken to her and learnt that the doctors had not expected Bowden to come through the last winter, which had been spent on the Sussex Coast at St Leonard's. 'Every medicine had failed. It is quite cruel to see him lie inhaling medicated air – it seems such a mockery.'[4] At the height of his illness Bowden's father had died; of course, Bowden could not attend the funeral. As he sat writing in the room at Roehampton, Newman listened to his friend's coughing, knowing it would continue through the night. In the morning he administered Holy Communion and wrote a postscript to his letter. 'That coughing last night was a bad discharge – but what it means we cannot tell till the doctor comes.'[5]

Surprisingly Bowden held on, becoming weaker and weaker, until the second week of September. When the lease expired Elizabeth Bowden moved her husband to Clifton where Newman visited him. 'He was sadly altered. Fever has come on and perspirations. He certainly would not get from Clifton, except that he has in a way set his heart on waiting God's time at St Leonard's.'[6] Keble was given an account of a typical day.

> He does not like not to come downstairs while he can, though it is a great effort to him, particularly dressing. He lies on the sofa with Bible, Prayer Book, Breviary, and *Paradisus Animae* on a little desk before him; but his thoughts are so unsteady now, that he has wished much, but sought in vain

in Bristol, some sacred emblem or picture which might meet his eyes without effort. I took him the *Paradisus* by accident for another purpose two months ago, and he has seized upon it with great delight, and says it is a great comfort to him. He made me read Compline, Terce and Sext with him. Besides that he manages to get through the Morning and Evening Prayer, I believe – and sometimes the Penitential Psalms in the Breviary. Morning is his best time for eating, and he takes his principal meal then. His worst time is between six and eight in the evening. He gets out, or did, but a day makes a change now, in a Bath Chair – but he cannot bear the beautiful scenery at Clifton – it tries him. At length the hours have passed away, and no more expedients are needed. Evening comes, and he seems to have some quiet sleep of a night which recruits him, and he lies very tranquilly in bed. So he is lifted upstairs by his two servants, making a sort of low interjection, not of pain but of relief, 'lo, lo, lo,' or the like, and says, as he told me, 'Well, another crest has been topped, another billow is over,' calling the days his billows, with an allusion to 'Who would count the billows past?' He made me come and see what he called his 'procession' – his wife first with the candle, then he in the arms of the two men. While going up, he turned about his head, to be sure I was looking.[7]

Newman felt he had never known such pain, though he knew how one can forget past feelings. He admitted to Keble of being in very great distress. He had been so very close to Bowden for above twenty-seven years, and he was his oldest friend.

On his return to Littlemore he waited anxiously for news, and with an added sense of guilt; Bowden had wished he would stay and Newman had slipped away without his knowing. The expected news reached him on 14 September. Thinking Bowden had died at Clifton he made plans to depart, but was surprised to learn that he had, in fact, died in London at 17 Grosvenor Place, the house he had recently inherited from his father.

Newman, 'full of wrong and miserable feelings', set off for London. Bowden had led a blameless life, and he had made a blessed end; he really had believed in the Movement and, as Newman expressed it, he was one who really 'fed on our ordinances and got strength from them'.[8] When he saw the same devotion continued in a whole family, the little children finding quite a solace for their pain in the daily prayer, Newman began to feel it was impossible not to be at ease in the Church in which one had been brought up, because it was 'a place of refuge and temporary rest because of the steepness of the way'.[9]

Newman's friend was laid out in the principal drawing room; the furniture was the same, the ornaments on the mantelpiece those Newman had known as a youth in the happy times he had spent in Bowden's company; there was the music, the laughter and the seemingly endless talk. There on the wall was the portrait of John at the age of four with his younger sister by Hoppner. When the artist had asked the small boy how he would like to be drawn he had replied 'drawing a church', so Fulham Church was there in the background, and he with a pencil and paper. Newman found he could only feel faithless and hopeless. He would remain with the family at least until after the funeral, maybe for longer. Elizabeth Bowden was heroic, 'her whole bearing is quite out of the way. It forces itself upon one at such a time when one has not much heart to be thinking of such things.'[10]

Keble was able to offer some comfort.

Just now you are stunned with the blow but, as to being hard-hearted, I have too sad and shameful experience how soft-hearted people who cry easily may soon let go the good thoughts which come to them from such death beds, and have their hearts harded in another sort of manner. But really and truly may not one accept such a calm departure as this as a pledge of mercy and comfort in one's own cares and perplexities? The gleam has gone behind the cloud, but we hope for a sight of it again at no very long distance.[11]

Nevertheless, Newman sobbed bitterly over the coffin to think that his friend had left him still dark as to what the way of truth was, and what he ought to do in order to please God and to fulfil his will.

Meanwhile a storm-cloud of great moment was darkening over Oxford and in particular over the head of William George Ward. With Newman's voice virtually silenced after the stir caused by the publication of Tract 90, Ward had become the voice of the Movement. His articles in the *British Critic* became more and more outspoken. Ward was far more indiscreet than Hurrell Froude had ever been. There was something theatrical, Falstaffian even, about this awkward, shabbily dressed and ungainly clerical figure who taught mathematics at Balliol and penned extensive articles which Thomas Mozley, the editor of the *British Critic*, referred to as 'monstrous cobwebs'.

When the magazine came to an end in the autumn of 1843 Ward felt that he was silenced. He had set out to answer a pamphlet by Palmer which had denounced the 'Romanising tendency' of the Movement and condemned the obvious direction in which it seemed to be going. Ward's rambling reply extended to some 600 pages; it was published in the summer of 1844 during the long vacation with the title 'Ideal of a Christian Church, considered in Comparison with Existing Practice'. Only the Roman Church, Ward argued, satisfied the condition of what a Church ought to be; the English Church, in spite of all its professions, utterly and absolutely failed to fulfil them.

In October, a new academic year beginning, the storm broke. During several months of ever-rising tension a new Vice-Chancellor was elected: Dr Symons, the Warden of Wadham, who had never disguised his hostility to the Movement. Early in the new year Convocation assembled in the Sheldonian Theatre on a snowy February day to consider the proposals put to it by the Hebdomadal Board: to condemn Ward's book, and deprive him of his degree. There was also a third proposal: to censure formally the principles of Tract 90. If Ward should be smitten, why not also smite his mentor? Such was the thought of men like Dr Faussett and Dr Ellerton of Magdalen. When this third proposal was about to be put to the vote the Proctors exercised their right of veto, as they had warned they would do. Their *Nobis procuratoribus non placet* might only delay matters until their term of office was over, but in any event, the matter was from then on dropped. It was indeed fortunate that each of the Proctors was Newman's friend.

In his book *The Oxford Movement* Richard Church, who had himself been one of the Proctors, described the events of February 1845 as Oxford's greatest shock.

> The routine of Oxford had been broken as it had never been broken by the fiercest strifes before. Condemnations had been before passed on opinions, and even on persons. But to see an eminent man of blameless life, a fellow of one of the first among the Colleges, solemnly deprived of his degree and all that the degree carried with it, and that on a charge in which bad faith and treachery were combined with alleged heresy, was a novel experience, where the kindnesses of daily companionship and social intercourse still asserted themselves as paramount to official ideas of position. And when, besides this, people realised what more had been attempted, and by how narrow a chance a still heavier blow had been averted from one towards whom so many hearts warmed, how narrowly a yoke had been escaped which would have seemed to subject all religious thought in the University to the caprice or the blind zeal of a partisan official, the sense of relief was mixed with the still present memory of a desperate peril.[12]

Surprisingly Ward did not seem over-worried by the proceedings, and, as if to add a touch of humour to it all, in spite of having long been a strong advocate for clerical celibacy, within a week announced his engagement.

At Littlemore Newman was busily working on his 'Essay on the Development of Christian Doctrine'. He had begun his task a few months earlier. 'I came to the resolution of writing an essay on Doctrinal Development, and then, if at the end of it, I found my convictions in favour of the Roman church were not weaker, of taking the necessary steps for admission into her fold.'[13] As Richard Church was to put it, 'It was no secret what was coming.'[14]

All that was going on at Oxford was watched by Wiseman with the keenest interest. Surely, now the flood-gates were opening; soon the converts must come surging in? This time there would be certainties: the sad story of Mr Sibthorpe might be forgotten.

Richard Sibthorpe, a Fellow of Magdalen, the Vicar of St James's, Ryde, in the Isle of Wight, and a very popular preacher, had visited Oscott in the October of 1841. After only a few days' conversation Wiseman had easily convinced him he should become a Catholic and received him into the Church. Foregoing the usual period of preparation, only six months later Sibthorpe was ordained to the priesthood, but after two years he had evidently seen the error of his ways and returned to the Church of England. It was a bitter blow for Wiseman at the time, though Sibthorpe was to return to the Catholic Church many years later.

Happily there were the cases of William Lockhart and Bernard Smith to stay the mind on. Smith, also of Sibthorpe's college, had been one of Pugin's successes. The zealous architect had travelled to Leadenham in Lincolnshire to oversee the re-decoration of the church roof. The Vicar had been so charmed by Pugin's enthusiasm and his obvious sincerity that he had agreed to meet Wiseman. The result was that he too was received into the Church at Oscott in 1844 and, entering the College as a student, was now training for the priesthood.

Wiseman was expecting to hear news of Newman's conversion almost daily. He had followed carefully the difficulties of Ward, which Frederick Lucas, the editor of *The Tablet*, had called 'The Oxford Farce'. He had heard of the fate of Canon Oakeley, the Vicar of Margaret Street Chapel, who had been at Ward's side to give support during the proceedings in the Sheldonian, and had been asked by his bishop to resign his living. Still no news came from Littlemore. Wiseman did not wish to act personally, but he wished desperately to know how matters were progressing, if at all. In July he decided that Bernard Smith might go to Littlemore; as an old friend, who had once been Newman's curate, there might seem nothing odd about the visit. When Smith arrived Newman greeted him coldly and soon left the room, but Dalgairns, St John, Bowles and Stanton received him with undisguised friendship, wishing to know in detail how he had fared at Oscott; what life was like there, since they each knew it was only a short while before they would be in the same position themselves. Newman reappeared for a moment and invited Smith to remain for dinner; realising the significance of the visit he had decided a sign might be a clearer indication than any form of words. When Newman entered for dinner and stood for a moment in the centre of the small refectory Smith, knowing how meticulous his Vicar had always been about clerical dress, could not help noticing that Newman was wearing grey trousers, a sign that he no longer regarded himself as a clergyman in Anglican Orders. The sign was obvious: Newman now knew himself to be a layman. 'I know the man,' Smith reported later to Wiseman, 'and I know what it means. He will come, and soon.'[15]

In fact, there were two more months to wait, but from that day onward matters moved with great speed. It was soon known that Ward and his wife had asked to be received. Both Dalgairns and St John realised they could not wait any longer and each, on holiday from Littlemore, entered the Church separately: Dalgairns at Aston, where Father Dominic Barberi received him on Michaelmas Day; and St John, at Prior Park. Meanwhile Stanton was taking a holiday at Chorley in Lancashire, and was planning to be received by one of the Jesuits at Stonyhurst. This left only Bowles and Newman of the Littlemore community, but when Dalgairns returned he brought the news that Father Dominic would be staying for a night at the beginning of October. Newman wrote immediately to Stanton asking him to return home so that the three of them could be received together.

On 3 October Newman wrote to the Provost to resign his Oriel fellowship. Hawkins was away at the time and so did not read the letter until 6 October. Here was confirmation of all the rumours that had been rife in Oxford for weeks. 'Where I could speak officially or as a friend,' Hawkins answered, 'I should do what I could do to dissuade any member, much more any minister, of the Church of England, from what you know I cannot but regard as a very grievous error.' He continued to hope that Newman might still at least be saved from some of the worst errors of Rome, such as praying to human mediators or falling down before images, 'because in you, with all the great advantages with which God has blessed you, I must believe such errors to be most deeply sinful'.[16] Hawkins had no choice but to accept the situation: the form of Newman's letter had been correct.

Ambrose St John returned to the college from Prior Park as a Catholic on 7 October. In the afternoon of the following day he set off across the fields with Dalgairns towards the Oxford 'Angel' to meet Father Dominic from the coach. It was a Wednesday: the sky was the colour of pewter and it rained ceaselessly as the two accompanied the little Italian priest, his shabby habit soaked through, the short distance out to Littlemore. The guard of the waggon, also dripping wet, expected some sort of a tip from his foreign passenger. 'I will remember you in my Mass,'[17] Father Dominic replied.

When he reached the college, the priest was encouraged to sit down by the fire to dry out his habit, but he had not been there for very long before Newman entered the room. Father Dominic rose, but Newman, pale and shaking, flung himself on his knees before him, broke down and begged to be received into the Church of Christ.

'What a spectacle it was for me to see Newman at my feet!' Father Dominic wrote to a friend afterwards. 'All that I have suffered since I left Italy has been well compensated by this event, and I hope the effects of such a conversion may be great.'[18]

Stanton had also arrived from Lancashire, but Father Dominic was unable to spend any time with him until Newman had made his general confession.

The effect of the proceeding was such that the penitent was left prostrate and Stanton and St John had to help him out of the small oratory. When he entered Bowles's room Father Dominic bowed to a small print of the Pietà that hung on the wall. 'My dear brother,' he said, 'I am surprised that you should dwell in a Church which has no ideas.'[19] He heard Bowles's confession and then went into Stanton.

The next day, as he himself recorded, all three were received into the Church.

> These three made their profession of faith in the usual form in their private oratory, one after another, with such fervour and piety that I was almost out of myself with joy. I afterwards gave them all canonical absolution and administered to them the Sacrament of Baptism sub conditione. On the following morning I said Mass in their oratory and gave Communion to Messrs. Newman, St. John, Bowles, Stanton and Dalgairns. After Mass, Mr Dalgairns took me to the house of Matthias Woodmason, Esq., a gentleman of Littlemore; I heard his confession and that of his wife and two daughters, and received all into the Church.[20]

In such a simple and practical manner, confident in the formularies of his Church, did this saintly Passionist Father, whom Newman would always consider his 'Father in God', receive the remaining members of the Littlemore household into full communion with the Church of the Apostles.

Father Dominic Barberi remained at Littlemore until Saturday, 11 October, and after his departure Newman visited the Woodmasons, and later called upon Ward and his wife who were living nearby. Among the callers at the college was Robert Newsham, the Jesuit priest, who for almost thirty years had been in charge of the Catholic Chapel in St Clement's and would now be the converts' parish priest. The next morning the small group went to the public Mass in the little church close to Magdalen Bridge for the first time.

Apart from frequent visits to St Clement's, the daily routine at the college remained much as before, though there was an added feeling of excitement. Many letters arrived as the news reached Newman's many friends. To those closest to him he had written personally – most letters, some thirty in all, dated 8 October. Each friend was informed in the simplest terms what he was about to do, but he offered no explanation; only to Elizabeth Bowden and Catherine Froude did he write slightly more extensively. He knew he would be causing pain, particularly to members of his family.

Jemima wrote suggesting her brother should consider the influence he had now lost. Newman replied that he had never thought of any influence he might have had; he had never mastered what that was. Anyway, he could not see how he could have lost influence, or 'thrown it away' as his sister said, if he was answering a call to duty.

> With what conscience could I have remained? How could I have answered it at the last day, if, having opportunities of knowing the Truth which others have not, I had not availed myself of them? What doom would have been mine, if I had kept the Truth a secret in my own bosom, and when I knew which the One Church was, and which was not part of the One Church, I had suffered friends and strangers to die in an ignorance from which I might have relieved them! impossible. One may not act hastily and unsettle others when one has not a clear view – but when one has, it is impossible not to act upon it.[21]

Jemima would never understand, but, unlike Harriett, she would not break off contact with her brother. Newman told her he had no distinct views about remaining at Littlemore; while he was undecided about the future he would remain. He had always looked upon Littlemore as being under the special protection of St Mary, and so many providential circumstances had brought him there that he feared in some way to move.

It was only possible to attend Mass at St Clement's twice during the week, since Newsham also ran a school at Dorchester, some nine miles distance from Oxford. Newman knew how the daily attendance at Mass might have given him greater support, but he accepted the situation, and was grateful that there was a Mass on a Tuesday and Thursday besides on a Sunday. On 21 October Newsham received John Walker into the Church. Walker, a Fellow of Brasenose College, had been at Littlemore for about a month after resigning his curacy at Benefield, in Northamptonshire. Then, on 29 October, Canon Oakeley was also received – an event at which Father Dominic Barberi was present, and he stayed at Littlemore for the night. No doubt he would have found the fare as basic as before: 'no delicacies, no wine, no ale, no liquors, and seldom meat', as he had informed a friend after his previous visit, adding with a note of irony, 'A Capuchin monastery would appear a great palace when compared with Littlemore.'[22]

On the following morning Newman and St John went to Mass and Communion with Father Dominic before he left by coach for Aston and, on the same day, a letter arrived from Wiseman suggesting that Newman and his friends should visit him at once so that they might receive the Sacrament of Confirmation on All Saints' Day. There was no time to lose. In the morning of 31 October St John and Walker accompanied Newman through Gloucester on the journey to Oscott. Arriving at 8.30 in the evening Newman wished to make his confession; a priest was called. It was Father George Spencer.

It is customary for Catholics to take on a special name, or names, at their

Confirmation. In the cases of those who think carefully about such things, as opposed to those who merely like the sound of the names, the choice is usually significant: Newman took the name Mary. Wiseman administered the Sacrament to him, and to St John, Walker and Oakeley besides. There were, as Wiseman informed Russell, ten quondam Anglican clergymen present. Had this ever happened before since the Reformation, he wondered. Among the ten were Dalgairns, Stanton and Bowles, who had received the same rite on the previous Sunday, and Spencer and Smith were the Masters of Ceremony. After the service 'much conversation on the past and future ensued',[23] unlike the previous evening when Newman arrived. Then Wiseman had found it difficult to make conversation beyond inquiring about the journey. However, Smith and Spencer had been more forthcoming.

Although it was decided that Oakeley should remain at Oscott for the time being, Newman and the two others left on the following Monday morning, but not before he had opened up his mind thoroughly to the bishop, which prompted Wiseman to assure Russell that the Church had not received, at any time, a convert who had joined her in more docility and simplicity of faith than Newman. During the brief visit the two men had walked out to see the Old College buildings, and they had evidently lingered there long enough for the Littlemore party to miss the Cheltenham train at Birmingham, with the result that they returned home via London.

The next few months were to see in some measure the fulfilment of Wiseman's hopes as more and more Anglicans sought admission to the Church. As for Newman, Wiseman soon offered him the Old College buildings, which seemed made for the 'Littlemorians', as he called them. It would be a pity in some ways to abandon so important a post as Oxford, but Newman had explained that he wished to give his young friends a good Catholic training and education, which could not be so easily done at Littlemore. At the time, Newman was to speak of 'the cruel suspicions of those who think there is heresy at the bottom of us'. A problem had arisen, because many of the Old English Catholics simply did not believe in the sincerity of these new arrivals: their faith could not possibly have any substance. They had left their own Church, it was thought, out of necessity and had adopted Catholicism as a matter of expediency, so that they were regarded with much the same kind of suspicion as St Paul had been when he arrived in Jerusalem after his conversion. Wiseman was sympathetic to this attitude, for he felt very much troubled by it himself. The root cause was the English Catholics' long isolation from the centre; from the time of his first return to England in 1835 he had tried to encourage closer ties with Rome and to win the English Catholics over to a deeper devotion to the Holy See. If the new converts were to have the influence on the culture and learning of the English Church that he was certain they should have, it was important that they obtained Rome's full acceptance. Newman certainly, but possibly his friends also, must go to Rome.'

Wiseman's resolution to keep the new converts close to him might have increased suspicion, but it turned out in the long run to have been for the best. In February 1846 the Littlemore community moved to Old Oscott, which they quickly renamed Maryvale. Newman's last days at the college at Littlemore naturally caused him much pain. A visit from Pusey made him particularly sad. 'How right I was in saying it was better not to meet!'[24] Newman told St John. The day before he left Littlemore he wrote to Pusey, rather than visit him as Pusey had wished. Newman had heard that Pusey was speaking about his changed manner; a sharpness had been noticed since his reception. This supposed deterioration was used to dissuade others from joining the Church of Rome. Look how Newman and his friends have changed for the worse. 'Such misunderstandings must be just now,' Newman wrote. 'What good then is there in meeting to mistake each other? It is the same with writing. I cannot write so as to please even myself.'[25]

Day after day he packed from morning to night with Bowles's help, sending the boxes off to Oscott where St John was already in residence. There were many parishioners to visit. 'I have had a very trying time, parting with the people,' he told Henry Wilberforce. 'I came into this house by myself – I quit it by myself. Very happy times I have had here ... Perhaps I shall never have quiet again – Shall I ever see Littlemore again?'[26] To Elizabeth Bowden he spoke of consolation in spite of the pain. 'Whatever odium attaches to my name with men in general, there are many individual hearts which feel a sympathy with me, and kindness towards me, which is keener and more lasting than the vague, ignorant disapprobation of the world.'[27]

Newman left Littlemore for good on 22 February 1846. It was a Sunday: he attended Mass at St Clement's for the last time and said farewell to Newsham. At 4 o'clock a fly came to the college to take him and his luggage to the Observatory, the home of Manuel Johnson, which had long been a familiar meeting-place for the Tractarians. Johnson had invited several of Newman's friends to dine, including Copeland. After dinner Church and Pattinson called, and some time during the evening Newman slipped out to say goodbye to James Ogle, who had been his private tutor, and whose daughter, one of five, had married Johnson. Ogle, who was embarrassed by the situation, had said kindly: 'Depend on it, you will come back to us.'[28] Newman was reminded of St Peter's words when Our Lord asked him whether he and the rest would go away, 'Lord to whom shall we go?' It would indeed be like turning away from heaven itself.

Later, Pusey came to offer his farewell. So it was that Newman's last night at Oxford was made less lonely by uneasy friendship. The following morning he set off with Bowles for Maryvale. Travelling by way of Leamington they reached Birmingham, where St John, who had set off to meet them, missed them completely; but in the evening the small community of six was gathered safely together at Maryvale: Newman, St John, Stanton, Bowles, Walker and John Morris, who had not yet been received, and Dr Acqueroni, the scholarly Italian priest whom Wiseman had chosen to be their chaplain. Two days later was Ash Wednesday, and the beginning of Lent.

On Ash Wednesday Newman received an apologetic letter from Pusey in which he admitted that he had said disparaging things about the converts. 'I only wished, through you, to beg pardon of any you hear of, of whom I have said any thing which pained them, either personally or collectively, because, whether right or wrong, I was not the person to say it,'[29] he wrote. Newman saw an opportunity to prick Pusey's conscience in reply, but also to give a warning. On 26 February he wrote:

> Thank you for your affectionate note. I will but say that I cannot conceive, and will not, that the subject of so many prayers as are now offered for you, beginning at Rome, and reaching to Constantinople and England, should ultimately remain where you are. And I am confirmed in this expectation by observing how very much you have changed your views year by year. I think the year can hardly be named which you ended with the same view of the Roman Catholic religion as you began it. And every change has been an approximation to that religion.
>
> This, my dearest Pusey, is an earnest which satisfies me about the future, though I don't tell others so – nor am I anxious or impatient at the delay, for God has His own good time for everything – What does make me anxious, is, whenever I hear that, in spite of your evident approximation in doctrine and view to the Roman system, you are acting in hostility against it, and keeping souls in a system which you cannot bring out into words, as I consider, or rest upon any authority besides your own.
>
> Excuse this freedom, and do not let me pain you. I am in a house, in which Christ is always present as He was to His disciples, and where one can go in from time to time through the day to gain strength from Him. Perhaps this thought makes me bold and urgent.[30]

The reservation of the Blessed Sacrament in the Chapel, which was next to Newman's room, gave him a peace he had not expected. 'It is such an incomprehensible blessing to have Christ in bodily presence in one's house, within one's walls, as swallows up all other privileges and destroys, or should destroy, every pain. To know that He is close by – to be able again and again through the day to go to Him,'[31] he told Wilberforce. After a week he wrote along similar lines to Elizabeth Bowden. What a difference now he felt from the confusion and desolation of those last days at Littlemore. Here too he was in the midst of confusion and disorder, but he was enjoying a blessing few Catholics could expect to have, but still he was favoured with the Presence and he could not help speaking of it.

> I mean, the surpassing privilege of having a Chapel under the very roof in which I live and Christ in it. It has been sometimes objected that some of us have gone over for the privileges we hoped to gain in the Catholic Church. That has not been our case here. We went over not realizing those privileges which we have found by going. I never allowed my mind to dwell on what I might gain of blessedness – but certainly, if I had thought much upon it, I could not have fancied the extreme, ineffable comfort of being in the same house with Him who cured the sick and taught His disciples, as we read of Him in the Gospels, in the days of His flesh. When I have been in Churches abroad, I have religiously abstained from acts of worship, though it was a most soothing comfort to go into them – nor did I know what was going on; I neither understood nor tried to understand the Mass service – and I did not know, or did not observe, the tabernacle Lamp – but now after tasting of the awful delight of worshipping God in His Temple, how unspeakably cold is the idea of a Temple without that Divine Presence! One is tempted to say what is the meaning, what is the use of it?[32]

By 10 March many but not all of the books were out on shelves; for a fortnight the carpenters had been busy and were not near done. Details of the progress were outlined to Copeland. 'One bookcase, with the Fathers all in it, is up – the modern divines are up too. History is in preparation – Exegetics have a place – Classics are a difficulty.'[33] Hagiology and Liturgies had to have their place. The library, however, was only part of their labour and, as Newman had always anticipated leaving the country for a while, it would not be long before the books might have to be moved all over again. 'It is well to be a pilgrim,' he told Copeland, 'and with the Blessed Sacrament ever upon one's footsteps, as it now dwells under our very roof, one cannot be much of an exile any where.'[34]

Of the people with whom he corresponded at this time some were destined to follow his example and become Catholics. Elizabeth Bowden was received in the July of that year, and four years later Henry Wilberforce resigned his living at East Farleigh and was received with his wife and all his children. It was never the same with Pusey.

'O my dear Henry, this world is such a vanity,' Newman wrote to Wilberforce, 'let us look at things as we should wish to have looked at them at the last.

> When I go into Chapel, my prayer for you is that He should touch your conscience, Carrissime; but every thing in its own order – and I am not impatient. What does distress me is, when a person is setting himself to oppose the movement, as is Pusey. It is one thing not to see one's way to move,

another to stop and turn back those who are moving. You will say that I have done so before now – not absolutely, I think – I have only said 'Pause –' 'do not act hastily' – but Pusey says 'Trust in me that you are safe' and 'to move would be a mortal sin'.[35]

Wilberforce replied that he dreaded to be influenced. He knew the power of Newman's mind and he was certain that had Newman turned Quaker he would have felt he must be right. In the meantime he would do much as Pusey, dissuading all he could. 'I see no other honest or safe line in my state of mind and my position,'[36] he wrote.

A few days later the first snow of the winter fell, but it did not linger. Some hedgerows were already in leaf. At Maryvale stoves were put up in the Chapel and gallery, but the old range had been removed as the kitchen was being improved. The busy sound of sawing and hammering meant that shelves were still being put up in the library. On Friday, 20 March Newman recorded that snow had again fallen and he was feeling very cold. Much was occupying his mind, though. On that same day he informed his friend Maria Giberne, whom he knew he could trust, that the Pope had sent him a silver crucifix and a particle of the True Cross. 'I wish about the True Cross to be a secret,' he warned, 'because Protestants would scoff.' Newman noticed the deepest significance in the gift.

> It is a singular coincidence that the certificate of the grant of the sacred Relic is dated on the day that No 90 came out five years ago – and the news of it came to me on the anniversary of the Heads of Houses bringing out their manifesto against it – so that the process of condemnation was just as long as the time it has taken to do me honour. What makes this specially acceptable is this – that it is an indirect approval of my book – at least a negative approval – for, if the book had any thing in it very dangerous or unsound, I suppose this honour would not have been paid me.[37]

Maria would have understood. At first she had been greatly disturbed by Newman's conversion, but just before Christmas she too had been received at the London House of the Jesuits by Father Brownbill, to whom Newman had introduced her. Maria was a firm link with the past: her sister had been married to Newman's first mentor, Walter Mayers. She herself, a competent portrait painter, had been staying in the Newman household in the January 1828, and had shared in the family's sorrow over Mary's illness and death. She would remain one of Newman's closest friends for life.

11

The Development of Christian Doctrine

$$\boxed{1845\text{--}47}$$

The book Newman referred to as having received 'at least negative approval' from Rome was his *An Essay on the Development of Christian Doctrine*. As he said in the Postscript to the Advertisement for the First Edition, his first act on his conversion had been to offer his work for revision to the proper authorities; but the offer was declined on the grounds that it was written and partly printed before he was a Catholic, and that it would come before the reader in a more persuasive form if it were read as the author wrote it.

Newman had taken the manuscript to Oscott with him at the time of his Confirmation in the hope that Wiseman would look at it. After seeming to ignore it altogether, Wiseman did read it but offered no revision. 'Now as to the book, of which his friends speak as a wonderful work,' Wiseman had written to Dr Murray, 'you will see by his account that it is not one written lately, but the work of a long time; he tells me that no one would believe how much thought and labour it had cost him.' Wiseman went on to outline the scheme of the book, in which he again emphasised that it had all been written while Newman had been an Anglican, when he did not contemplate joining the Church immediately.[1] It gave the history only of the mode in which he was led to his own convictions. However, at the end the author stated that now he was a Catholic and held his faith on the authority of the Church, and believed in all things she teaches.

The essay began with a definition of 'development' as a natural growth, as opposed to a corruption or process of decay. Just as a full-grown oak tree bore no resemblance to the acorn from which it grew, but is nevertheless the natural result of growth, a development of the life in the seed of its origin, so each Christian dogma and doctrine had been gradually defined.

Newman argued that time was necessary for the true comprehension and perfection of great ideas. It had certainly taken time for the Church to define the Doctrine of the Blessed Trinity. The Gospels gave the seed of revelation, but no one would deny that many passages became clear only in the light of the doctrine's definition. Revelation was a Heavenly gift. 'He who gave it virtually has not given it, unless He has also secured it from perversion or corruption, in all such developments as may come upon it by the necessity of its nature. That intellectual action through successive generations, which is the organ of development, must be in its determinations infallible.'[2] Yet ideas grow, or develop, gradually, and through the power of the Holy Spirit the fullness of their meaning becomes clear. The problem was how to tell a truly genuine development from a corruption or an accretion. Newman applied certain tests.

> To find what corruption or perversion of the truth is, let us enquire what
> the word means when used literally of material substances. Now, it is plain,
> first of all, that corruption is a word attached to organised matter only; a
> stone may be crushed to powder, but it cannot be corrupted. Corruption,
> on the contrary, is the breaking up of life preparatory to its dissolution. The
> resolution of the body into its component parts is the stage before its
> dissolution; it begins when life has reached its perfection, and it is the sequel,
> or rather the continuation, of that process towards perfection, being at the
> same time the reversal and undoing of what went before ... Taking this
> analogy as a whole, I venture to set down seven Notes of varying cogency,
> independence and applicability, to discriminate healthy developments of an
> idea from its state of corruption and decay, – as follows:
>
> There is no corruption if it retains one and the same type, the same
> principle, the same organization; if its beginnings anticipate its subsequent
> phases, and its later phenomena protect and subserve its earlier; if it has power
> of assimilation and revival and a vigorous action first and last.[3]

Newman continued his essay with a wide-ranging review of how Catholic doctrine had grown from the days of the Apostles down through the centuries until his own time. What were often seen by Protestants as 'Roman corruptions' of the primitive Creed, were really logical developments of the original deposit of Faith. This was not to deny that corruption had crept in: the Church had been beset with heresy from the beginning. Error and heresy had often threatened the very life of the Church, but such were never true developments, but corruptions, rather, of brief duration, that quickly ran themselves out and ended in death. The Church had remained firm through all these attacks, for she held to the mystery of revealed truth, and had maintained unblemished her central doctrine of God the Father, of His co-eternal Christ, and His co-eternal Spirit. 'And is it not utterly incredible that with this thorough comprehension of so great a mystery, as far as the human mind can know it, she should be at that very time in the commission of the grossest errors in religious worship and should be hiding the God and Mediator, whose incarnation she contemplated with so clear an intellect, behind a crowd of idols?'[4]

Newman had much to say about the issue that had been a personal stumbling block, as it has been, and, indeed, may be for many Protestants still: the Catholic Church's devotion to the Blessed Virgin. The ecclesiastical recognition of the place which Mary holds in the economy of grace, Newman argued, was a natural development of the definition of our Lord's proper divinity. The Council of Ephesus in the year 430 determined that the Blessed Virgin was Theotocos, the Mother of God, but the title had been applied to Mary from primitive times, and was already familiar to Christians. Here Newman's immensely wide reading came to his aid as he listed instance after instance from the Fathers. 'Run through all creation in your thoughts, and see if there be equal to, or greater than, the Holy Virgin Mother of God,' wrote St Proclus. St Augustine had sown the seed of the Doctrine of the Immaculate Conception when he had written that all have sinned 'except the Holy Virgin Mary, concerning whom, for the honour of the Lord, I wish no question to be raised at all, when we are treating of sins'.[5]

In order to do honour to Christ, in order to defend the true doctrine of the Incarnation, in order to secure a right faith in the manhood of the Eternal Son, the Council of Ephesus had declared Mary to be the Mother of God. Thus it was, Newman argued, that all heresies of that day, the Arian, the Nestorian and the Monophysite, had tended in a most wonderful way towards Mary's exaltation; and the School of Antioch, the fountain of primitive rationalism, 'led the Church to determine first the conceivable greatness of the creature, and then the incommunicable dignity of the Blessed Virgin'.[6]

Towards the end of the essay Newman returns to the subject once again. 'It has been anxiously asked,' he wrote, 'whether the honours paid to St Mary, which have grown out of devotion to her Almighty Lord and Son, do not, in fact, tend to weaken that devotion; and whether, from the nature of the case, it is possible so to exalt a creature without withdrawing the heart from the Creator.

> The point to consider here was: Had the honours paid to Mary weakened devotion to her Son? Was it a matter of fact, or was it only presumption or conjecture?
>
> Here I observe, first, that, to those who admit the authority of the Fathers of Ephesus, the question is in no slight degree answered by their sanction

of the Theotocos, or 'Mother of God', as a title of St Mary, and as given
in order to protect the doctrine of the Incarnation, and to preserve the faith
of Catholics from a specious Humanitarianism.[7]

If a survey were taken of European Christian communions, Newman
claimed, it would be found that it was not those characterised by devotion
towards the Blessed Virgin that had ceased to adore her Eternal Son, but
those very bodies which (being unfettered by State law) have renounced that
devotion. The regard for His glory, which was professed in that keen jealousy
of her exaltation, had not been supported by the event.

> They who were accused of worshipping a creature in His stead, still worship
> Him; their accusers, who hoped to worship Him so purely, they, wherever
> obstacles to the development of their principles have been removed, have
> ceased to worship him altogether.[8]

Next Newman noted how the tone of devotion paid to Mary was altogether
distinct from that which is paid to her Eternal Son and to the Holy Trinity,
as must certainly be allowed on inspection of the Catholic services. To Our
Lord the tone was 'severe, profound, awful, as well as tender, confiding and
dutiful, Christ is addressed as true God, while he is true Man; as our Creator
and Judge, while He is most loving, gentle and gracious. On the other hand,
towards Mary the language employed is affectionate and ardent, as towards
a mere child of Adam; though subdued, as coming from her sinful kindred.'
In illustration Newman contrasts the tone of the *Dies Irae* with that of the
Stabat Mater.

It was pointless to object, he continued, that in this contrast of devotional
exercises, from the infirmity of human nature, the human will supplanted
the Divine; for the question was simply one of fact. It had to be asked whether
the character of much of the Protestant devotion towards Our Lord had
been that of adoration at all, and not rather such as might be paid to an
excellent human being, no higher devotion than Catholics paid to St Mary
but differing from it, however, in often being familiar, rude, and earthly.
Carnal minds would ever create carnal worship for themselves; and to forbid
them the service of the Saints would have no tendency to teach them to
worship God.

> Moreover, it must be observed, what is very important, that great and constant
> as is the devotion which the Catholic pays to the Blessed Mary, it has a special
> province, and has far more connexion with the public services and the festive
> aspect of Christianity, and with certain extraordinary offices which she holds,
> than with what is strictly personal and primary in religion.[9]
> *Unica spes mea Jesus, et post Jesus Virgo Maria.* Amen.[10]

141

It was a general pretext of heretics, Newman argued, that they were but serving and protecting Christianity by their innovations; and it was their charge against the Catholic Church, that her successive definitions of doctrine had but overlaid and obscured it. One thing shines out from Newman's essay which must have helped to bring him to his great decision, that is his understanding that the Church founded by Christ must have a visible Head upon earth. Nowhere can the Church be found except under the jurisdiction of the Holy See.

> If Christianity is both social and dogmatic, and intended for all ages, it must, humanly speaking, have an infallible expounder. Else you will secure unity of form at the loss of unity of doctrine, or unity of doctrine at the loss of unity of form; you will have to choose between a comprehension of opinions and a resolution into parties, between latitudinarian and sectarian error ... You must accept the whole or reject the whole; attenuation does but enfeeble and amputation mutilate; it is trifling to receive all but something which is as integral as any other portion. Thus it would be trifling indeed to accept everything Catholic except the Head of the Body of Christ upon earth.[11]

At first Wiseman had thought of Newman setting out for Rome at the end of June when he expected to be there himself; for a while he would undertake personally to 'educate' his famous convert. Since he was going to be in the city on business, it would be little trouble to steer Newman in the right direction. For Wiseman was quite certain the Maryvale community should become Oratorians and had already discussed the possibility with their leader. At this time also Faber, who had been received a few weeks after Newman in the previous year, had returned from Rome 'full of spirits and money' and had set about the task of establishing a community in Birmingham. His fellow converts were mostly young men from his former parish in Huntingdonshire; calling themselves the Brothers of the Will of God, they had soon attracted attention and had been pelted in the streets, something Newman felt would bring Faber great satisfaction.

As it happened, Newman's departure was delayed until the end of September, by which time, at the age of forty-five, he had been a Catholic for almost a year. On 6 June, together with the members of his community, he received tonsure and minor orders at Oscott. The delay in departure also meant that he was able to accompany St John and Bowles to Coventry for the consecration of William Ullathorne as Vicar Apostolic of the Western District. This energetic Benedictine, whom Newman was to describe as 'a straightforward Englishman', was a member of an Old Catholic family and a descendant of St Thomas More. He was five years younger than Newman, and he had spent many years organising the Church out in Australia. In 1841 he had returned to take charge of the Mission at Coventry, and after only two years as Bishop of the Western District, he was transferred back to the Central District, and became the first Bishop of Birmingham when the Hierarchy was restored in 1850.

Ullathorne's consecration happened to take place on the same day, 21 June, that Giovanni Maria Mastai-Ferretti was crowned as Pope Pius ix in Rome. Wiseman's friend, Pope Gregory xvi, had died at the beginning of the month. So it was that when Newman entered St Peter's to hear Mass on Thursday, 29 October, he found it was being said by the new Pope, one who had the reputation of being a liberal and whose pontificate was destined to be the longest in history.

The journey had begun on 7 September when Newman and St John set sail by steamer from Brighton to Dieppe. Travelling quickly through France and crossing the Alps by the Simplon, much of the way on foot, the two arrived at Milan on Sunday 21 and attended Mass at the Cathedral.

'I still think Milan is the most interesting place I ever was in,' he wrote home to William Penny, who had joined the community at Maryvale. 'It is so very great a blessing to be able to go into the churches as we walk in the city – always open with large ungrudging kindness – full of costly marbles to the sight, and shrines, images, and crucifixes all open for the passerby to make his own by kneeling at them – the Blessed Sacrament every where, and indulgences abundant.'[12] What a change in attitude from his first visit to Rome!

The Cathedral had moved him more than he could remember St Peter's having done, but in 1833 he had abstained from all services. Now, as he told Henry Wilberforce, it was most wonderful to see the Divine Presence looking out almost into the open streets from the various churches. He visited St Ambrose's Church – where the body of the saint lies – and he knelt at those relics 'which have been so powerful, and whom I have heard and read of more than other Saints from a boy. It is thirty years this very month, as I may say, since God made me religious, and St Ambrose in Milner's history was one of the first objects of my veneration.'[13] St Augustine too had been converted in Milan; his mother, St Monica, had come there to seek out her son. Above all, there too the great Athanasius, in his exile, had come to meet the Emperor. Newman also visited the tomb of St Charles Borromeo, the great archbishop of Milan, who had given such generous help to the English College at Douai and in 1580 had been visited by Ralph Sherwin and Edmund Campion on their way back to England and a martyr's death. Newman felt he had never been so moved by a place before. 'I never knew what worship was, as an objective fact, till I entered the Catholic Church, and was partaker in its offices of devotion.' Now he would say the same about its cathedral assemblages:

A Catholic Cathedral is a sort of world, every one going about his own business, but that business a religious one; groups of worshippers and solitary ones – kneeling, standing – some at shrines, some at altars – hearing Mass and communicating – currents of worshippers intercepting and passing by each other – altar after altar lit up for worship, like stars in the firmament – or the bell giving notice of what is going on in parts you do not see and all the while the canons in the choir going through their hours, Matins, Lauds or Vespers, and at the end of it the incense rolling up from the high altar, and all this in one of the most wonderful buildings in the world and every day – lastly, all of this without any show or effort, but what every one is used to.[14]

While he was in Milan Newman met up with two English priests, Francis Amherst and George Talbot, who had been ordained by Wiseman on 6 June. In spite of their being at Oscott so recently, Newman did not seem to have known of their plans. He received communion from Talbot's hand in St Ambrose's Church on Sunday, 27 September, but the two were never to become friends, as the future would tell.

The Collegio di Propaganda would be Newman's and St John's home until their ordination at the end of the following May. When they arrived in Rome the accommodation at the College was not ready, because the Italians had decided to decorate two rooms specially for their important English students. Instead the first three weeks were spent at Buy's, which Newman described as a wretched place, a palace of filth where the carpet was a nest of fleas and there were milk pans for slop bowls. It must have brought back memories of his time in Sicily. As the only two adult members of the College they were not required to dress as Propagandists, nor as clergy, but as gentlemen. However, they did wear the College dress for a while, which consisted of a dress coat with a sort of undergraduate's gown hanging behind, black stockings which must be without wrinkle, and a large heavy cocked hat. To add to this they wore buckles at the knees and buckles on the shoes: it was like 'dressing up black-a-moors in muslin'. Soon Newman preferred to wear a cassock and a biretta, though the cassock dragged in the mud.

When the rooms in College were completed they were found to consist of an anteroom made from the end of a corridor which had been blocked off by a glass partition, and their bedrooms which were opposite each other and led off a connecting passage. All the furniture was new and the wallpaper and curtains were far grander than necessary. 'We are treated like princes, much to our distress,' Newman told Elizabeth Bowden. 'It is really quite absurd, considering our habits, but they will not believe that we like plainer things, and are surprised to find we can bear in daily things to do as they do.'[15]

During the first few weeks not only was the weather appalling, but both Newman and St John caught colds and were forced to spend some time in bed. St John, it seems, had caught a chill while visiting one of the catacombs. Coping as best they could, they were soon well enough to attend lectures in dogmatic and moral theology; and they met as many people as possible. Newman was surprised to find that Maria Giberne was in Rome trying to establish herself as a portrait painter, and George Ryder and his family, who had been received recently into the Church, were lodging in the city also.

From home came news that Father Spencer had joined the Passionists; it would be good news for Father Dominic. Cardinal Acton had taken Newman to visit the Passionists' House in Rome: 'very clean and beautifully situated'. They had seen the various remains, clothes and other personal effects, of the founder, the Venerable Paul. 'Suppose we all become Passionists,'[16] Newman suggested to Dalgairns. Letters from Maryvale suggested that the community was lacking direction and sorely missing its superior.

Suddenly, on Sunday, 22 November Newman and St John were summoned to the Pope at half an hour's notice. It had been a very wet day, as Newman told Bowles. 'The state of Rome in moderately wet weather is indescribable. I never saw any city with the tenth part the quantity of dung in the streets as Rome – When the rain comes this is formed into a thickish fluid.'[17] That Sunday they had returned to the College with the skirts of their mantillas tinged 'with the nastiest stuff'; a hasty attempt was made to rinse out the dirt, since the Rector had told them to confront the Holy Father just as they were. Riding in Monsignor Brunelli's carriage they set off for the Vatican. Newman saw the Pope as 'a vigorous man, with a very pleasant countenance'; as he bent down to kiss the slippered foot he banged his chin on the Pope's knee. Otherwise the interview went well, the Pope was very kind. With a quickness in his movements, he ran across the room to open a closet from which he produced a beautiful oil painting of the Mater Dolorosa, and presented it to Newman.

As Christmas approached, and the snow froze on the Roman roofs though the streets were as dry as a bone, 'the sounds sharp as in a frost in England', Newman began to feel happier than he had ever been in his life before. There was something dreamlike about it; all was so quiet, so safe, so happy that he felt he had always been there, as if there had been no violent rupture or vicissitude in the course of his life. 'I was happy at Oriel, happier at Littlemore, as happy or happier still at Maryvale – and happiest here,' he told Henry Wilberforce. 'At least, whether I can rightly compare different times or not, how happy is this very thing that I should ever be thinking the state of life, in which I happen to be in, the happiest of all. There cannot be a more striking proof how I am blest.'[18]

On 31 December Newman told Dalgairns that they had visited the Chiesa Nuova, the Church of St Philip Neri. They had heard Mass and communicated in the small room where St Philip had had his ecstasies. The Casa adjoining the church Newman considered the most beautiful thing of the kind to be seen in Rome, though perhaps a little too comfortable, 'fine galleries for walking in summer, splendid orange trees'.

> If I wished to follow my bent, I should join them, if I joined any – They
> have a good library, and handsome sets of rooms apparently. It is like a College
> with hardly any rule. They keep their own property, and furnish their own
> rooms.[19]

It spoke to him of home. Was not this what Wiseman wished for him? It seemed Wiseman might be right.

'It is curious and very pleasant that, after all the thought we can give the matter, we come round to your Lordship's original idea, and feel we cannot do better than be Oratorians,'[20] Newman wrote to Wiseman early in January 1847. The statement did not commit him to a final decision, but it brought to an end the anxious period when St John and he had considered at various times their small community joining the Jesuits, the Redemptorists, or the Dominican Third Order. Wiseman's 'original idea' had always returned to take pride of place. A few days after his letter was written he had been present when Cardinal Acton had received Edward Caswell and his wife into the Church. Caswell, another Oxford man, had been Perpetual Curate of Stratford-sub-Castle near Salisbury, and had attributed his conversion to his reading of Newman's *Development of Christian Doctrine*. No one knew at the time how Caswell's future would be bound up with the English oratory Newman was now busy planning.

From this time onward Newman paid almost daily visits to St Peter's and the Chiesa Nuova where he had formed a close bond with Augustine Theiner, a scholarly Oratorian and a convert from German Rationalism. Though he was considered an 'unmethodical talker', he talked well enough to give much encouragement towards the fulfilment of the Englishmen's aspirations.

Newman studied the rule of St Philip Neri diligently. In outline it seemed ideally suitable: 'a body of priests labouring in the conversion of great towns, yet with time for literary work'.[21] St Philip in many ways reminded him of Keble. 'I can fancy what Keble would have been, if God's will had been he should be born in another place and age; he was formed on the same type of extreme hatred of humbug, playfulness, nay, oddity, tender love for others, and severity, which are the lineaments of Keble.'[22] From a child St Philip had given himself up to religion and had laboured entirely in the Eternal City for the good of the poor. As a contemporary of St Ignatius

Loyola and St Charles Borromeo he had played an important part in the strengthening of the Counter-Reformation Church.

One Sunday in January 1847 Newman had heard a sermon by Father Ventura, a Sicilian priest who was said to rival Lacordaire as an orator. The subject was, somewhat surprisingly, the Irish Famine. The famine had begun in 1845 with the failure of the potato crop, and had continued with a second failure the following year. The seriousness of the situation had brought down the Peel Government, and was only slowly faced up to when Lord John Russell came into office in July 1846. The famine caused an up-heaval of gigantic proportion, for the crop failed for a third year, though by that time the Government had largely come to grips with the disaster, but not before thousands of Irish emigrated, many to England, which would have a more profound effect on the Catholic congregations there than the steady flow of converts from the Church of England.

There would clearly be much to do when the Oratorians returned home.

During the early months of 1847 Dr Ullathorne visited Rome and Newman saw him several times. Later in the year Wiseman himself arrived. Newman had kept up a steady correspondence with the Bishop, seeking his advice, and outlining his hopes. 'I can do nothing without Rome on my side,'[23] he wrote. There was so much jealousy in England, it was essential that he should have Rome's support. In Rome the opinion of most churchmen seemed to be that the only people doing anything in England were those connected with Wiseman. 'Now the conviction has more and more come to me,' Newman insisted, 'that it is very expedient for a person like me, a convert, and a writer, (and so pledged in a way to certain opinions) to be a theological professor or the like.'[24] Yet he realised that his *Development of Christian Doctrine* was opposed by some eminent Roman professors, and Dr Grant of the Scotch College had been speaking against it. He need not have feared, for it was not long before the Pope was encouraging the Oratorian venture, and did all he could to find Newman premises where he and his friends could study for the noviciate.

It was not long before Dalgairns, Bowles, Stanton and William Penny had arrived in Rome, together with Robert Coffin, who had resigned as Vicar of St Mary Magdalen's, Oxford, and become a Catholic in 1845, largely through Newman's influence. Since his conversion he had been tutor to Ambrose Phillipps's children at Grace Dieu.

Ordination to the priesthood for Newman and St John came on Trinity Sunday, 30 May in the Chapel of the College at the hands of Cardinal Fransoni, the Cardinal Prefect of Propaganda. Soon it was rumoured in the city that back in England Dr Pusey had become a Catholic. Newman thought it would be simply a miracle; he did not know why miracles should not take place, but, as he wrote to Elizabeth Bowden, all human probabilities and laws were against Pusey's changing, and he was right.

After some talk of the community moving to Malta, the Pope decided it should remain in Rome and be trained by Carlo Rossi, a brilliant Oratorian of Newman's own age. On 28 June Newman left the Collegio di Propaganda for good and moved to rooms in the monastery adjoining the Basilica of Santa Croce in Gerusalemme, some two miles outside the city. When the community walked down to St Peter's on the evening of the Feast of St Peter and St Paul, it was like being back at Littlemore, and jokes were made about walking into Oxford.

By the third week in July it was rumoured that Wiseman was about to be created a Cardinal. 'We should gain greatly by it, and I almost think Catholicism in England would gain,'[25] Newman wrote. Although the possibility was no doubt in the Pope's mind, nothing transpired just yet. On 9 August the Pope visited his Oratorian novices at a time when Wiseman happened to be there. Such attention made Newman feel he was under special protection; not only had the summer been kind, but he felt St Mary and St Philip were close at hand, though 'Lead Thou me on' was quite as appropriate to his state as ever, as he told Henry Wilberforce, 'for what I shall be called to do when I get back, or how I shall be used, is quite a mystery to me'.[26]

The Pope had entrusted Wiseman with the task of establishing better diplomatic relations with the British Government, and on 19 August, a few days after he had ordained Stanton, he sent for Newman and told him he was returning to England more quickly than expected, and therefore could not accompany St John and him to Monte Porzio as planned.

During the last weeks of August Newman and St John visited the Oratory at Naples. The Gerolamini, as the novices there were called, were 'nice and modest'. 'We have got on very well with them. I think we have got a good many ideas ... we shall ask them all the questions we can think of,'[27] Newman wrote back to Bowles. At Naples they also met more important Oratorians, the Superior of the house of Messina, and a Palermitan father, who invited them to Palermo. In the event there was no time to go over to Sicily, but the Oratorian Archbishop, Antonio Caracciolo, who had been formerly the Superior of the house at Palermo, received them warmly. At least such introductions served to give Newman the feeling of belonging.

On the journey home a visit was made to Monte Cassino, where Newman said Mass at St Benedict's altar, and spent one night there, during which he felt too ill to dine in the refectory, but was entertained to supper in his room in the company of an Irish-born monk, Dom Bernard Smith, whose name must have reminded Newman of his former curate. At this time also St John seemed tired out and possibly sickening for something; a few days after they returned to Rome he was taken ill and had to be seen by a doctor.

However, their return brought them news of the future: the brief for setting up an Oratory in England had been drawn up. It was made out for Birmingham – and Maryvale was to be the Mother House of the whole kingdom. It was certain, as Newman told Elizabeth Bowden, that important changes were about to take place in the state of Catholicism in England, and the Oratorians must in some way or other be brought nearer to London, even though their home would continue to be Maryvale. 'The Pope seems to have given Dr Wiseman his whole confidence; and except that he is now engaged in important ways in England, I suppose he would have kept him here as a Cardinal at once.'[28]

On 10 October the Pope appointed Newman the first Superior of the English Oratory with the power to appoint four Deputies; this meant that although the base would be Birmingham there could be other houses established. Already there had been overtures from Father Thomas Doyle, one of the priests from St George's, Southwark, in the hope that the Oratorians might settle there. Newman had written explaining that his numbers were likely to be too small for the needs of a district such as St George's.

Towards the end of Newman's time at Rome an unlikely visitor arrived in the person of Archdeacon Manning. For two days in the first week of December the two walked about the city just as they had done at Oxford all those years ago. It will have been interesting for him to learn of Manning's recent visits to Germany and Switzerland, but it was a difficult time for Newman. He was trying to see as many people as possible to say goodbye, yet Manning was Henry Wilberforce's brother-in-law and Newman knew how he admitted already to feeling 'less able to say Rome is wrong'. So he managed to find time for Manning, even on his last day in Rome, Sunday, 5 December. He said Mass in the morning at the Chiesa Nuova, thinking it might be the last time he would be in the church of the founder of the Order to which he had now dedicated his life.

On the journey home Newman and St John visited the Holy House at Loretto, where they said Mass and bought a rosary for Stanton, as he had requested. At Fano they called on Wiseman's mother, and then by way of Bologna, Padua and Verona, finding time to make brief visits to the shrines of St Dominic and St Catherine, they crossed over the Brenner Pass and made their way during the next three days to Munich where they took tea with Ignatius Döllinger, the eminent German theologian, and had what Newman described as 'some profitable talk'. Returning to England on Christmas Eve, they put up at Hatchett's for the night, and the following day offered their Festal Mass at Elizabeth Bowden's private chapel. Later they went to Golden Square to have lunch with Wiseman, whose Christmas news was that Faber and his community had offered to become Oratorians. That evening the Bowdens were expected at their cousins, so, as Newman's diary records, he returned to Piccadilly where St John and he dined together soli in the Coffee Room at Hatchett's. It was, as he informed Jemima a few days later, a reminder of 1828 when he had preached the Whitehall Sermon and had posted down after it to Brighton. 'No great encouragement to pass Christmas Day in London.'[29]

12

The Oratory of St Philip

1847–49

'You may fancy the joy with which St John and I heard the news that you proposed we should be one,'[1] Newman wrote to Faber on 31 December. He had no doubt that Faber himself would be an asset, but he held some reservation about Faber's 'youths', who seemed to have something fanatical about them. He wondered whether they would have any notion of what Oratorianism really was. 'In many respects it differs from what you are at present,' Newman added. 'It is not so near ascetic – indeed it is not ascetic. It is not poetical – it is not very devotional. Now it is a question what your youths will say to this.'[2] How many of these young men, Newman wondered, were fit to become priests? An Oratory had fewer lay brothers than Faber's present community, and those there were usually had secular offices: gardener, cook, manciple, and so forth.

An Oratorian ought, like a Roman legionary, to stand in his place and fight by himself, though in a company – instead of being a mere instrument of another, or a member of a phalanx – Or he is an Athenian, as described in Pericles's Oration, as contrasted with a Spartan. I am so desirous of our coming together, that I wince while I put down these objections, but no good will come of it, if we don't consider the matter first in all its bearings.[3]

One thing in favour of the amalgamation was that Faber had offered 'his house, his money, his all', but this did not turn out to be as straightforward as it seemed. Certainly, Wiseman had seen the situation as Providential. He had heard how Faber had suddenly come to his decision. The idea had come to him while he was making his morning meditation.

I rose at five and made my meditation. It was full of distractions; but I took

151

pains with it, although I had no particular sweetness in it, nor was there anything signal about it in any way. Towards the conclusion, when making my colloquies, and repeating my petition for counsel and prudence, when nothing was further from my thoughts, all on a sudden I felt an interior call to join the Oratory of St Philip, and in one instant all perplexity of the faculties of my soul which I had experienced for some weeks was calmed.[4]

Wiseman had already written to Faber suggesting that, as he was still officially their Superior, the community should travel up to London to take their vows at Golden Square on 8 December, the Feast of the Immaculate Conception. His letter reached the Wilfridians, as Wiseman called them, the day following Faber's sudden inspiration. It was vital to inform Wiseman of the change of plan immediately, so Faber and Father Hutchinson, another convert who had accompanied him to Rome, set off immediately for London. As if to set a seal on the venture, when they arrived at Wiseman's house, they were confronted by Richard Stanton in his Oratorian habit. After a lengthy conference Wiseman gave his formal consent to the idea, but it would have to wait for Newman's return and, what was more, his approval.

Ideally, Wiseman would have liked the first Oratory to be established in London now that their number was likely to be much larger, but Newman's brief from the Pope had fixed this at Birmingham, and Newman's name alone was introduced into it, his name only. As Newman informed Henry Wilberforce, it would be impossible to change without the Pope's interference; besides Wiseman's moving to London had taken place after the brief had been drawn up.

Wiseman moved to the London District on the unexpected death of Bishop Griffiths, which heralded an end to the old order of Catholic administration in England. Griffiths was succeeded by Bishop Walsh, whose weak health had already meant that Wiseman, his coadjutor, was doing most of his work. For some time Rome had been considering restoring the Catholic Hierarchy but, it was suggested, the decision to do so had been delayed partly because Pope Gregory xvi thought Dr Griffiths would be unsuitable as the first Archbishop. Whether this is true or not, there had been much talk of the restoration before Griffiths's death, and even more afterwards, because the new Pope was equally anxious to bring it about. England was now on the Roman map.

Whatever Dr Griffiths's shortcomings, his death received an honourable mention in *The Times* which spoke of his being 'an amiable gentleman, benevolent pastor, and discreet ecclesiastical ruler'. Such a mention in that newspaper was likely to have been the first ever accorded to a Vicar Apostolic. Such politeness would not often be accorded to Wiseman who took up residence at Golden Square in September 1847. It was not long before the new coadjutor Vicar Apostolic felt a certain loneliness, for he knew even some of the London clergy were divided over the wisdom of his appointment. At least he could rely on the loyalty of the Superior of the English Oratorians.

Newman arrived back at Maryvale and the English Oratory was formally established on the Feast of the Purification, 2 February. Twelve days later the Wilfridians were admitted, and Faber became a novice under Newman. As Newman himself had only served a brief noviciate he decided that Faber should only be a novice for five months, and Newman was happy for him to be absent from the house for certain periods of time to preach. Because he did not enjoy the best of health, Newman thought he should spend some time by the seaside.

At about this time Newman received a letter from Anthony Hanmer, the curate at Tiverton, Devon, who asked Newman whether he was satisfied with the move he had made in becoming a Catholic. Perhaps Hanmer had heard rumours that Newman was regretting his situation and was contemplating returning to Anglicanism. Newman replied that to ask about satisfaction was like asking you what you thought of, or how you liked your mother and father.

> I will say that from the time I became a Catholic, the shadow of a misgiving
> has not crossed my mind that I was not doing God's will in becoming one
> – not a shadow of regret (it quite makes me smile to fancy it) that I am not
> still an Anglican. Most people know in a measure what I gave up to become
> a Catholic, and they can fancy that probably it was much more than they
> happen to know, yet were the loss a hundred fold, it would indeed have been
> a cheap bargain. It is coming out of shadows into truth – into that which
> is beyond mistake a real religion – not a mere opinion such that you have
> no confidence that your next door neighbour holds it too, but an external
> objective substantive creed and worship. The thought of Anglicanism with
> nothing fixed or settled, with Bishop contradicting Bishops within, and the
> whole world against it, without, is something so dreary and wretched, that
> I cannot speak of it without the chance of offence to those who still hold it.[5]

Hanmer had spoken against making 'ventures in faith' which Newman answered with the example of Abraham. Had not he made a venture when he went out, 'not knowing whither he went? – he had not even the opportunity, which you have, of asking persons who had gone before him'.[6] The point had been made and Hanmer did not delay much longer; he was received into the Church at Spanish Place some eighteen months later.

Naturally the whole process of conversion had occupied Newman's mind for years. There was something miraculous about it but, on looking back, the steady progression towards certainty had an inevitability and seemed almost obvious. While he was in Rome he had written a short novel which had now appeared anonymously as *Loss and Gain: The story of a Convert*. In the person of his hero, Charles Reding, Newman follows the process once again. Reding is training for the Anglican ministry at Oxford during the Tractarian controversy. Apart from a close friend, Willis, who soon goes over to Rome, all Reding's companions are anti-Catholic, but in spite of their confidence Reding passes through an agony of doubt, and after two years of struggle he finds himself at the threshold of the Church. Writing this in Rome, where Newman became more and more deeply aware of the Real Presence in the Blessed Sacrament, he lets Willis defend the sacrifice of the Mass by arguing that it was not a Roman superstition, as Reding still feared.

> I declare to you to me nothing is so consoling, so piercing, so thrilling, so overcoming, as the Mass, said as it is among us. I could attend Masses for ever and not be tired. It is not a mere form of words – it is a great Action, the greatest action that there can be on earth. It is not the invocation merely, but, if I dare use the word, the evocation of the Eternal. He becomes present on the altar in flesh and blood, before whom angels bow and devils tremble ... Each in his place, with his own heart, with his own wants, with his own thoughts, with his own intention, with his own prayers, separate but concordant, watching what is going on, watching its progress, uniting in its consummation; – not painfully and hopelessly following a hard form of prayer from beginning to end, but like a concert of musical instruments, each different, but concurring in a sweet harmony, we take our part with God's priest, supporting him, yet guided by him. There are little children there, and old men, and simple labourers, and students in seminaries, priests preparing for Mass, priests making their thanksgiving; there are innocent maidens, and there are penitents; but out of these many minds rises one eucharistic hymn, and the great Action is the measure and the scope of it.[7]

Although *Loss and Gain* has some passages of great power and beauty, it has to be admitted that much of the dialogue tends to be tedious. Certainly, Newman wrote much of it lightheartedly, and one can imagine the laughter shared with St John as the tale began to take shape. As Newman explained many years later he had written his *Loss and Gain* in answer to a novel someone had sent him from home, in which the Oxford converts had been lampooned. This was *From Oxford to Rome*, a novel by Miss Harris which enjoyed a certain popularity at the time, but as Newman was to put it: 'Its contents were so wantonly and preposterously fanciful, as they were injurious to those whose motives and actions it professed to represent, but a formal criticism or grave notice of it had seemed out of place.'[8] The suitable answer lay in another tale 'drawn up with a stricter regard to truth and probability, and with at least some personal knowledge of Oxford, and some perception of the various aspects of the religious phenomenon'. It was a challenge he met admirably, and one of his friends visiting Santa Croce in 1847 remembered finding Newman chuckling over a passage he had just written. Perhaps it was this one, where Reding returns to Oxford after the long vacation.

'Have you heard the news?' said Sheffield; 'I have been long enough in college to pick it up. The kitchen man was full of it as I passed along. Jack's a particular friend of mine, a good honest fellow, and he has all the gossip of the place. I don't know what it means, but Oxford had just now a very bad inside. The report is that some of the men have turned Romans; and they say there are strangers going about Oxford whom no one knows anything of. Jack, who is a bit of a divine himself, says he heard the Principal say that, for certain, there were Jesuits at the bottom of it; and I don't know what he means, but he declares he saw with his own eyes the Pope walking down High Street with the priest. I asked him how he knew it. He said he knew the Pope by his slouching hat and his long beard; and the porter told him it was the Pope.'[9]

When *Loss and Gain* was first published and the identity of the author became known, Faber informed him that the Puseyites thought he had sunk lower than Dickens.

Newman's letters during the Spring of 1848 continued to inform his friends of the progress of his Oratorian plans. Although he remained at Maryvale, Faber's community was still at St Wilfrid's, Cheadle, where the new chapel was being completed. The cost of keeping up both houses caused Newman much anxiety, and he became increasingly certain that Cheadle was not a place which would answer the purpose of an Oratorian Mission, but a Mission there had to be, because the Earl of Shrewsbury had endowed Faber on that understanding. Anxiety at home was matched with anxiety abroad as news came of the deteriorating political situation in Rome. On 21 March the Oratorians began a Novena to Our Lady for the Pope who was under threat by the revolutionaries. Later in the year, as the situation in the city deteriorated further, the Blessed Sacrament was exposed all day for the Pope's safety. On 16 November Newman's 'confidential friend and benefactor' Monsignor Palma, who had helped him adapt the Oratorian Rule for England, was shot through the window of his room at the Quirinal. On 2 December, writing to Jemima from St Wilfrid's, Cheadle, to where the whole community had now moved, he spoke of that good man's death, and the effect it must be having on the Pope, who was himself so bravely answering to his symbol in St Malachi's prophecy, *Crux de cruce*.

Palma's death must to the Pope be a most cruel blow – he was one of his most confidential friends.
One penalty of being a Catholic is that it gives one a communion of sorrows

and fears, all over the world; one suffers in many countries at once. How a Pope bears it, who has the weight of the whole world upon him, I cannot fancy, except that he has so many prayers for him in every country. I know in a little way what responsibility is, – and know that it is almost physical pain upon my mind, and especially when it involves the concerns of others – But it is to me marvellous how a Pope can stand it. There was a report that it had brought on some return of the epileptic fits he had when a youth – but I have heard nothing lately to confirm it. Poor Palma was a hard-working man, – always at some good work – with a number of penitents, and poor clients. His one request from us again and again for his great services to us was 'Pray for me', and he said it so earnestly that it was as if he foresaw something was coming. It was this day year as near as possible the very day, I think, that I took leave of him, and tomorrow that he got St John and me a private interview with the Pope. I have not been so overcome since dear Bowden's death – but it is all well.[10]

Newman thought it most likely that Palma had been saying his Office when the shot struck him, since he could remember how he used to say it walking up and down his room, and he knew the gallery very well into which his rooms opened. He had been a true friend and, apart from St John, the only friend he had had in Rome. He never had another.

When Newman spoke of responsibility giving an almost physical pain to his mind he was thinking of the increasingly difficult time he was having with Faber, or Father Wilfrid as he was known in the community. When the Wilfridians had first arrived Newman had understood they were offering their House at Cheadle without conditions, but it transpired that they stood to lose the £7,000 Faber and his companions had sunk into the property if they vacated it. The result was that increasing pressure was put on Newman to vacate Maryvale and move to Cheadle, which eventually he was forced to do, though it saddened him greatly in spite of the fact that he knew it would only be a temporary measure, since St Wilfrid's could never be suitable as an Oratory: that must be in Birmingham.

On 18 January 1849 Lord Shrewsbury wrote to Newman insisting that the Oratorians should remain at St Wilfrid's and serve the surrounding area; he even suggested that the Rule should be altered. Surely the Bishop would wish it? Newman replied that the Congregation of the Oratory did not willingly take charge of country missions. Its fundamental principle was to labour for the good of souls in great towns, nor could it bestow itself on other objects consistent with its duty to St Philip and the Holy Father who by his brief had established it in England. If they were to do as Lord Shrewsbury had suggested they would cease to be Oratorians, and the Bishop had no power to dispense with their Rule. Newman acknowledged that his reply might seem ungracious, but there must be an alternative plan which would succeed in reconciling his Lordship's wishes for the spiritual welfare of the neighbourhood with Newman's duty to the Oratory. So it turned out, but the matter would continue to cause much anxiety for some time yet.

The last letter Newman wrote from St Wilfrid's was addressed to Henry Wilberforce on 24 January informing him of the impending move to 40 Alcester Street. 'I am now on the point of starting for Birmingham',[11] he wrote. Father Ambrose and several others of the community had already departed for their new home. It was hoped to open the Oratory on the Feast of the Purification, exactly twelve months after the Congregation had been set up. 'How much has passed, how much has been done in that year! What may not the present bring forth!'[12]

Two days before the Chapel was due to open little was ready and the benches were not in place. John Bowden had entered the Order on 25 January at St Wilfrid's, but had been taken ill almost immediately. Faber had written to say that Brother Edward, as Bowden was now called, was looking 'pale, worn and ill'. Newman became anxious; in fact, the whole group of young men, the Giovani, was giving him concern, but, as he told Faber, it was important to trust in God, Our Lady and St Philip, and above all to love one another. Not only were there young novices at St Wilfrid's, but also several boys whose education Newman had undertaken including Charles Bowden and Henry and George Ryder. Henry, a boy of remarkable gifts, would eventually join the Order as Father Ignatius, and at Newman's death succeed him as Superior.

The Chapel opened as planned; Father Ambrose celebrated and Newman preached. With the Bishop's permission collections would be made in the Chapel until the community was formally established in Birmingham. The lack of money would always be a problem. Later on the same day Newman wrote a detailed letter on the subject to Coffin, the Father Rector, still at St Wilfrid's. Perhaps it would be necessary to dispense with the services of John Wenham as tutor to the boys. The full care of the boys was Wenham's business, or at least that was the intention, although Wenham's health was not good. Newman had been insistent that Wenham should go out with his pupils, particularly as the Ryders wished to go fishing. Accidents could happen; a few days later Juniper, the pony, bolted throwing Brothers Lawrence and John out of the cart. As to discipline, Newman laid down special orders for that.

'I do not at all relish the notion of corporal punishments, nor the threat of them,' he told Faber. 'And by the bye I ought to have mentioned to Wenham one thing, that I heard he had pulled Lisle's ears, which had better not be done ... Boys' persons should be sacred.'[13] In the event Wenham's time as tutor did not last long, and he left to become the priest at Mortlake, and eventually the Provost of Southwark.

On the first Sunday evening there was a congregation of between five and six hundred, and some forty children came forward of their own accord to seek instruction. A week later a policeman informed the Fathers that there had been between six and seven hundred present at the evening service. 'Our Congregations are good and attentive,' Newman told Elizabeth Bowden. 'And we are trying to put our house to rights – but oh what weary work that is – I have had a clearing out from Oriel, a clearing out from Littlemore – a getting in to Maryvale, a getting in and out at Rome, a getting in to St Wilfrid's and now a getting into Birmingham. I intend to be here for good – but what can one promise oneself?'[14] Birmingham would be for good, but there was one more move to make when the community moved from Alcester Street to their present home in Edgbaston.

However busy the small group of priests became at Alcester Street there was not sufficient work for many more who wanted to join them from St Wilfrid's. The confessionals were 'not thronged yet'. Gradually it became obvious that the future lay in opening a house and church in London. It was equally obvious to any observer that there would never be room for Newman and Faber in one house. To read Newman's letters to Faber during the months prior to the latter's departure for the capital fills one with admiration for his patience and overbounding charity, for there was often a barb in Faber's letters which must have hurt Newman deeply. Almost as soon as he had reached Alcester Street Faber was informing him how the young men of the community had taken a positive dislike to Father Ambrose while he had been their novice master.

> When I spoke to the Gordons [Brother Joseph and Brother Philip] about
> a particular friendship growing up between them, the answer was that you
> set the example with Father Ambrose. When I spoke to Brother Francis
> [Francis Knox] about Birmingham some weeks ago, his answer was a strong
> expression of aversion to Father Ambrose, and repugnance to live in a 'small'
> community with him. – My dearest Padre, I know how all this will pain you;
> you know what my feelings of love are for dear Father Ambrose; but do
> not trust me only; make Father Bernard speak to you openly about it.[15]

Newman replied that he believed Faber as much as he would Dalgairns.

> As to particular friendships, I have much wished a definition of what is meant.
> St James and St John had a sort of a particular friendship among the Apostles
> – so must brothers in a Congregation ever – i.e. there must be feelings between
> them which are not between others. The point, I conceive, is that they should
> not show it, – should not act upon it. The only way of hindering the fact,

is for them to be in separate Congregations – this applies to Brs Joseph and Philip, you and F. Antony, me and F. Ambrose. Again what is more striking, think of our Lord's love for St John.[16]

Newman felt that in acts he had been most strictly impartial, and it was out of circumstances that he had been brought closer to Father Ambrose than to others. He could not hide the fact unless he actually ceased to love Father Ambrose as well as he did. 'All I can do is to try to love others as well – which if I omit to try to do is certainly a fault.'[17] Was it not a fact that Faber himself was more intimate and familiar with Father Antony Hutchinson than with others. The unlucky difference was that Father Antony was more popular than Father Ambrose. It was depressing to have to go on like this; Faber's letters with some complaint or another arrived almost daily. Even Bishop Ullathorne found Faber's approach often threatening in tone, and certainly lacking in respect for the Bishop's position.

A few weeks later Faber was complaining to Newman over the cost of food.

Your accounts are a perfect mystery to me. How do you manage 14½ months with £6 worth of meat per calendar month and no puddings? Meat is no cheaper at Birmingham than in London, or oughn't to be. We once had a piece of veal for pies; lamb we have never tasted; we have had beef and mutton principally. Say you get your meat, average 6d per lb, i.e. 40 lbs per £1 – you have 240 lbs for 30 days; then deduct bone, fat, waste in boiling etc; the whole with deducting waste, gives 16 lbs a man for 30 days minus 4, i.e. 26 days, a little more than half lb per diem (no waste deducted remember) for Brothers Frederick and Bernard. How do they live, Padre mio? And no puddings![18]

Yet it is from Faber's letters that we sometimes gain an unusual insight into Newman's character, particularly his sense of humour which has often seemed lacking. For instance, he recalled the time Newman made shadow rabbits on the wall which so scandalised his host at a dinner. When the host snubbed him Newman's response was to fall asleep in his chair. Faber was a man who desperately needed to be appreciated and he knew that Newman was the bond of union among those who otherwise would not have come together. He would need Newman's full support in the immediate future, since by the Pope's brief Newman was Superior of the whole Oratorian Community in England. The problem was that every member of that Community wished for as much of their Superior's time as possible; for as Father William had put it simply to Newman, 'You know it is not to be Oratorians, but to be with Newman that we are met together – we came not seeking the Oratory but you.'[19]

When the time came for the London Oratory to be opened Newman travelled to King William Street the day before and, in Father George Talbot's company, took the opportunity to visit St George's, Southwark while the Fathers and Brothers prepared for the important service. Pugin's new cathedral, with its tower reminiscent of Salisbury's, had been opened by Wiseman in the previous July. The inclusion of a rood screen had aroused a bitter controversy between supporters of the Gothic and Italianate styles of church decoration in which the Oratorians had taken the Italianate side. As Newman put it, for Oratorians, a product of the sixteenth century, to assume the architecture simply and unconditionally of the thirteenth would be as absurd as their putting on them the cowl of the Dominican or adopting the tonsure of the Carthusians. Oratorians did not want a cloister or chapter room but an Oratory. Certainly there was nothing Gothic about the Oratory chapel at King William Street; it had been formerly the upper floor of the Lowther Assembly Rooms which the Fathers leased together with two adjacent houses in the street itself.

The scaffolding was not taken out of the chapel till the evening before the opening, and the workmen were still finishing off almost up to the time the ceremony began. Newman slept particularly well on his first night, and on the morning of 31 May Wiseman presided at the Mass and preached a sermon 'so singularly touching' that it was believed no dry eyes could be found among those who heard it. Newman described Wiseman's offering as 'in composition and logic a perfect sermon'. He had delivered it from the altar with great feeling, although it was so intolerably hot in the chapel that the Bishop was 'wetted through to his alb' which was so dyed blue with his cassock that it had to be discarded and burnt. It was perhaps a blessing that Newman had left his chasuble at home, and he refused to be Assistant Priest at the Mass because of the heat. 'I should have been quite knocked up,'[20] he told Father Ambrose. The acoustic in the room had been bad, partly, he thought, owing to the skylights, causing the priests to 'sound thin in Mass' and rendering less than perfect the performance of the music Capes had composed specially for the occasion.

The Oratorians soon had a large following in London, for during the decade between 1840 and 1850 the Catholic population almost doubled. It seems unbelievable but there were more Catholics in London in 1850 than the total population of Rome.

On 17 July Faber reported to Newman that a great number of prostitutes were coming to confession. 'There is almost a *necessitas peccandi* [necessity for sinning] on the poor things if we can't get refuge for them,'[21] he wrote. He intended to give money, half the contents of the poor box, to the Good Shepherd nuns 'with an understanding that we might pack off such penitents at once'.[22] There were problems of another sort in caring for the poor: the conditions were dreadful for the paint had driven the fleas out of the chapel and they had come into the house. Brother Chad was said to have been catching them in handfuls. 'What remains uneaten of me tomorrow will write to you,'[23] Faber joked. On the Feast of the Assumption, 15 August, he told Newman,

> We have had a wonderful day ... I wish we had counted the penitents of
> the last two days; they must have been several hundreds. I think I absolved
> sixty at one sitting last night; the communions have been marvellous ... Mr
> Wickway of Oxford Street has called today to apologise for leaving our Chapel.
> He says he came last Sunday (he was one of our ½ crown offertory men)
> but he could not breathe and became giddy, and in company with two other
> gentlemen who felt ill at the chest through the effluvia he left the chapel.
> He spoke very kindly and with regret at losing our sermons, and returning
> to St Patrick's, Soho, but he assured me that all considered our chapel
> dangerous in respect of cholera.[24]

Cholera did break out later that summer among a gang of some 800 Irish hop-pickers in Kent, in fact in Henry Wilberforce's parish at East Farleigh. People were dying fast and the only priest was at Tunbridge Wells, a distance of fourteen miles away, and he had his hands full. Faber informed Wiseman of the situation on 18 September. Father Knox had travelled to Kent with the Holy Oil and put himself up at a public house.

> We heard from him yesterday; he has more than 100 dying – Father Rowe
> has been over to help him, and put him on a system, and has been most
> kind; there are 10,000 hoppers in Kent, and the pestilence breaking out in
> almost all the villages amongst them: they lie in sheds, men and women piled
> up anyhow. Yesterday I received a letter from Henry Wilberforce himself,
> begging for lay brothers to come and clean and tend the sick.[25]

Soon both Faber and Dalgairns were also in Kent. Faber told the Bishop he had informed Newman of his move. 'I have heard nothing from the Padre, except that the Birmingham Oratory has taken Bilston and its cholera,'[26] he said.

This was true: Newman's diary for Saturday, 15 September records that Father Ambrose and Brother Aloysius had accompanied him to Bilston to assist the priests of the Mission there who had sought the Oratorians' aid. For some days he had been suffering from a severe cold and an acute ear infection so that a blister was applied behind the ear, and he had been suffering deafness for almost three weeks. For several days he had been unable to say Mass. When he had left the Oratory the parishioners were in a state of great anxiety 'every one crying as if we were going to be killed'.[27] However, when he arrived on the scene at Bilston not only did his deafness cease, but also the situation turned out to be far better than had been feared; in fact, the epidemic was virtually over. The following day he wrote in his diary: 'Cholera expiring nothing to do.'[28]

But the epidemic had led to an unexpected grief. Instead of returning straight home to Alcester Street Newman visited St Wilfrid's where he found Edward Caswell and his brother, the former deeply distressed by the sudden death of his wife who had been carried off in fourteen hours by the most violent cholera. Louisa Caswell's body was brought from Torquay to St Wilfrid's for burial and Newman was the chief celebrant at her Requiem Mass. As for Caswell, his loss meant that he would soon join the Order and remain close to Newman's side for the next thirty years. The day before the funeral Newman had written:

> We are all in God's hands, and he orders us about, each in his own way; happy for us, if we can realise this, and submit as children to a dear Father, whatever He may please to do with us.[29]

'A parish is an onus, but it creates a local mass of affection,'[30] Newman wrote. The congregation at Alcester Street continued to grow. Sometimes so many people arrived for a service that some had to be turned away. The Chapel, which had once been a gin distillery, could hold barely six hundred when filled. The Fathers gave lectures on a Monday and a Thursday which were well attended, and confessions were heard every morning and evening and at all hours during the day on demand. There was an evening school for about 100 children, and there was a need for even more. 'We might have 200, had we hands,'[31] Newman told Maria Giberne. Many adults were under instruction and a steady flow of converts was received into the Church. In the same letter Newman said that he felt his destiny had now been fixed; he would probably remain in Birmingham until he died. Perhaps he would live to see prejudice against Catholics go away, for at present it was strong beyond measure – especially in bad people.

> They profess to think the priest may forgive all sins, and for money – This is a dreadful trial on poor girls, who are looking out for service – it quite distresses one to convert them, for this reason – It is throwing all kinds of obstacles in their way – they don't get places – they don't get married – It is a dreadful problem, how best to provide for them. It obliges one to consent to their marrying Protestants. The poor factory boys seem to have no prejudice against us – many of them literally profess no religion, and numbers of them have not been baptized. We have a good many Irish come to us, very few indeed in our district, but they have found us out, and come to us though we cannot go to them.[32]

On 30 September Newman gave Ward an account of how things were prospering more and more. The Fathers were being talked of and their congregation was growing. 'If a blessing still goes with us, and St Philip is not tired of us, in two or three years time, we shall be in a very respectable position in the place,'[33] he said. It seemed St Philip had already granted a special favour. A poor factory girl, a convert of Father Ambrose's, who did not seem to have had much faith in him or any faith at all, and had had a severe illness, was suddenly brought back from the point of death by the application of St Philip's relics. 'She says she heard a voice within her say "Dust and ashes, get up and walk." She sent down here to say "might she come down to service? and if Father Ambrose knew all, he would let her".'[34] It had been a rainy evening, and the latter part of the message had not been given, so Newman had said no. However, it seems the girl came anyway. This was the first of three graces through St Philip which took place during the next few months.

A few days later, the news of the healing began to circulate. 'Had we a large Church, I think at this moment we could do anything – but all things will be given us in the right time,' Newman informed Elizabeth Bowden. The congregation forcibly pushed back the door, and the porch was crowded. At the service of Benediction the priest brought the monstrance out into the street to bless the people kneeling on the pavement opposite. There was no possibility of acquiring a larger church at the moment: 'There is hardly a rich Catholic in Birmingham; and those who have money, either wish to give it to other objects, or would exact conditions of us which we might not care to concede,'[35] he told Maria Giberne, who had been busy copying paintings for the church, including the Madonna from the Santa Croce which, Newman told her, would be put up as soon as possible.

Towards the end of October Newman had a new book of sermons ready for publication with the title *Discourses to Mixed Congregations*. Here he assembled, with only slight revision, the sermons he had preached since he had returned from Rome, and he dedicated them to Wiseman.

> I present for your Lordship's kind acceptance and patronage the first work
> which I publish as a Father of the Oratory of St Philip Neri. I have sort
> of claim upon your permission to do so, as a token of my gratitude and
> affection towards your Lordship, since it is to you principally that I owe it,
> under God, that I am a client and subject, however unworthy, of so great
> a Saint.[36]

These sermons, although in many ways different from those he had preached at Oxford, are among Newman's best. The years of frustration and anxiety are past and the new convert feels himself unrestrained, free and certain. Yet he knows he speaks to a different kind of audience. As Faber was to put it, the sermons were 'a determinate effort to lift up the old Catholic tone and standard'. Newman speaks to his 'mixed' congregation, made up largely of the poor, with tenderness; there is nothing high-brow here, and he shares with them the mystery, the excitement and the confidence of the infallible doctrine of the Church. 'I should have fancied the doctrine of infallibility was implicit in every act of the Holy See and of the Church, as the necessary account of those acts – as if a man said, "Why is a dead fish heavier than a live one", he implies the fact,' he wrote to Faber on 20 October.

> Catholics never say that all doctrines must have been passed in Council. The very idea of tradition is something unwritten, which happens to be consigned to Decrees and Canons when it is, in this or that particular, doubted. No one ever doubted that infallibility is a doctrine of the Roman Church. If the doubt arose and grew among us the Church would be sure to be down upon it.[37]

The sermons, or as Newman chose to call them, Discourses, when published, made a deep impression on Catholics and Protestants alike: many Puseyites became Catholics because of them, men like Thomas Allies, and H.F. Bellasis. Even Benjamin Jowett, that great bulwark of Broad Church Anglicanism, admitted that 'Romanism had never been so glorified before'.

Something new was happening in England. The work he had to do there, as Newman had assured Wiseman all those years before, had now surely begun.

> When a body of men come into a neighbourhood to them unknown, as we are doing, my brethren, strangers to strangers, and there set themselves down, and raise an altar, and open a school, and invite, or even exhort all men to attend them, it is natural that they who see them, and are drawn to think about them, should ask the question, What brings them hither? Who bids them come? What do they want? What do they preach? What is their warrant? What do they promise? – You have a right, my brethren, to ask the question.[38]

He sets himself the task of answering the question in many of its aspects. Yet perhaps there was a class of persons to whom the new Catholic missioner might seem to have been sent more than to others, to whom he could naturally address himself, and on whose attention he had a sort of claim. Here Newman was thinking of many he left behind in the Church of England, men like his dear Henry Wilberforce, to whom he had recently written, 'I can't understand at all how you dare to keep your living – you have no right to it at all.'

To such men Newman had this to say:

> There are those, I say, who, like ourselves, were in times past gradually

led on step by step, till with us they stood on the threshold of the Church.
They felt with us that the Catholic Religion was different from anything else
in the world; and though it is common, (for no two persons exactly felt alike,)
yet they felt they had something to learn, their course was not clear to them,
and they wished to find out God's will. Now, what might have been expected
of such persons, what was natural in them, when they heard that their own
friends, with whom they had sympathised so fully, had gone forward, under
a sense of duty, to join the Catholic Church? Surely it was natural, – I will
not say, that they should at once follow them, (for they had authority also
on the side of remaining,) but at least it was natural, that they should weigh
the matter well, and listen with interest to what their friends had to tell them.
Did they do this in fact? alas, they did just the contrary: they said, 'Since
our common doctrines and principles have led you forward, for that very
reason we will go backward: the more we have hitherto agreed with you,
the less can we now be influenced by you. Because you have gone, therefore
we make up our minds once for all to remain. Your arguments are clearly
a temptation, because we cannot answer them. We will turn away our eyes,
we will close our ears, lest we should see and hear too much. You were so
singleminded when you were with us, that party spirit must now be your
motive; so honest in your leaving us, that notoriety is now your aim. We
cannot inflict a greater mortification on you than by taking no notice of you
when you speak; we cannot have a better triumph over you, than by keeping
others from you when they would address you. In a word, you have spoiled
a promising cause, and you deserve of us no mercy!' Alas, alas! let them
go and say all this at the judgment seat of Christ! Take it as the best advantage,
my brethren, and what is the argument based upon but this, – that all inquiry
must be wrong, which results in a change of religion? The process is
condemned by its issue; it is a mere absurdity to give up the religion of our
birth, the home of our affections, the seat of our influence, the well-spring
of our maintenance. It was an absurdity in St Paul to become a Christian;
it was an absurdity in him to weep over his brethren who could not listen
to him. I see now, I never could understand before, why it was the Jews
hugged themselves in their Judaism, and were proof against persuasion. In
vain the Apostles insisted, 'Your religion leads to ours, and ours is a fact before
your eyes; why wait for what is already present, as if it were still to come?
do you consider your Church perfect? What do you profess to have attained?
why not turn at least your thoughts towards Christianity?' 'No,' said they,
'we will live, we will die, where we were born; the religion of our ancestors,
the religion of our nation, is the only truth; it must be safe not to move.
We will not unchurch ourselves, we will not descend from our pretensions;
we will shut our hearts to conviction, and will stake eternity on our position.'
O great argument, not for Jews only, but for Mahometans, for Hindoos! great

argument for heathen of all lands, for all who prefer this world to another, who prefer a temporary peace to truth, present ease to forgiveness of sins, the smile of friends to the favour of Christ! but weak argument, miserable sophistry, in the clear ray of heaven, and in the eye of Him who comes to judge the world with fire![39]

If there were any to whom these remarks may more or less apply, Newman continued, let them not do him the injustice of thinking that he aimed at their conversion out of any party purposes of his own. What would he and his fellow priests gain from their joining them but an additional charge and responsibility.

But who can bear to think that pious, religious hearts, on which the grace of God has been so singularly shed, who so befit conversion, who are intended for heaven, should be falling back into the world out of which they have been called, and losing a prize which was once within their reach! Who that knows you, can get himself to believe that you will always disappoint the yearning hopes of those whom once you loved so much, and helped forward so effectively. *Dies venit, dies Tua*, the day shall come, though it may tarry, and we will in patience wait for it. Still the truth must be spoken, – we do not need you, but you need us; it is not we who shall be baffled if we cannot gain you, but you will come short, if you be not gained. Remain, then, in the barrenness of your affections, and the decay of your zeal, and the perplexity of your reason, if you will not be converted. Alas, there is work enough to do, less troublesome, less anxious, than the care of your souls. There are thousands of sinners to be reconciled, of the young to be watched over, of the devout to be consoled. God needs not worshippers; He needs not no objects of His mercy; He can do without you; He offers His benefits and passes on; He delays not; He offers once, not twice and thrice; He goes on to others; He turns to the Gentiles; He turns to open sinners; He refuses the well-conducted for the outcast; 'He hath filled the hungry with good things, and the rich He hath sent empty away.'[40]

Newman had known that the situation at East Farleigh was not happy. From what he could gather, Henry Wilberforce was teetering on the brink of becoming a Catholic. 'You know how things lie with you all, which is a secret from me,'[41] he had written to Henry at the end of July. He had heard how the tremendous devotion of the Fathers during the cholera epidemic had affected him, perhaps even more than the conversion of the Ryders. Certainly Henry's wife, Mary, had been affected by her sister's conversion. Henry's disposition and unsettled state had come through clearly to Newman. 'I have heard something about you this morning,' he had written on 19 September, 'which makes me say, "Send for me, and I will come to you at once ...

Do not let anything stand between conviction and its legitimate consequence." '[42]

It seems that Newman's letter on that day had been prompted by one he had received from Sophia Ryder who had been visiting East Farleigh and had reported on Henry's uncertain state. His religious position had brought him to the edge of despair, until Manning, his brother-in-law, had comforted him and confirmed his faith in the Church of England. In spite of this Henry Wilberforce continued to correspond with Newman, who replied on 1 October, 'I think I quite understand your state of mind, and earnestly trust and believe that God is leading you forward to the sure rest of His True Fold,'[43] he wrote. There were some months to pass before matters would come to a crisis. In fact, Mary Wilberforce was the first to make a move. In April Newman wrote to her while he was staying at King William Street. 'I really had hoped that, while I was in London, I might have had the great comfort of making you a Catholic ... It makes me very melancholy to think you are delaying, and you will, I am sure, let me say so. You say that you ought to trust those who can study the question – but this would be as good a reason for taking the step as not – for I suppose there are those who have studied it who have become Catholics. I will not believe that your own heart does not tell you where the truth is.'[44]

In view of Newman's own delays his attitude seems a little insensitive to Mary Wilberforce's natural hesitation at making the move without her husband, but he was now more aware of how seriously the Church regarded the sin of resisting the known truth. It was, as he said to her, too serious a matter not to speak plainly, though he did know how difficult it was to make the final step. Nevertheless, after the birth of her youngest son, Wilfrid, in the following June, she was received without her husband by Father Brownbill at Farm Street. On 7 July Newman noted in a letter to Sister Mary Monica Lockhart, a nun at the Convent at Greenwich, 'I see Henry Wilberforce has resigned his living.'[45]

Soon Wilberforce was visiting Birmingham and planning to move his Catholic family into a house next door to the Oratory.

13

The Difficulties of Anglicans

$$\boxed{1849\text{--}50}$$

On 18 February 1849, ten days after the Italian Republic had been proclaimed in Rome, Bishop Thomas Walsh died in London. Ever since his move from the Midlands he had been too old and infirm to take an active part in the administration of the District and had left more and more of the running of it to Wiseman. Towards the end he became chronically ill, unable to keep any food down. On 12 February Wiseman noted, 'The Bishop is not positively worse, but the vomiting continues, and if not stopped, must prove fatal. In the meantime his weakness increases, and I doubt his power to rally.'[1]

Before the end came the old man was mercifully granted some respite so that he was able to receive Holy Viaticum besides the other last rites. The Requiem was held at Moorfields, but it was fitting that his body should be returned to Birmingham for burial and Newman and several others from Alcester Street were present at the funeral at St Chad's Cathedral on 2 March.

Bishop Walsh had been associated with the area since he had been appointed secretary to Dr Stapleton, Vicar Apostolic of the Midland District, in 1801; subsequently he became spiritual father to the pupils of Sedgley Park, and later he was Vice-President, and then President of St Mary's, Oscott. While still at Oscott in 1825 he had become coadjutor to Bishop Milner and had succeeded him in the following year. The College at Oscott and the two cathedrals at Birmingham and Nottingham, besides numerous churches and religious foundations, bore witness to his ideals and his unswerving faith, but his last years were dogged by ill-health, and he had succeeded Dr Griffiths in London very much against his wish. It had been a great comfort to him to know that Wiseman would remain close by him as his coadjutor and move to London with him.

Nevertheless Bishop Walsh had been regarded in Rome as the right man to become the first English Archbishop and leader of the restored Hierarchy; when Cardinal Barnabo was drawing up a list of possible leaders he had proposed that whether living or dying Bishop Walsh should be the first Archbishop. In fact, the Bishop's death was to bring about a dramatic turn of events, for only now would Wiseman enjoy complete freedom and authority. It seems Cardinal Barnabo had foreseen this situation and it was some relief to him personally, against much opposition from some of the Old English Catholics, to see Wiseman safely in a position where his diplomatic skill might prove invaluable.

The question of re-establishing a Catholic Hierarchy in England, to replace the Vicars Apostolic, with bishops exercising ordinary jurisdiction over territorial dioceses, had been debated in Rome for many years and the events leading up to it were later fully described by Bishop Ullathorne who spent much time in Rome as plenipotentiary of the English bishops. Ullathorne came to look upon that time as the most important and most eventful of the labours of his episcopal life. He had been an ideal choice, because his time as a missionary in Australia had brought him to the forefront during the negotiations which had established the Hierarchy there, and he was well known to Propaganda and to Pius IX himself.

He had arrived in Rome early in the summer of 1848 after a hazardous journey through France. In Paris he had stopped his coach in order to mingle with the crowd and watched the funeral procession of the revolutionaries killed at the barricades. During his time there he witnessed the massing of the National Guard, the entrance of the army that came to quell the rising, and finally the arrest of the leaders of the Revolution. Once in Rome, over a nine-week period of meetings and discussion he gained agreement that the Hierarchy would indeed be restored. He was assured that the official documents were already in preparation and that no time would be lost.

But much time was lost, for on the very night Ullathorne left Rome revolution broke out, and within a short time the Pope's Minister, Count Rossi, and Monsignor Palma would be murdered, the Republic proclaimed, and the Pope forced to flee from Rome to Gaeta in the carriage of the Bavarian Ambassador and disguised as his physician. Compared with such events the restoration of the English Hierarchy seemed insignificant, a matter that must of necessity be postponed, though an Englishman caught in Rome during the ensuing siege might have taken hope from the action of Dr Thomas Grant, the future Bishop of Southwark, who was then Rector of the English College. Making certain his students were safely evacuated to Monte Porzio, his first act after their departure had been to hang the Union Jack out of the window. As his biographer explained,

He had a British subject's devout belief in the inviolability of that sacred ensign, and in its power of striking terror into the hearts of outer barbarians, and protecting the walls shadowed by its presence. His responsibility was increased by having the papers of the Inquisition, and other important documents belonging to the Holy Father, confided to his care.[2]

Who would doubt that England deserved a Catholic Hierarchy now!

However, it seemed to many that with the Pope's flight and forced exile the power of the papacy might be irretrievably lost. The opposite turned out to be the case, for when Pius ix returned to Rome in April 1850 his authority seemed strengthened, something which came as no surprise to Newman who in the following month began to deliver a series of lectures at the London Oratory.

How different is the bearing of the temporal power upon the spiritual! Its promptitude, decisiveness, keenness, and force are well represented in the military host which is its instrument. Punctual in its movements, precise in its operations, imposing in its equipments, with its spirits high and its step firm, with its haughty clarions and its black artillery, behold, the mighty world is gone forth to war, with what? With an unknown something, which it feels but cannot see, which flits around it, and flaps against its cheek, with the air, with the wind. It charges and it slashes, and it fires its volleys, and its bayonets, and it is mocked by a foe who dwells in another sphere, and is far beyond the force of its analysis, or the capacities of its calculus. The air gives way, and it returns again; it exerts a gentle but constant pressure on every side; moreover, it is of vital necessity to the very power which it is attacking. Whom have you gone out against? A few old men, with red hats and stockings, or a hundred pale students with eyes on the ground, and beads in their girdle; they are as stubble; destroy them: – then there will be other old men and other male students instead of them. But we will direct our rage against one; he flees: what is to be done with him? Cast him out upon the whole world! but nothing can go on without him. Then bring him back! but he will give us no guarantee for the future. Then leave him alone; his power is gone, he is at an end, or he will take a new course of himself; he will take part with the State or the people. Meanwhile, the multitude of interests in active operation all over the great Catholic body rise up, as it were, all around, and encircle the combat, and hide the fortunes of the day from the eyes of the world: the unreal judgments are hazarded, and rash predictions, till the mist clear away, and then the old man is found in his own place, as before, saying Mass over the tomb of the Apostles.[3]

Newman had his doubts as to the wisdom of giving this series of lectures intended to draw wavering Anglicans into the Church, but prompted by

Wiseman he had agreed, though, as he told Faber, he wrote them 'intellectually against the grain' more than he could recollect ever doing in the past.

'I was writing yesterday my Lecture up to its delivery,'[4] he told George Ryder. He had been awake much of the night with 'a face-ache', and as he sat, or stood, writing he had a head ache, and it was a fast day besides. It was clear Wiseman was right that there were some Anglicans influenced by the Tractarians who were holding back from conversion, men like Henry Wilberforce and his brother Robert, and Manning himself; but these men, who were to become Catholics during that year, were as much swayed by events in the Church of England as by anything Newman might have said in his lectures. This year, 1850, was also that of the celebrated Gorham Judgment, by which Dr Phillpotts, the Bishop of Exeter, was required by law to institute the Revd George Gorham as the incumbent of Bramford Speke, when it was clear Gorham held a strong Calvinist view of baptismal regeneration at odds with traditional Anglican doctrine. The Bishop refused and Gorham was inducted by commission. It was one more sign that the Church of England, whatever its claims to apostolicity, was a National Church and answerable at all times to Parliament. As Manning wrote at the time,

> A Theology of 300 years is in conflict with a Faith of 1800 years. I was born in the 300. My mature thoughts transplant me into the 1800. This is the real balance, but people will not look at it. I believe a man might hold what he likes in the English Church if he would be quiet and uphold the Church. The dishonesty is to be honest.[5]

Newman felt that the Movement of 1833 had failed in that it had not prevented the promotion of Bishops and others who denied or explained away the grace of Baptism. 'Nor has it hindered the two Archbishops of England from concurring in the royal decision that within the national communion baptismal regeneration is an open question,'[6] he said. Perhaps there had been some good done, but it was difficult to define. On the other hand, it had given a hundred educated men to the Catholic Church. Yet the huge creature from which they went forth showed no consciousness of its loss, but shook itself, and went about its work as before.

Newman argued that the Movement of 1833 had not been drawn from the National Church, neither was it pointed in the direction of the National Church, nor was it a party in the National Church; it did not move in the direction of a branch Church either or create a sect within it. It had been an attempt to prove apostolicity and this it had failed to do. The Church of England would rise and prosper with the nation and see the 'systematic promotion of men heterodox, or fiercely latitudinarian, in their religious views, or professedly ignorant of theology, and glorying in their ignorance'.[7]

The fact that in some Catholic countries the Church seemed to keep its people behind in the advance of civilisation was not inconsistent with the Church's sanctity.

> She has her mission, and do it she will, whether she be in rags, or in fine linen; whether with awkward or with refined carriage; whether by means of uncultivated intellects, or with the grace of accomplishments ... Not till the State is blamed for not making saints, may it fairly be laid to the fault of the Church that she cannot invent a steam engine or construct a tariff.[8]

England surpassed Rome in ten thousand matters of this world, Newman said, but there was always some doubt about the divine nature of a National Church. It was his intention to examine that doubt and look at things as they are, neither indulging the imagination nor allowing the mind to dream.

> I have said, we must not indulge our imagination in the view we take of the National Establishment. If, indeed, we dress it up in ideal form, as if it were something real, with an independent and continuous existence, and a proper history, as if it were in deed and not only in name a Church, then indeed we may feel interest in it, and reverence towards it, and affection for it, as men have fallen in love with pictures, or knights in romance do battle for high dames whom they have never seen. Thus it is that students of the Fathers, antiquarians, and poets, begin by assuming that the body to which they belong is that of which they read in times past, and then proceed to decorate it with that majesty and beauty of which history tells, or which their genius creates. Nor is it an easy process or a light effort by which their minds are disabused of this error. It is an error for many reasons too dear to them to be readily relinquished. But at length, either the force of circumstances or some unexpected accident dissipates it; and, as in fairy tales, the magic castle vanishes when the spell is broken, and nothing is seen but the wild heath, the barren rock, and the forlorn sheep-walk: so it is with us as regards the Church of England, when we look in amazement on that we thought so unearthly, and find so commonplace or worthless. Then we perceive that aforetime we have not been guided by reason, but biased by education and swayed by affection. We see in the English Church, I will not merely say no descent from the first ages, and no relationship to the Church in other lands, but we see no body politic of any kind; we see nothing more or less than an Establishment, a department of the Government, or a function or operation of the State, – without a substance, – a mere collection of officials, depending and living in the supreme civil power. Its unity and personality are gone, and with them its power of exciting feelings of any kind. It is easier to love or hate an abstraction, than so common-place a frame-work or mechanism. We regard it neither with anger, nor with aversion, nor with contempt, any more than with respect or interest. It is but one aspect of the

State, or mode of civil governance; it is responsible for nothing; it can appropriate neither praise nor blame; but, whatever feeling it raises is to be referred on, by the nature of the case, to the Supreme Power whom it represents, and whose will is its breath. And hence it has no identity of existence in distinct periods, unless the present Legislature or the present Court can affect to be the offspring and disciple of its predecessor. Nor can it in consequence be said to have any antecedents, or any future; or to live, except in the present moment. As a thing without a soul, it does not contemplate itself, define its intrinsic constitution, or ascertain its position. It has no traditions; it cannot be said to think; it does not know what it holds, and what it does not; it is not even conscious of its own existence. It has not love for its members, or what are sometimes called its children, nor any instinct whatever, unless attachment to its master, or love of its place, may be so called. Its fruits, as far as they are good, are to be made much of, as long as they last; for they are transient, and without succession; its former champions of orthodoxy are no earnest of orthodoxy now; they died, and there was no reason why they should be reproduced. Bishop is not like bishop, more than king is like king, or ministry like ministry; its Prayer-book is an Act of Parliament of two centuries ago, and its cathedrals and its chapter-houses are the spoils of Catholicism.[9]

It distressed him, Newman continued, to find that the Movement of 1833 had been considered merely as a party within a Church which would only exist so long as the people wanted it; but it could never be forgotten that that which determines its existence will determine its voice. It was as little bound by what it did or said formerly 'as this morning's newspaper by its former numbers, except as it is bound by Law; and while it is upheld by the Law'. Such a Church would not be weakened by the subtraction of individuals, nor fortified by their continuance, since its life was an Act of Parliament.

Of course the presence or departure of individuals will be one out of various disturbing causes, which may delay or accelerate by a certain number of years a change in its teaching: but after all, the change itself depends on events broader and deeper than these; it depends on changes in the nation. As the nation changes its political, so may it change its religious views; the causes which carried the Reform Bill and Free Trade may make short work with orthodoxy.[10]

It was, however, a very common difficulty for those Anglicans who might consider submitting to the Catholic Church to think that they were weakening the communion they left, which, with whatever defects, they saw in matter of fact to be a defence of Christianity against its enemies. To them Newman had this to say: 'No, my brethren, if the National Church falls, it will be

173

because it is national; because it left the centre of unity in the sixteenth century, not because you leave it in the present. Cranmer, Parker, Jewell, will complete their own work; they who made it, will be its destruction.'[11]

Newman delivered his last lecture in the series on 4 July. On the same day Wiseman wrote to Dr Russell at Maynooth:

A painful secret had been confided to me since early in May by the Cardinal Secretary of State, and it is only today that I hear the matter has reached London as a report, and a letter from Rome received a few days ago shows me that it has oozed out, and so will soon be public. I feel, therefore, authorised to write confidentially about it, till it is publicly known as a certainty. The truth, then, is that I leave England (for ever) next month.[12]

Wiseman had received the news with shock that the Pope had decided to make him a Cardinal and this meant as a matter of course that he must live in Rome at the Pontifical Court. Suddenly, it seemed, all his hopes for overseeing personally the conversion of England were dashed. As he put it, he would be bound in golden fetters for life. All his life's wish to labour for England, in the midst of the strife with heresy, was suddenly thwarted: he was wanted in Rome and a successor would be provided for the London District.

In this order I must hear the voice of God, and I at least have one consolation, that in accepting, in obedience, the unwelcome dignity, I am sacrificing everything that is dear to me, and, perhaps, destroying my own work, in which too much of selfish or earthly complacency may have mingled. It was only in February '49 that, by the death of good Dr Walsh, I first became properly a free agent, acting on my own responsibility, and in May 1850 I am again thrown into a vague and indefinite position.[13]

It was even humiliating, he said, to think that he was forsaking the position at the helm in the capital of this great Empire while the Church was bearing all before it, surely a much nobler position than to be one of a Congregation of Cardinals 'in which one may have the power of giving one voice in favour of the right'.

What most men would consider an honour had depressed him and crushed him, he confessed. It had buried him for ever in this life, but such was Wiseman's faith that he thought the humiliation must only do him good. Was it not like a farmer seeing the fields in which he had taken such a pride, and on which he had expended all his labour, swept over by a flood which would efface all his work? It was surely a judgment and a chastisement and must be submitted to as such. 'While, therefore, I bow to the mandate, and

174

to the Divine Will, I cannot but feel in it a reproof that my work has been badly done, and must be taken from me and given to others.'[14] He had never felt so much in need of good prayers as now, but although, as he told Faber, he had found it hard to resign himself to the situation, he knew the maxim of St Philip Neri that one cannot go wrong by obedience.

Wiseman left England, as he thought, for good, on 16 August. A fortnight earlier he had travelled to Birmingham to see Bishop Ullathorne, whom he thought would almost certainly succeed him and become the first Archbishop of Westminster in the proposed Hierarchy. Ullathorne lived in a house designed specially for him by Pugin, which one visitor described as the most gloomy place he ever saw. Face to face in Ullathorne's room Wiseman broke down and cried like a child.

He reached Rome on 5 September and on the same day was received by the Pope. The result of the meeting came as a great surprise. 'On my arrival I found the Pope, all the Cardinals, and Propaganda of the same mind,' he wrote to his friend Henry Bagshawe, 'that if possible, and if compatible with the Cardinalitial dignity, I ought to return.'[15] This sudden turn around shocked Wiseman almost as much as the thought of remaining in Rome had done, but his feeling of dejection soon gave way to one of great excitement; the work he had begun could now continue with even more vigour. It was important to let the faithful at home know of the great honour the Holy Father had bestowed on their Community, and he wrote a Pastoral Letter to be read out in all the churches of his new diocese of Westminster. He gave the Pastoral, dated 7 October, the exultant title 'Out of the Flaminian Gate of Rome' and sent it back to England, some five days before he himself set off for home, visiting many places including Venice and Vienna, where on All Saints' Day he dined with the Emperor. It was while he was in Vienna that he experienced a rude awakening: as he drove through the town, leaning back in his carriage and feeling a sense of deep pride over the events of the past month, he began to browse through a copy of *The Times* and was shocked to find his own name in the leading article. What he read sickened him.

'We are not surprised that Dr Wiseman, who has long been distinguished as one of the most learned and able members of the Roman Catholic priesthood in this country, should have been raised to the purple,'[16] he read. So far so good; but then he went on to read that, in the opinion of the writer, the Pope's creating a diocese out of Westminster and appointing Wiseman its Archbishop was 'the grossest act of folly and impertinence which the Court of Rome has ventured to commit since the Crown and people of England threw off his yoke'.[17] Wiseman was described as 'a new-fangled Archbishop' and 'an English subject, who has thought fit to enter the service of a foreign Power and accept its spurious dignities'. Rome clearly had designs on England, the writer insisted; but the Pope and his advisers had mistaken England's complete tolerance for indifference to its designs.

> They have mistaken the renovated zeal of the Church in this country for a return towards Romish bondage; but we are sorry that their indiscretion has led them to show the power which Rome would exercise if she could, by an act which the laws of this country will never recognise, and which the public opinion of this country will deride and disavow, whenever His Grace the titular Archbishop of Westminster thinks fit to enter his diocese.[18]

Wiseman's first action on reading all this was to write immediately to Lord John Russell, the Prime Minister, whom he had made a special point of visiting before he had left England in August. Lord John had hoped that Wiseman might have been able to resolve the question of the British Government's relations with the Holy See. In his letter from Vienna written on 3 November Wiseman reminded the Prime Minister of their meeting; he was anxious to explain that at the time he really had not known he would return. 'I am anxious that no impression should remain on your Lordship's mind that I had the slightest intention to deceive you',[19] he wrote. He regretted the distorted views the English papers had presented. The restoration of the Hierarchy had not been a sudden decision; the measure had not only been prepared but also printed three years previously, and Lord Minto had been shown it by the Pope himself. He was also anxious to point out that his own elevation to the College of Cardinals was entirely an ecclesiastical matter, and he had no secular or temporal delegation whatever. His duties, Wiseman said, would remain what they had always been, to promote the morality of those committed to his charge, especially the masses of the poor; and to keep up those feelings of good-will and friendly intercommunion between Catholics and their fellow countrymen which, he flattered himself, he had been the means of somewhat improving. Lastly, he said, he was confident that time would soon show what a temporary excitement may conceal:

> that social and public advantages must result from taking the Catholics of England out of that singular and necessarily temporary state of government in which they have been placed, and extending to them the ordinary more definite form which is normal to their Church, and which has already so beneficially been bestowed upon almost every colony of the British Empire.

Wiseman was right to think the excitement might be 'temporary', but it was fierce enough while it lasted and there were several anxious weeks when it seemed the ferocity of the Gordon Riots might be repeated. Fortunately Wiseman remained abroad and was largely ignorant of the extent of the opposition his elevation had aroused. In his absence Ullathorne did what he could to calm the situation; in a letter to *The Times* on 22 October, he emphasised that there was no Papal aggression, as was claimed, and the setting up of the new dioceses was a private matter which only concerned Catholics. It was little different from there being an Anglican bishop in Gibraltar which had a predominantly Catholic population, he said; there the Catholics had made no fuss.

Four days later Ullathorne was enthroned as the first Bishop of Birmingham in St Chad's Cathedral. Newman had been invited to preach at the pontifical Mass, and he rose to the occasion delivering one of his most memorable sermons, 'Christ on the Waters'. The first part of the sermon contains passages of great beauty, but as he wrote Newman had been fully aware of the controversy raging in the country. It was a triumphal moment, he said; the Church was coming out of prison as collected in her teaching, as precise in her action, as when she went into it.

> She comes out with pallium, and cope, and chasuble, and stole, and wonder-working relics, and holy images. Her bishops are again in their chairs, and her priests sit round, and the perfect vision of a majestic hierarchy rises before our eyes.[20]

Such words could only have been met with hostility by the non-Catholic population of England; but they were not meant for them. This was, as Wiseman and Ullathorne had said, a private matter; yet Newman took the opportunity once again to insist that it had been the Catholic faith the people of England had held for a thousand years and that the claim to continuity between the pre- and post-Reformation churches, which even he at one time had accepted, just was not true. The people of England now looked down in contempt on what they had once been, and upon the religion which reclaimed them from paganism.

'A change again came over the land,' Newman continued: 'a thousand years had well-nigh rolled, and this great people grew tired of the heavenly stranger who sojourned among them.

> They had had enough of blessings and absolutions, enough of the intercession of saints, enough of the grace of the sacraments, enough of the prospect of the next life. They thought it best to secure this life in the first place, because they were in possession of it, and then to go on to the next, if time and means allowed. And they saw that to labour for the next world was possibly to lose this; whereas, to labour for this world might be, for what they knew, the way to labour for the next also. Anyhow, they would pursue a temporal end, and they would account any one their enemy who stood in the way of their pursuing it. It was a madness; but madmen are strong, and madmen are clever; so with the sword and the halter, and by mutilation and fine and imprisonment, they cut off, or frightened away from

the land, as Israel did in the time of old, the ministers of the Most High, and their ministrations ... And so they turned to enjoy this world, and to gain for themselves a name among men, and it was given unto them according to their wish. They preferred the heathen virtues of their original nature, to the robe of grace which God had given them; they fell back, with closed affections, and haughty reserve, and dreariness within, upon their worldly integrity, honour, energy, prudence, and perseverance; they made the most of the natural man, and they 'received their reward'.[21]

The separation of England from the Catholic Church, Newman claimed, was the work of the devil; it had been as if God had forsaken the land, allowing the evil one to triumph.

And the just Judge of man made as though He would do what men anticipated. He retired, as I have said, from the field; he yielded the battle to the enemy; – but He did so that He might in the event more signally triumph. He interfered not for three hundred years, that His enemies might try their powers of mind in forming a religion instead of His own. He gave them three hundred years' start, bidding them do something better than He, or something at all, if so be they were able, and He put Himself to every disadvantage. He suffered the daily sacrifice to be suspended, the hierarchy to be driven out, education to be prohibited, religious houses to be plundered and suppressed, cathedrals to be desecrated, shrines to be rifled, religious rites to be interdicted by the law of the land. He would owe the world nothing in that revival of the Church which was to follow. He wrought, as in the old time by His prophet Elias, who, when he was to light the sacrifice with fire from heaven, drenched the burnt-offering with water the first time, the second time, and the third time; 'and the water ran round about the altar, and the trench was filled up with water'. He wrought as He Himself had done in the raising of Lazarus; for when He heard that His friend was sick, 'He remained in the same place two days': on the third day He said plainly 'Lazarus is dead, and I am glad, for your sake, that I was not there, that you may believe'; and then, at length, He went and raised him from the grave. So too was it in His own resurrection; He did not rise from the cross; He did not rise from His mother's arms; He rose from the grave, and on the third day.[22]

Three days: three hundred years; three ages had passed away, Newman continued, the bell had tolled once, and twice, and thrice; the intercession of the Saints had had effect; the mystery of Providence had been unravelled; the destined hour had come.

And, as when Christ arose, men knew not of His rising, for He rose at midnight and in silence, so when His mercy would do His new work among us, He wrought secretly, and was risen ere men dreamed of it. He sent not His Apostles and preachers, as at the first, from the city where he had fixed His throne. His few and scattered priests were about their own work, watching their flocks by night, with little time to attend to the souls of the wandering multitudes around them, and with no thoughts of the conversion of the country. But He came as a spirit upon the waters; He walked to and fro Himself over the dark and troubled deep; and, wonderful to behold, and inexplicable to man, hearts were stirred, and eyes were raised in hope, and feet began to move towards the Great Mother, who had almost given up the thought and the seeking of them. First one, and then another, sought the rest which she alone can give. A first, and a second, and a third, and a fourth, each in his turn, as grace inspired him, – not altogether, as by some party understanding or political call, – but each drawn by divine power, and against his will, for he was happy where he was, yet with his will, for he was lovingly subdued by the sweet mysterious influence which called him on. One by one, little noticed at the moment, silently, swiftly, and abundantly, they drifted in, till all could see at length, that surely the stone was rolled away, and that Christ was risen and abroad. And as He rose from the grave, strong and glorious, as if refreshed with His sleep, so, when the prison doors were opened, the Church came forth, not changed in aspect or in voice, as calm and keen, as vigorous and as well furnished, as when they closed her.[23]

Then, as Newman thought of William Ullathorne, newly enthroned, he thought too of the great bishop-saint to whom he himself owed so much, who more than any other human agent had been responsible for his standing there on that day, though in time they were separated by fifteen hundred years:

It is told in legends, my Brethren, of that great saint and instrument of God, St Athanasius, how that when the apostate Julian had come to his end, and persecution with him, the saintly confessor, who had been a wanderer over the earth, was found to the surprise of his people in his cathedral at Alexandria, seated on his episcopal throne, and clad in the vestments of religion.[24]

Had Newman ended on that note it would have been compelling enough, but the times required something further. The fierce opposition which such an occasion aroused needed to be met head on, and so he divided his sermon into two parts. In the second part he set out to confront the Protestant mind and explain it to itself in the simplest terms. He was not called upon, he said, to make a formal refutation of the Protestant charge that the Catholic Church was evil, but he would trace the operation of the charge.

It was not surprising, he said, because for eighteen centuries the Church had 'answered to the instance of that miraculous protection which was manifested in the fisher's boat in Galilee',[25] that it had hardened many men's hearts, for there was no argument so strong 'but the wilful ingenuity of man is able to evade or retort it'.[26] Even Our Lord had been accused of casting out devils in the name of Beelzebub, the prince of the devils. If they have called the good-man of the house Beelzebub, how much more them of His household!

> The world, then, witnesses, scrutinizes, and confesses the marvellousness
> of the Church's power. It does not deny that she is special, awful, nay,
> supernatural in her history; that she does what unaided men cannot do. It
> discerns and recognizes her abidingness, her unchangeableness, her
> imperturbability, her ever youthful vigour, the elasticity of her movements,
> the consistency and harmony of her teaching, the persuasiveness of her claims.
> It confesses, I say, that she is a supernatural phenomenon; but it makes short
> work with such a confession, viewed as an argument for submitting to her,
> for it ascribes the miracle which it beholds, to Satan, not to God.[27]

This was an initial assumption of Protestants: the Catholic Church was not the spouse of Christ, but the child of the evil one; her supreme head was not the vicar of Christ, and pastor and doctor of His people, but the man of sin, and the destined deceiver and son of perdition. Newman argued that it was plain that the very evidences, which really demonstrated the Church's divine origin, were plausibly used against her just as they had been used against Our Lord, as tokens of reprobation. Antichrist, when he comes, will be an imitative or counterfeit Christ, Protestants argued, therefore he will *look* like Christ to the many, otherwise he would not *be* counterfeit, but if Antichrist looks like Christ, Christ, of course, must look like Antichrist. The idolatrous sorceress, if she is to have any success in her enchantments, must feign a gravity, an authority, a sanctity and a nobleness, which really belong to the Church of Christ alone; no wonder, then, since Satan·is to be able to persuade men that she is like the Church, he is also able to persuade them that the Church is like her.

Newman demonstrated how, when men assumed that the Church came not from above but from below, it did not matter how much more numerous and striking the evidences of the Church's divinity might be: they could much the more conclusively be used as charges against it.

> Does she claim to be sent by God? but Antichrist will claim it too. Do
> men bow before her, 'and lick up the dust of her feet'? but, on the other
> hand, it is said of the apocalyptic sorceress also, that the kings of the earth
> shall be made 'drunk with her wine'. Does the Church receive the homage
> of the islands, and the ships of the sea? The answer is ready; for it expressly

said in Scripture that the evil woman shall make 'the merchants of the earth rich by the abundance of her delicacies'.[28]

Continuing in this vein Newman concluded that to the Protestant the Church just could not be thought of as good.

> Good forsooth it cannot, shall not be; rather believe anything than that it comes from God; believe in a host of invisible traitors prowling about and disseminating doctrine adverse to your own, believe us to be liars and deceivers, men of blood, ministers of hell, rather than turn your minds, by way of solving the problem, to the possibility of our being what we say we are, the children and servants of the true Church. There never was a more successful artifice than this, which the author of evil has devised against the Maker, that God's work is not God's but his own. He has spread this abroad in the world, as thieves in a crowd escape by giving the alarm; the men, in their simplicity, run away from Christ as if Christ were he, and run into his arms as if he were Christ.[29]

Newman did not deny, however, that there had been appalling scandals in the Church's history:

> She has her reproaches, she has her shame; no Catholic will deny it ... If there was a Judas among the Apostles, and a Nicholas among the deacons, why should we be surprised that in the course of eighteen hundred years, there should be flagrant instances of cruelty, of unfaithfulness, of hypocrisy, or of profligacy, and that not only in the Catholic people, but in high places, in royal palaces, in bishop's households, nay in the seat of St Peter itself? Why need it surprise, if in barbarous ages, or in ages of luxury, there have been bishops or abbots, or priests who have forgotten themselves and their God, and served the world or the flesh, and have perished in that evil service? What triumph is it, though in a long line of between two and three hundred popes, amid martyrs, confessors, doctors, sage rulers, and loving fathers of their people, one, or two, or three are found who fulfil the Lord's description of the wicked servant?[30]

The Church had ever had the reproach and shame of being a mother of children unworthy of her, Newman said. 'She has good children; she has many more bad.'[31] This being so there had always been and always would be an abundance of materials in the lives and the histories of Catholics, ready to the use of those opponents, who, starting with the notion that the Holy Church is the work of the devil, wished to have some corroboration of their leading ideas. 'I can only say that, taking man as he is, it would be a miracle were such offences altogether absent from her history.'[32] But what other religious body could compare with the Church in duration and extent? her influence had extended throughout the whole world.

> There are crimes enough to be found in the members of all denominations: if there are passages in our history, the like of which do not appear in the annals of Wesleyanism or of Independency, or the other religions of the day, recollect there have been no Anabaptist pontiffs, no Methodist kings, no Congregational monasteries, no Quaker populations. Let the tenets of Irving and Swedenborg spread, as they never can, through the world, and we should see if, amid the wealth, and power, and station which would accrue to their holders, they would bear their faculties more meekly than Catholics have done.[33]

The visible prerogatives of Catholicism, Newman said, made men suspicious of it, while its scandals were sure to fill them with dread and horror. He then went on to outline how most English minds had in the course of three hundred years come to think there was nothing good in the religion which they once thought the very teaching of the Most High. Most men, by nature, dislike labour and trouble; if they labour, as they are obliged to do, they do so because they are obliged. They exert themselves under a stimulus or excitement, and just as long as it lasts. Thus they labour for their daily bread, for their families, or for some temporal object which they desire; but they do not take on them the trouble of doing so without some such motive cause.

> Hence in religious matters, having no urgent appetite after truth, or desire to please God, or fear of the consequences of displeasing Him, or detestation of sin, they take what comes, they form their notions at random, they are moulded passively from without, and this is what was commonly meant by 'private judgment'. 'Private judgment' commonly means passive impression. Most men in this country like opinions to be brought to them, rather than to be at pains to go out and seek for them. They like to be waited on, they like to be consulted, they like to be their own centre. As great men have their slaves or their body servants for every need of the day, so, in an age like this, when everyone reads and has a voice in public matters, it is indispensable that they should have persons to provide them with their ideas, the clothing of their mind, and that of the best fashion. Hence the extreme influence of periodical publications at this day, quarterly, monthly, or daily; these teach the multitude of men what to think and what to say. And thus it is that, in this age, every one is, intellectually, a sort of absolute king, though his realm is confined to himself or to his family; for at least he can think and say, though he cannot do, what he will, and that with no trouble at all, because he has plenty of intellectual servants to wait on him. Is it to be

supposed that a man is to take the trouble of finding out truth himself, when he can pay for it? So his only object is to have cheap knowledge; that he may have his views of revelation, and dogma, and policy, and conduct,– in short of right and wrong, – ready to hand, as he has his table-cloth laid for his breakfast, and the materials provided for the meal. Thus it is, then, that the English mind grows up in its existing character. There are nations naturally so formed for speculation, that individuals, almost as they eat and drink and work, will originate doctrines and follow ideas; they, too, of course have their own difficulties in submitting to the Church, but such is not the Englishman. He is in his own way the creature of circumstances, he is bent on action, but as to opinion he takes what comes, only he bargains not to be teased or troubled about it. He gets his opinions anyhow, some from the nursery, some at school, some from the world, and has a zeal for them, because they are his own. Other men, at least, exercise a judgment upon them, and prove them by rule. He does not care to do so, but he takes them as he finds them, whether they fit together or not, and makes light of the incongruity, and thinks it a proof of common sense, strong shrewd sense, to do so. All he cares for is that he should not be put to rights; of that he is jealous enough. He is satisfied to walk about, dressed just as he is. As opinions come, so they must stay with him; and, as he does not like trouble in his acquisition of them, so he resents criticism in his use.

When, then, the awful form of Catholicism, of which he has already heard so much good and so much evil – so much evil which revolts him, so much good which amazes and troubles him – when this great vision, which hitherto he has known from books and from rumour, but not by sight and hearing, presents itself before him, it finds in him a very different being from the simple Anglo-Saxon to whom it originally came. It finds in him a being, not of rude nature, but of formed habits, averse to change and resentful of interference; a being who looks hard at it, first of all, because, if listened to, it would give him much trouble. He wishes to be let alone; but here is a teaching that purports to be revealed, which would mould his mind on new ideas, which he has to learn, and which, if he cannot learn thoroughly, he must borrow from strangers. The very notion of a theology or a ritual frightens and oppresses him; it is a yoke, because it makes religion difficult, not easy.[34]

Newman continued by saying that the Englishman, no doubt in good faith and sincerity of heart, thought he knew more about God's dealings with men than anyone else; he measured all things in heaven and earth by the floating opinions which had drifted into his mind. He was satisfied and sure of his principles; he conceived them to be dictates of the simplest and most absolute sense, and it did not occur to him for a moment that objective truth claimed to be sought, and a revealed doctrine required to be ascertained. He himself was the ultimate sanction and authority of all that he held.

> Putting aside, then, the indignation which, under these circumstances, he naturally feels in being invited to go to school again, his present opinions are an effectual bar to his ever recognizing the divine mission of Catholicism; for he criticizes Catholicism simply by those opinions themselves which are antagonists of it, and takes his notes of truth and error from a source which is already committed against it. And thus you see that frequent occurrence, of really worthy persons unable to reconcile their minds, do what they will, to the teaching and the ways of the Catholic Church. The more they see of her members, the more their worst suspicions are confirmed. They did not wish, they say, to believe the popular notions of her anti-Christian character; but, really, after what they have seen of her authorities and her people, nothing is left to them but an hostility to her, which they are loth to adopt. They wish to think the best of every one; but this ecclesiastical measure, that speech, that book, those persons, those expressions, that line of thought, those realized results, all tend one way, and force them to unlearn a charitableness which is as pernicious as it is illusory. This, My Brethren, they speak; alas, they do not see that they are assuming the very point in dispute; for the original question is whether Catholics or they are right in their respective principles and views, and to decide it merely by what is habitual to themselves is to exercise the double offence of accuser and judge.[35]

Yet multitudes of sober and serious minds and well-regulated lives, Newman continued, looked out upon the Catholic Church and shrank back from her presence on no better reasons than these.

> They cannot endure her; their whole being revolts from her; she leaves, as they speak, a bad taste in their mouths; all is so novel, so strange, so unlike the Anglican prayer book, so unlike some favourite author of their own, so different from what they would do or say themselves, requires so much explanation, is so strained and unnatural, so unreal and extravagant, so unquiet, nay, so disingenuous, so unfeeling, that they cannot even tolerate it. The Mass is so difficult to follow, and we say prayers so very quickly, and we sit when we should stand, and we talk so freely when we should be reserved, and we keep Sunday so differently from them, and we have such notions of our own about marriage and celibacy, and we approve of vows, and we class virtues and sins on so unreasonable a standard; these and a thousand such details are, in the case of numbers, decisive proofs that we deserve the hard names which are heaped on us by the world.[36]

Then Newman spoke of the unbalanced and unfair standard Protestants set against the Catholics. If a Protestant excluded Catholic books from his house he would be considered a good father and master; yet if a Catholic should do the same with Protestant tracts he would be accused of 'being afraid of the light'. A Protestant may ridicule a portion of the Scripture under the name of the Apocrypha; but he would not allow a Catholic to denounce the Protestant translation of the Bible.

> Protestants are to glory in their obedience to their ecclesiastical head; we may not be faithful to ours. A Protestant layman may determine and propound all by himself the terms of salvation; we are bigots and despots, if we do but proclaim what a thousand years have sanctioned. The Catholic is insidious, when the Protestant is prudent; the Protestant frank and honest, when the Catholic is rash and profane. Not a word we say, not a deed that we do, but is viewed in the medium of that one idea, by the light of that one prejudice, which our enemies cherish concerning us; not a word or deed but is grafted on the original assumption that we certainly come from below, and are the servants of Antichrist.[37]

The Englishman tended to think nothing true that was strange to him, Newman continued. There was no calumny too gross for his credulity, no imputation on Catholic practice so monstrous which they would not drink up greedily like water. The Catholic Church was distrusted, feared, hated, and ridiculed.

> We are fair game for all comers. Other men they view and oppose in their doctrines, but us they oppose in our persons; we are thought morally and individually corrupt, we have not even natural goodness; we are not merely ignorant of the new birth, but are signed and sealed as the ministers of the evil one. We have this mark on our foreheads. That we are living beings with human hearts and keen feelings, is not conceived; no, the best we can expect is to be treated as shadows of the past, names a thousand miles away, abstractions, commonplaces, historical figures, or dramatic properties, waste ground on which any load of abuse may be shot, the convenient conductors of a distempered political atmosphere – who are not Englishmen, who have not the right of citizens, nor any claim for redress, nor any plea for indulgence, but who are well off, forsooth, if they are allowed so much as to pollute this free soil with their odious presence.[38]

So it was that Catholics were thrown back on themselves; for anything they could do on the stage of the world was turned against them as an offence. Yet, Newman concluded, the Church could rejoice on that day for it was conscious always of its divine prerogatives and high destiny. The weight of calumny and reproach was its cross. St Antony, the first monk, who lived his long life in the Egyptian desert, had had 'abundant experience of conflicts with the evil one'. He told his children that bad spirits make a noise and clatter and shout and roar, because they have nothing else to do; it is their way of driving us from our Saviour. There was only one thing Newman feared and that was the 'presence of sin in the midst of us'.[39] The success of the Church lay not with the Pope, or bishops, or priests, or monks; but with each individual.

> Pray that we may not come short of that destiny to which God calls us; that we may be visited by his effectual grace, enabling us to break the bonds of lukewarmness and sloth, to command our will, to rule our actions through the day, to grow continually in devotion and fervour of spirit, and, while our natural vigour decays, to feel that keener energy which comes from heaven.[40]

It was barely two weeks before Guy Fawkes' Day, 5 November. If ever spirits made a 'noise and clatter' they made it then. St George's Cathedral had been barricaded and was guarded by the police against attack. Outside the Oratory in King William Street a jeering mob gathered and threw fireworks on to the chapel roof; instead of the usual guy an effigy of Wiseman was burnt. 'No Popery!' was the constant cry in Fleet Street where fourteen guys were burnt beside a giant effigy sixteen feet high and dressed in what were supposed to represent a cardinal's robes. In other cities and towns there was disturbance; in Birmingham Newman's Oratory was besieged, though at the sight of the Fathers there were often cheers, unlike Father Ignatius Spencer in Liverpool who was wearing his Passionist habit and was hooted at and assaulted in the street. 'I got two blows on the head,' he wrote in his diary, which he counted a blessing.

As for Wiseman, he was resting at Liège before crossing over to England, as yet unconscious of the popular fury his elevation had aroused.

14

The Catholic Hierarchy

$$\boxed{1850\text{--}52}$$

Resisting any attempt on the part of his friends to postpone his crossing, Wiseman arrived back in England on the morning of 11 November. As his own house was being decorated and the painters were still working there, he decided to stay with Henry Bagshawe, his friend and co-editor of the *Dublin Review*, who lived in Fitzroy Square. Immediately he summoned his Vicar General, Dr Whitty, to his presence. He was grateful to Whitty for his letter warning him of the state of things at home which had reached him at Bruges.

'On my speaking of the Protestant excitement,' Whitty recalled, 'one of the first things he showed me was a foolscap sheet of paper lying on the desk before him.

> I stooped down to look at it, and saw the words 'An Appeal to the English People', together with two or three lines. 'Yes, I know the excitement', he said, 'is great. But I am writing something here which I think will calm it.' 'Well,' said I to myself, 'you are indeed a sanguine man to expect that yours or any writing can calm this storm.'[1]

In fact, Wiseman's Appeal, whose full title was *An Appeal to the Reason and Good Feeling of the English People on the subject of the Catholic Hierarchy*, did much to calm the situation when it appeared as a thirty-one page pamphlet; it was also printed more or less in full in five London daily papers, including *The Times* on the morning of 20 November. Dr Whitty compared its effect with the blowing up of the *Orient* at Aboukir: 'It did not indeed put an end to the battle, but it created a pause for a full week at least – a silence of attention.'[2]

Of his own Westminster diocese Wiseman spoke with particular feeling, for he knew what an affront the assumption of that title had seemed to the Establishment. He pointed out how the diocese consisted of two very distinct parts. One comprised the stately Abbey, with its adjacent palaces and royal parks. To that portion the duties and occupation of the Anglican Dean and Chapter were mainly confined, and they would remain undisturbed. However, Wiseman said with a certain amount of irony that he would feel perfectly free to continue going there just as he had frequently done in the past. 'I may visit the old Abbey, and say my prayers by the shrine of the good St Edward; and meditate on the olden times, when the church was filled without a coronation, and multitudes hourly worshipped without a service.'[3] Yet, he continued, that splendid monument, its treasures and art, and its fitting endowments, formed the part of Westminster which would not concern him; for there was another part which stood in frightful contrast, though in immediate contact with that magnificence.

> Close under the Abbey of Westminster there lie the labyrinths of lanes and courts, and alleys and slums, nests of ignorance, vice, depravity, and crime, as well as squalor, wretchedness and disease; whose atmosphere is typhus, whose ventilation is cholera; in which swarms a huge and almost countless population, nominally, at least, Catholic; haunts of filth which no Sewerage Committee can reach, corners which no Lighting Board can brighten. This is the part of Westminster which alone I covet, and which I shall be glad to claim and visit as a blessed pasture in which sheep of Holy Church are to be tended, in which a bishop's godly work has to be done.[4]

No one was more impressed with the Cardinal's action than Newman. He had been relieved that Wiseman's friends had not succeeded in deferring his arrival. 'I was afraid he would not come,' Newman told Thomas Allies. 'We must not show any sort of fear.'[5] He felt that the quicker the appointments were made for the dioceses the better, but he had been anxious on hearing rumours that the measure was thought by many in the government to be contrary to Common Law. What annoyed him particularly was the action of the Prime Minister. 'I should like Lord John, a creature of the people, brought to account for calling the religion of one third of the British Empire a superstition and a mummery. Whether it is prudent at the moment I don't know,' he said, 'but it would be a proper counter-movement to frighten him.'[6]

Wiseman himself felt Lord John had let him down badly by expressing so forcefully his anti-Catholic sympathies in his reply to the Bishop of Durham who had complained of the Pope's 'insolent and insidious' action. Before he had departed for Rome there had seemed no doubt in Wiseman's mind that the Prime Minister had offered encouragement, but it may have been that Lord John felt he had nothing to lose since at that time Wiseman was unlikely to return.

In his letter to the Bishop, which had become public the day before Guy

Fawkes' Day, Lord John had affirmed his reliance on the people of England 'so long as the glorious principles and the immortal martyrs of the Reformation shall be held in reverence by the great mass of a nation which looks with contempt on the mummeries of superstition, and with scorn at the laborious endeavours which are now making to confine the intellect and enslave the soul'.[7]

'At the present crisis,' Wiseman wrote in his Appeal, 'the Catholics of England had no right to expect any co-operation from the Government of the country – they asked for none; but they had the right of every citizen to impartiality.

> They naturally might have expected that he to whom was entrusted the helm of the State would keep himself above those influences of party feeling which disqualify the mind for grave and generous counsels; which preserve himself uncommitted by any hasty or unofficial expression of opinion; would remain on the neutral ground of his public responsibility, to check excess on every side, and moderate dangerous tendencies in any party. Instead of this, the head of Her Majesty's Government has astonished, not this country alone, but all Europe, by a letter which leaves us but little hope that any appeal to the high authority which rules over the empire would be received, to say the least, with favour.[8]

On 3 December Newman wrote to George Talbot: 'The Cardinal is firm and vigorous, the effect of his pamphlet has been enormous – the multitude, who dare not confess the truth, only extol his cleverness the more.'[9] It has often been claimed that Wiseman acted foolishly in his handling of the establishment of the Hierarchy, and that the fury aroused might have been avoided but for his tactlessness. Many Catholics thought so at the time. However, fury was surely inevitable. Wiseman showed great courage; he knew he had a divine message to deliver to the English people, a message he could hardly have put across had he crept back to his new diocese unannounced. The fact that his carriage was pelted with dung in the streets of Southwark would have meant little to one who was living proof that, after three hundred years of enforced silence, the Catholic Church had come to proclaim anew the Faith which had been long since abandoned and utterly forgotten by the masses of the people, most of whom adhered to little or no faith. Well might the Anglican Bishop of London have spoken of the Catholic priesthood as 'emissaries of darkness', and the Archbishop of York of the snare which Rome's ever-wakeful ambition was 'plotting for our captivity and ruin'. Similar statements issued from most of the Anglican Hierarchy during the months leading up to Christmas, but the fact was the people did listen to Wiseman's appeal. 'The people of this great country,' wrote Newman at the time, 'are such (moral) cowards, that nothing is likely so to prevail with them as firmness.

They will rush forward, if you retreat – but they will be cowed and fall back, if you calmly keep your ground. We must not budge an inch.'[10]

On Christmas Eve Newman again praised Wiseman in a letter to Charles Russell at Maynooth.

How wonderfully he has come out on this occasion! Never did any one in a more striking way show himself equal to an emergency. When the row first took place, and he had not yet reached England, an intimate friend of his, who had known him long, said, he thought it would be his death. Rather, it has turned out his life – I mean it has brought out his energies in so remarkable way, that one may say that, if he had only lived for this crisis, it would have been enough.[11]

Newman acknowledged that Wiseman still had a very difficult part to play, since the status of a Cardinal was not recognised by the government. This was a new problem to be worked out. It was important that Wiseman had 'a number of good advisers close about him who would sound the channel and ascertain the current hour by hour'.[12] Newman had also observed how Bishop Ullathorne had shown 'the same firm, bold front'.[13] Both Wiseman and Ullathorne were men who would rather have gone to prison than recede. As a result of the firm stand taken by the Cardinal there was a new influx of converts, mostly Puseyites who had also been censured by Lord John and the bishops for 'leading their flocks to the brink of the precipice'.[14] On Guy Fawkes' Day there had been many 'No Puseyites' placards among those denouncing Wiseman and the Pope. In the first week of the following April Newman travelled north to receive converts from the clergy of St Saviour's Church in Leeds. The church had been built by Pusey, and was served by a college of unmarried clergy in an attempt 'to show Tractarianism at work amid the horrors of an industrial town'.[15] Several members of the college had become Catholics in 1847, but this last exit from St Saviour's, in spite of a desperate visit by Pusey himself, was the direct result of the Bishop of Ripon and Dr Hook, the Vicar of Leeds, objecting to the sacramental teaching being given there. One of the college, William Neville, joined the Oratory at Birmingham and later became Newman's literary executor.

On 6 April, Passion Sunday, Henry Manning and Newman's friend the lawyer James Hope were received into the Church by Father Brownbill in London. 'So ended one life,' Manning wrote, 'and I thought my life was over. I fully believed that I should never do more than become a priest; about which I never doubted, nor ever wavered. But I looked forward to live and die in a priest's life, out of sight.' To Robert Wilberforce he wrote on the day of his reception:

You will not be surprised that I now tell you of the happy step James Hope and I have taken this day. With the fullest conviction, both of reason and of conscience, we have sought admittance into what we alike believe to be the one true fold and Church of God on earth.

Pray for me that I may be thankful for the peace which overflows even in the midst of human sorrow. So it must be, for so He foretold; but all is well if we may do His will and see his face at last.[16]

News of Manning's conversion travelled fast to Birmingham. In a postscript to his letter to Faber on the same day Newman added without comment: 'So Manning is received.'[17]

While all the excitement of the 'Papal aggression' had lasted Newman had remained at Birmingham. 'Every one has his place; mine is where I am. I should be thrown away in a more prominent one. I have ever been as I am, and am too old to take up a new line.'[18] He acknowledged that his position was the reverse of Wiseman's. Wiseman was made for the world, and in the present crisis he had risen to the occasion.

'Highly as I put his gifts,' Newman wrote, 'I was not prepared for such a display of vigour, power, judgment, and sustained energy, as the last two months have brought out.

> I heard a dear friend of his say, before he had got back to England, that the news of the opposition would kill him: how he has been out! It is the event of the time. In my own remembrance there has been nothing like it. It is an anxious thing, that he is the only one among us equal to the work Providence has laid upon him; yet, again, not anxious, because he is in the hands of Providence, and because Providence ever works with few instruments.[19]

It was important, Newman thought, that the Cardinal should keep out of society as much as possible. His line of action was perfectly distinct from that of ordinary great people; he was in a different sphere. Hard men of the world, in high station, would be delighted to dream a Cardinal felt satisfaction in their company. Newman had heard how Wiseman had been pleased by the attention shown him at the Royal Academy dinner. This was natural enough, he realised, but nevertheless there was little time for such things. Great men, like Pythagoras, should keep in their cave, not wear off the bloom of their popularity.

In Newman's 'cave' many changes had occurred during the past few months. Towards the end of August the Pope had conferred on him a doctorate of divinity. Ullathorne had visited the Oratory to admit him to the doctorate and had eaten with the brethren. At the end of September, after making a final visit to St Wilfrid's, Newman prepared to hand the house over with much of its furniture to the Redemptorists, though they soon decided they did not want it after all, and it was eventually handed over to the Passionists. On 9 October the London and Birmingham houses were separated from each other on a permanent basis. Not long after this both Coffin and Penny left the Order; Coffin to join the Redemptorists, becoming after a while their Provincial and later Bishop of Southwark; Penny to become a secular priest. Both men remained close friends of Newman.

Before all the names of the new bishops were finally announced there were rumours that Newman himself would be made a bishop. 'No one can seriously wish it, who is loyal to St Philip,' he wrote to Faber, 'and there are no lengths to which I would not go to prevent it.' He would have preferred to lose hundreds of pounds in embassies to Rome first, he said.

What the Church needed more than anything in Newman's view was sound theology. 'We want theology, not bishops,'[20] he said, but he was happy to do anything he could do to help the situation once the storm over the Hierarchy had broken. In February 1851 the Ecclesiastical Titles Bill was introduced into Parliament in an attempt to prevent the new bishops from taking the names of towns or cities. Under its terms a fine of £100 could be imposed on any archbishop, bishop or dean who used a territorial title and any endowment could be forfeit. The bill did not become law until the July, but it had no bite and was never enforced. Soon there were Bishops of Nottingham, Clifton, Beverley, Hexham, Liverpool, Northampton, Plymouth, Salford, Shrewsbury, Southwark, and Newport and Menevia, which formed one diocese in Wales, besides Ullathorne's Birmingham and Wiseman's Metropolitan See fixed at Westminster. In the event few people complained, and those who did could do very little to alter the situation.

Newman had been less alarmed than amused by the 'Papal aggression' panic aroused in the nation. During the summer of 1851 he agreed to deliver a series of weekly lectures at the Corn Exchange, in Birmingham. In these lectures, addressed to the brethren of his own Oratory, Newman returned to the offensive, attacking once again the anti-Catholic prejudice of the Protestant Establishment, those heirs of the traditions of the reign of Elizabeth I: the country gentlemen, the Whig political party, the Church Establishment, and the Wesleyan Conference. How was it, he asked, that the Establishment could remain impervious to heresy, schism, infidelity and fanaticism, but should one 'fling upon the gale the faintest whisper of Catholicism',[21] then a connatural foe was recognised instinctively?

> I am going to enquire why it is that in this intelligent nation and in the nineteenth century, we Catholics are despised and hated by our own countrymen. Why they are prompt to believe any story, however extravagant, that is told to our disadvantage; as if, beyond a doubt, we were everyone of us, either brutishly deluded or preternaturally hypocritical, and they

themselves, on the contrary, were in comparison of us, absolute specimens of sagacity, wisdom, uprightness, manly virtues and enlightened Christianity. I am not enquiring why they are not Catholics themselves, but why they are so angry with those who are.[22]

The first lecture was delivered on Monday, 30 June and it seems likely that Manning and Henry Wilberforce were present, for they were both staying at the Oratory at the time. The Corn Exchange in High Street had desks and counters around the sides, although the floor was open. Newman, raised on a dais, remained seated to lecture with his text on a reading desk placed slightly to his left. Using a metaphor from a military campaign he told his audience how Protestants were relying on old pictures and old maps made years and years ago, which had been handed down to them by their fathers, instead of deigning to look at Catholics themselves, instead of attempting to learn anything of them first-hand. It seemed a point of faith with them to rely on inaccurate information. All this was different from actual warfare in which ignorance was weakness: here, on the contrary, ignorance was power, and in truth a Protestant knew as little about Catholicism as well can be conceived. Looking back into an imaginary past, an English 'Elizabethan' Protestant had a view of Catholic monks, Jesuits, and their Church quite his own, unlike that of his more learned brethren abroad; and moreover, he was apparently ignorant of the existence of any view besides it, or that it was possible for any sane man to doubt it, or any honest man to deny it.

Week after week Newman developed his theme, but he was about to get himself into trouble. On 16 July he wrote to James Hope for legal advice:

Could you off hand answer me a question? Can I be had up for a libel, in criminal court or civil, for saying against Dr Achilli the contents of the article in the *Dublin Review*, since published as a pamphlet? I can't make out he has answered it. It contains the gravest charges, about his seducing women etc. with many of the legal documents proving them. I am too dull and stupid to say more.[23]

Hope answered by return of post that to publish libellous matter, even if it had been published before, did leave one open to action; but he thought it most unlikely that Newman would be in any danger since there was abundant proof of the allegations against Achilli. There was certainly abundant proof, and the documents were all in Wiseman's hands. Surely the situation was safe enough. Anyhow Newman was prepared to take the risk and in his fifth lecture delivered a fierce denunciation of this ex-Dominican apostate priest, a lecher and seducer, who had been making popular anti-Catholic speeches in Ireland and was about to follow a similar course in England.

It seemed Protestant prejudice was prepared to employ almost any means to put its point across. Even Palmerston, the Foreign Secretary, had taken an interest in Achilli, for which he received the formal thanks of a deputation from the council of the Evangelical Alliance. Achilli's immoral reputation was, of course, well known to the Catholics, and this had prompted Wiseman to attack him anonymously in the July issue of the *Dublin Review* in 1850.

On the occasion of Newman's lecture Elizabeth Bowden and her daughters were in the audience as their friend launched into an uncharacteristic diatribe. One wonders what effect such a woeful tale had on them.

> Ah! Dr Achilli: I might have spoken of him last week, had time admitted
> it. The Protestant world flocks to hear him, because he has something to tell
> of the Catholic Church. He has something to tell, it is true; he has scandal
> to reveal, he has an argument to exhibit. It is a simple one. That one argument
> is himself; it is his presence which is the triumph of Protestants; it is the
> sight of him which is a Catholic's confusion. It is indeed our great confusion,
> that our Holy Mother could have had a priest like him. He feels the force
> of the argument, and he shows himself to the multitude that is gazing on
> him. 'Mothers and families,' he seems to say, 'gentle maidens, innocent
> children, look at me, for I am worth looking at. You do not see such a sight
> every day. Can any Church live over the imputation of such a birth as I
> am?'[24]

Newman imagines Achilli speaking aloud to his audience, continuing with the passage which was to get him into trouble.

> I have been a Catholic and an infidel; I have been a Roman priest and
> a hypocrite; I have been a profligate under a cowl. I am that Father Achilli,
> who, as early as 1826, was deprived of my faculty to lecture, for an offence
> which my superiors did their best to conceal; and who, in 1827, had already
> earned the reputation of a scandalous friar. I am that Achilli, who in the
> diocese of Viterbo in February, 1831, robbed of her honour a young woman
> of eighteen; who in September, 1833, was found guilty of a second such crime,
> in the case of a person of twenty-eight; and who perpetrated a third in July
> 1834, in the case of another aged twenty-four. I am he, who afterwards was
> found guilty of sins, similar or worse, in other towns of the neighbourhood.
> I am the son of St Dominic who is known to have repeated the offence at
> Capua, in 1834 and 1835; and at Naples again, in 1840, in the case of a
> child of fifteen. I am he who chose the sacristy of the Church for one of
> these crimes, and Good Friday for another. Look on me, ye mothers of
> England, a confessor against Popery, for ye 'ne'er may look upon my like
> again'. I am that veritable priest, who, after all this, began to speak against,

not only the Catholic faith, but the moral law, and perverted others by my teaching. I am the Cavaliere Achilli, who then went to Corfu, made the wife of a tailor faithless to her husband, and lived publicly and travelled about with a wife of a chorus singer. I am that Professor in the Protestant College at Malta, who with two others was dismissed from my post for offences which the authorities cannot get themselves to describe. And now attend to me, such as I am, and you shall see what you shall see about the barbarity and profligacy of the Inquisitors of Rome.[25]

When he was made aware of what Newman had done Dr Achilli was persuaded by his Protestant sponsors to sue for libel. At first he thought to sue Wiseman for the original *Dublin Review* article, but as it had been published anonymously he thought he might have a better case against Newman. Achilli brought his action for criminal libel, though the case was not heard until June 1852. Newman wrote immediately to Wiseman requesting the documents to defend himself, thinking that the court would dismiss the case on the preliminary hearing, but he was surprised to receive no answer from the Cardinal, in spite of several requests. The fact was that Wiseman's papers had become such a muddle that he mislaid the vital documents. Father Gordon of the London Oratory visited Wiseman and found him in great distress. 'Father Newman is surprised not to have heard from you.' 'I dare not write to him,' was the reply; 'I have hunted in vain and cannot find the documents.'[26] They were eventually unearthed when it was too late and Newman had been committed for trial.

In order to prepare his defence several of Newman's friends travelled out to Italy to gather witnesses. Maria Giberne was particularly active on his behalf and persuaded many of the women 'wronged' by Achilli to come to England for the trial. Together with a number of London serving girls, they were able to give ample evidence of Achilli's immorality, but the jury, buoyed up by the prevailing anti-Catholic prejudice and swayed by the judge's summing up which had included a tirade against the Inquisition, remained unconvinced. All but one of the twenty-two charges against Achilli were 'not proved to their satisfaction', and Newman was found guilty. It was clearly a grossly unfair verdict and in its leading article on the morning following *The Times* said that a great blow had been given to the administration of justice in the country, and that Roman Catholics would henceforth have only too good reason for asserting that there was no justice for them in cases tending to arouse Protestant feeling among judges and juries.[27]

Newman was forced to wait until January 1853 for sentence to be passed. He had quite resigned himself to a term of perhaps a year's imprisonment but, when only a fine of £100 with costs was imposed, he considered he had been in some measure vindicated. As for Achilli, he found himself shunned and completely discredited; the audiences for his lectures soon dwindled away to nothing.

The costs of the trial amounted to some £12,000 and here Wiseman made up for his former failing by encouraging a subscription to pay it off. Money came in from admirers from all over the world: in fact, Newman was left with a surplus, which enabled him to buy a property at Rednal outside Birmingham. If the Achilli affair achieved anything, it was the realisation on the part of sane Englishmen that Protestant bigotry had gone too far, that prejudice had led to a gross miscarriage of justice. Newman had triumphed in spite of the humiliation of being dressed down by the judge, Lord Campbell, who compared his conversion unfavourably with that of Achilli. Englishmen could be thankful they had no Inquisition in their country. Achilli might have been an unfrocked priest; he might be a perjurer and a rampant fornicator, all forgivable sins to one who had had the good sense to become a Protestant.

Two weeks after the trial ended the newly restored Hierarchy gathered together at Oscott to attend the first Provincial Synod of Westminster. Not only the bishops, but also representatives from each of the new chapters and the religious orders were assembled. On Wednesday, 7 July Wiseman celebrated Mass and preached the inaugural sermon. For the Cardinal the occasion held a happy sense of homecoming, for he had always seen Oscott as the centre of his endeavours. In barely twelve years much had happened, and when he had assisted Bishop Walsh in completing Pugin's buildings he could hardly have guessed the speed with which events would unfold up to this moment. On the following Sunday Ullathorne celebrated, and Manning, recently returned from Rome, preached one of his first sermons as a Catholic priest.

'The Church in England in Synod takes up its work again after a silence of three hundred years,' he said.

> It reopens its proceedings with a familiarity as prompt, and a readiness as calm, as if it resumed today the deliberations of last night. Though centuries of time have rolled away since it sat in council, the last Synod in England is but the session of yesterday to the session of tomorrow.[28]

It is said the bishops were deeply impressed by the earnestness of manner, impressive delivery and ascetic appearance of Manning, whom they were seeing and hearing for the first time. But of all who spoke during the course of the Synod none spoke more movingly than Newman. He was in his fifty-first year and at the height of his powers. The abysmal Achilli business had not prevented him from overseeing the move of his beloved Oratory from Alcester Street to newly-built premises in Edgbaston, those in the Hagley Road, an

Oratory still today. Since the November of the previous year he had been Rector of the Catholic University of Ireland. After his trial he had hurried back to Dublin for the installation of Archbishop Cullen; now he was at Oscott for the opening of the second session of the Synod. When Dr Briggs, the eldest of the bishops present, celebrated Mass, Newman ascended into Pugin's pulpit and preached what many consider to be one of the most memorable discourses ever written, his sermon which he called 'The Second Spring'.

> But what is it, my Fathers, my Brothers, what is it that has happened in England just at this time? Something strange is passing over the land, by the very surprise, by the very commotion, which it excites. Were we not near enough the scene of action to be able to say what is going on, – were we the inhabitants of some sister planet possessed of a more perfect mechanism than this earth has discovered for surveying the transactions of another globe, – and did we turn our eyes thence towards England just at this season, we should be arrested by a political phenomenon as wonderful as any which the astronomer notes down from his physical field of view. It would be the occurrence of a national commotion, almost without parallel, more violent than has happened here for centuries, – at least in the judgments and intentions of men, if not in act and deed. We should note it down, that soon after St Michael's day 1850, a storm arose in the moral world, so furious as to demand some great explanation, and to arouse in us an intense desire to gain it. We should observe it increasing from day to day, and spreading from place to place, without remission, almost without lull, up to this very hour, when perhaps it threatens worse still, or at least gives no sure prospect of alleviation.[29]

Every party in the body politic, Newman continued, was undergoing the influence of this strange phenomenon, from the Queen upon her throne down to the little ones in the infant or day school. The ten thousands of the constituency, the sum total of Protestant sects, the aggregate of religious societies and associations, the great body of the established clergy in town and country, the Bar, even the medical profession, even literary and scientific circles, every class, every fireside, give tokens of this ubiquitous storm. What is it all about? against what is it directed? what wonder has happened upon earth? what prodigious, what preternatural event is the cause of so vast an effect?

> The physical world revolves year by year, and begins again; but the political order of things does not renew itself, does not return; it continues, but it proceeds; there is no retrogression. This is so well understood by men of the day, that with them progress is idolized as another name for good. The past never returns– it is never a good;– if we are to escape existing ills, it

must be by going forward. The past is out of date; the past is dead. As well may the dead live to us, as well may the dead profit us. This, then, is the cause of this national transport, this national cry, which encompasses us. The past has returned, the dead lives. Thrones are overturned, and are never restored; States live and die, and then are matter only for history. Babylon was great, and Tyre, and Egypt and Nineveh, and shall never be great again. The English Church was, and the English Church was not, and the English Church is once again. This is the portent, worthy of a cry. It is the coming in of a Second Spring; it is a restoration in the moral world, such as that which yearly takes place in the physical.[30]

Three centuries ago, Newman continued, the Catholic Church, that great creation of God's power, stood in this land in pride of place. It had the honours of near a thousand years upon it; it was enthroned in some twenty sees up and down the country; it was based in the will of a faithful people; it energised through ten thousand instruments of power and influence; and it was ennobled by a host of Saints and Martyrs.

Newman went on to mention many of the Saints by name, all of them bishops, beginning with St Augustine and finishing with St Richard of Chichester. He spoke too of the religious orders, the monastic establishments and the universities. The English Church had had wide relations all over Europe; its high prerogatives in the temporal state, its wealth, its dependencies, its popular honours – where was there, Newman asked, in the whole of Christendom a more glorious hierarchy? Mixed up with the civil institutions, with kings and nobles, with the people, found in every village and in every town – it seemed destined to stand so long as England stood, and perhaps to outlast England's greatness.

The long story of why the Church was blotted out was well known and there was no need to repeat it; but it was a fact, Newman insisted, that the vivifying principle of truth, the shadow of St Peter, the grace of the Redeemer had left it.

That old Church in its day became a corpse (a marvellous, an awful change!); and then it did but corrupt the air which once it refreshed, and cumber the ground which once it beautified. So all seemed to be lost; and there was a struggle for a time, and then its priests were cast out or martyred. There were sacrileges innumerable. Its temples were profaned or destroyed; its revenues seized by covetous nobles, or squandered upon the ministers of a new faith. The presence of Catholicism was at length simply removed, – its grace disowned, – its power despised, – its name, except as a matter of history, at length almost unknown. It took a long time to do this thoroughly; much time, much thought, much labour, much expense, but at last it was done. Oh, that miserable day, centuries before we were born! What a martyrdom to live in it, and see the fair form of Truth, moral and material, hacked piecemeal, and every limb and organ carried off, and burned in the fire, or cast into the deep! But at last the work was done. Truth was disposed of, and shovelled away, and there was a calm, a silence, a sort of peace; – and such was the state of things when we were born into this weary world.[31]

All those present at Oscott had been witnesses of the utter contempt into which Catholicism had fallen at the time they were born; some, like Newman himself, had known it as Anglicans, from without, but the majority there had known it as members of the Catholic Church. It was not out of place, Newman said, to bear witness from without. Drawing from his own experiences in childhood, he continued:

No longer the Catholic Church in the country; nay, no longer, I may say, a Catholic community; – but a few adherents of the Old Religion, moving silently and sorrowfully about, as memorials of what had been. 'The Roman Catholics'; – not a sect, not even an interest, as men conceived of it, – not a body, however small, representative of the Great Communion abroad, – but a mere handful of individuals, who might be counted, like the pebbles and detritus of the great deluge, and who, forsooth, merely happened to retain a creed which, in its day indeed, was the profession of a Church. Here a set of poor Irishmen, coming and going at harvest time, or a colony of them lodged in a miserable quarter of the vast metropolis. There, perhaps an elderly person, seen walking in the streets, grave and solitary, and strange, though noble of bearing, and said to be of good family, and a 'Roman Catholic'. An old fashioned house of gloomy appearance, closed in with high walls, with an iron gate, and yews, and the report attaching to it that 'Roman Catholics' lived there; but who they were, or what they did, or what was meant by calling them Roman Catholics, no one could tell; – though it had an unpleasant sound, and told of form and superstition. And then, perhaps, as we went to and fro, looking with a boy's curious eyes through the great city, we might come today upon some Moravian chapel, or Quakers' meeting-house, and tomorrow on a chapel of the 'Roman Catholics': but nothing was to be gathered from it, except that there were lights burning there, and some boys in white, swinging censers; and what it all meant could only be learned from books, from Protestant Histories and Sermons; and they did not report well of 'the Roman Catholics', but, on the contrary, deposed that they had once had power and had abused it. And then, again, we might, on one occasion, hear it pointedly put out by some literary man, as the result of his careful investigation, and as a recondite point of information, which few knew, that there was this difference between the Roman Catholics of England and the Roman Catholics of Ireland, that the latter had bishops, and the former were governed by four officials, called Vicars-Apostolic.[32]

Such was the sort of knowledge possessed of Christianity by the heathen of old time, Newman said; those who persecuted its adherents from the face of the earth, and then called them a *gens lucifuga*, a people who shunned the light of day. Such were the Catholics in England, found in corners and alleys and cellars and in the housetops, or in the recesses of the country; cut off from the populous world around them and dimly seen, as if through a mist or in twilight, as ghosts flitting to and fro, by the high Protestants, lords of the earth. At length so feeble did they become, so utterly contemptible, that contempt gave birth to pity; and the more generous of their tyrants actually began to bestow on them some favour, under the notion that their opinions were simply too absurd ever to spread again, and that they themselves, were they but raised in civil importance, would soon unlearn and be ashamed of them. 'And thus, out of mere kindness to us, they began to vilify our doctrines to the Protestant world, that so our very idiotcy or our secret unbelief might be our plea for mercy.'[33]

It was a great and awful contrast between the Church of St Augustine and St Thomas of Canterbury, and the poor remnant of their children in the beginning of the nineteenth century. It was a miracle, one might say, to have pulled down that lordly power; but there was a greater and a truer one in store. No one could have prophesied its fall, but still less would any one have ventured to prophesy its rise again ... Had it been prophesied some fifty years ago, would not the very notion have seemed preposterous and wild?

> What! those few scattered worshippers, the Roman Catholics, to form a
> Church! Shall the past be rolled back? Shall the grave open? Shall the Saxons
> live again to God? Shall the shepherds, watching by their poor flocks by night,
> be visited by a multitude of the heavenly army, and hear how their Lord
> has been new-born in their own city? Yes; for grace can, where nature cannot.
> The world grows old, but the Church is ever young. She can, in any time,
> at her Lord's will, 'inherit the Gentiles, and inhabit the desolate cities'.

Then Newman called upon the Mother of God, beginning with the quotation from the Canticles he had chosen for his text.

> 'Arise, make haste, my love, my dove, my beautiful one, and come. For
> the winter is now past, and the rain is over and gone. The flowers have
> appeared in our land ... the fig-tree hath put forth her green figs; the vines
> in flower yield their sweet smell. Arise, my love, my beautiful one, and come.'
> It is the time for thy Visitation. Arise, Mary, and go forth in thy strength
> into that north country, which once was thine own, and take possession of
> the land which knows thee not. Arise, Mother of God, and with thy thrilling
> voice, speak to those who labour with child, and are in pain, till the babe

of grace leaps within them. Shine on us, dear Lady, with thy bright countenance, like the sun in his strength, *O stella matutina*, O harbinger of peace, till our year is one perpetual May. From thy sweet eyes, from thy pure smile, from thy majestic brow, let ten thousand influences rain down, not to confound or overwhelm, but to persuade, to win over thine enemies. O Mary, my hope, O Mother undefiled, fulfil to us the promise of this Spring.

Yet Newman's last words were saved for his patron, St Philip. As he spoke to those assembled priests, who day by day offered up the Immaculate Lamb of God, who held in their hands the Incarnate Word under the visible tokens which He has ordained, Newman reminded them that when the English College at Rome had been set up 'by the solicitude of a great Pontiff in the beginning of England's sorrows',[34] there had been an old man who had passed the young Englishmen in the streets of the great city with the salutation *Salvete flores martyrum*!

My Fathers, my Brothers, that old man was my own St. Philip. Bear with me for his sake. If I have spoken too seriously, his sweet smile shall temper it. As he was with you three centuries ago in Rome, when our Temple fell, so now surely when it is rising, it is a pleasant token that he should have even set out on his travels to you; and that, as if remembering how he interceded for you at home, and recognizing the relations he then formed with you, he should now be wishing to have a name among you, and to be loved by you, and perchance to do you service, here in your own land.[35]

While Newman had been speaking Wiseman, in the presidential chair, wept; at times, giving up all effort at dignity and self-control, he was heard to sob openly like a child. The other bishops and clergy were nearly all in tears. As Bishop Ullathorne described: 'When the preacher came out from the Synod, they crowded upon him, giving full flow to ardent outpourings of their gratitude. It was an indescribable scene; a scene so overpowering to the gentle preacher, that Dr Manning rescued him from it, and quietly accompanied him to his room.'[36]

Many years later, in January 1880, shortly before his seventy-ninth birthday, when he was so frail that in the course of a few weeks he would fall twice and crack three ribs, and when he had been a Cardinal for only nine months, Newman accepted an invitation to preside at and deliver an address to the Catholic Reunion, in Birmingham. Still vigorous in mind, he chose that evening to recall the Michaelmas of 1850, 'an unhappy time', a time 'too violent, too unjust, sometimes too extravagant to last',[37] a time of fear and alarm when it could be prophesied in one English village he knew that, if the Papists ever got the upper hand, the streets of the village would flow with blood.

'Not long before these annual gatherings commenced, and close upon thirty years ago, Catholics had suddenly become very unpopular both in Birmingham and through the whole country,' he said. The misfortune had arisen from a singular misunderstanding. It was generally fancied that in some way or other the authorities at Rome were conspiring together against the religious liberties of England, and that, by appointing an English cardinal and English bishops, they intended or hoped, in some unjustifiable way or other, to propagate in this country the Catholic religion. This had not been the case, there had been no conspiracy, though it had never been concealed that the Church hoped to make people Catholics by fair and honest means. It was natural that such a hope should be opposed, and that people would be angry and afraid. It would be absurd and very wicked if it was said England was a heathen country and needed conversion as a heathen country needed it. There was widespread knowledge of Christianity and a love of the main truths, a zeal on their behalf, and an admirable prodigality of contributions in furthering them. There were a great many religious, a great many actively benevolent men among Protestants. This was not inconsistent, Newman insisted, with the Catholic Church holding that such men knew only half the Gospel; and as the Catholic Church was sure that it had the whole, this was a good enough reason why it should wish for conversions. In fact many conversions had already taken place during the past thirty years, and a great deal of ill-will had been felt towards the Church as a consequence; but that ill-will had been overcome, and a feeling of positive good-will had been created instead. This was because there was now hardly a family that did not have at least one member who had converted or was on intimate terms with another family which had: brothers, sisters or cousins, or connexions, or friends or acquaintances, or associates in business or work; such an interpenetration of Catholics with Protestants, especially in the great cities, could not take place without there being a gradual accumulation of experience, slow indeed, Newman said, but, therefore, the more sure, of individual Catholics, and what they really were in character, and whether or not they could be trusted in the concerns and intercourse of life.

The Cardinal continued:

I fancy that Protestants, spontaneously and before setting about to form
a judgment, have found them to be men whom they could be drawn to like
and love quite as much as their fellow Protestants might be – human beings
whom they could be interested in and could sympathise with, and interchange
good offices with, before the question of religion came into consideration.
Perhaps they even got into intimacy and fellowship with some one of them
before they knew he was a Catholic, for religious convictions in this day do
not show themselves in a man's exterior; and then, when their minds turned
back on their existing prejudices against the Catholic religion, it would be

202

forced upon them that the hated creed, at least, had not destroyed what was estimable and agreeable in him, or at least that he was a being with human affections and human tastes, whatever might be his inner religious convictions.[38]

As much as members of a Protestant country might dislike their relations being converted to a religion not their own, and angry as they might be with them at first, yet, as time went on, they found themselves taking their part when others spoke against them. They felt the cruelty as well as the baseness of the slanders circulated against Catholics when those slanders hurt those dear to them. This was the major change that had taken place since those 'unhappy times' thirty years before: Englishmen were much more friendly now to Catholics as individuals, but Newman did not think they were any more friendly towards the Catholic religion.

They do not, indeed, believe, as they once believed, that our religion is so irrational that a man who professes it must be wanting either in honesty or wit; but this is not much to grant, for the great question remains to decide whether it is possible for a country to continue any long time in the unnatural position of thinking ill of a religion and thinking well of believers in it. One would expect that either dislike of the religion would create an unfriendly feeling towards its followers, or friendliness towards its followers would ensure good-will towards the religion. How this problem will be solved is one of the secrets of the future.[39]

When *The Times* reported the Cardinal's address it could not deny the truth of much that he had said. There was no doubt that there was a better relationship between English Protestants and English Roman Catholics. No Englishman would wish to deny it.

It must be acknowledged, also, that Protestants confronted with Catholics in the communication of daily life were unable to continue to think the religion they professed immoral and debasing.[40]

Yet, it has to be said regretfully that today, more than a hundred years after Newman's death on 11 August 1890, how this problem will be solved is one of the secrets of the future still.

15

Chronology of Newman's Later Life

1852–90

1852 May	Newman, as Rector-elect of the proposed Catholic University, begins his lectures in Dublin on 'The Idea of a University'.
June	Convicted of libelling Achilli.
1854 March	Newman blesses the new London Oratory at Brompton.
June	Installed as Rector of the Catholic University in Dublin.
1856 April	Resigns as Rector, but is persuaded to remain non-resident Rector for another year.
	Publishes *Callista*, a novel about the early Church.
1857	Newman agrees to edit a new translation of the Bible. Project soon abandoned.
1858	Returns to Birmingham.
1859 May	Newman founds the Oratory School.
1860 April	Newman becomes editor of *The Rambler*.
July	Newman's article, 'Consulting the Faithful in Matters of Doctrine', delated to Rome. Newman resigns as editor.
1861–62	Difficulties at Oratory School lead to resignation of Fr Darnell as Head, and of other staff. School reorganised under Newman and Ambrose St John.
1864	Newman's controversy with Canon Charles Kingsley. Publishes *Apologia Pro Vita Sua* in which he traces the development of his religious opinions. The *Apologia*'s great success leads to new influence and a new wave of conversions.
1865 February	Wiseman dies and is succeeded by Manning as Archbishop of Westminster.
	Newman publishes *The Dream of Gerontius*.
1866 April	Newman plans to open an Oratorian house at Oxford. Plan blocked by Propaganda.
1870 June	First Vatican Council passes decree of Papal Infallibility. Newman publishes *A Grammar of Assent*.

1875	Publishes *Letter to the Duke of Norfolk on Papal Infallibility* in answer to Gladstone's pamphlet attacking Vatican decrees.
1877	Elected honorary fellow of Trinity College, Oxford.
1878	Pope Pius IX dies and is succeeded by Leo XIII.
1879 May	Newman created Cardinal.
1889	Newman says his last Mass on Christmas Day.
1890 August	Newman dies and is buried at Rednal.

References

ABBREVIATIONS

JHN: John Henry Newman.

LD: *Letters and Diaries of JHN*, ed. The Birmingham Oratory: vols I–VI (Oxford University Press, 1978–84); vols XI–XV (Thomas Nelson, 1962–64). Vols indicated by Roman numerals.

Cp: *Correspondence of JHN with John Keble and others 1839–1845*, ed. The Birmingham Oratory (Longmans, Green and Co., 1917).

Moz: *Letters and Correspondence of JHN*, ed. Anne Mozley in 2 vols (Longmans, Green and Co., 1891).

Wis: *Cardinal Wiseman*, Wilfrid Ward (Longmans, Green and Co., in 2 vols, 1897; new edition, 1900).

AW: JHN: *Autobiographical Writings* (Sheed and Ward, 1955).

Apol: JHN: *Apologia Pro Vita Sua* (1865), ed. M. J. Svaglio (Oxford University Press, 1967).

Ari: JHN: *The Arians of the Fourth Century* (1833) (Longmans, Green and Co., 1890).

Diff: JHN: *Lectures on certain Difficulties felt by Anglicans in submitting to the Catholic Church*, vol. I (1850); vol. II (1865) (James Duffy, 1857).

Dev: JHN: *Essay on the Development of Christian Doctrine* (1845) (New Ark Library, Sheed and Ward, 1960).

Ess: JHN: *Essays Critical and Historical*, vol. I (1828); vol. II (1840) (Longmans, Green and Co., 1919).

HS: JHN: *Historical Sketches* (Longmans, Green and Co., 1917).

LG: JHN: *Loss and Gain: The Story of a Convert* (1848) (Longmans, Green and Co., 1874).

Mix: JHN: *Discourses to Mixed Congregations* (1849) (James Duffy, 1862).

OS: JHN: *Sermons Preached on Various Occasions* (1857) (Burns Oates, 1874).

Prepos: JHN: *Lectures on the Present Position of Catholics in England (1851)* (Burns Oates, 1851).

VM: JHN: *Via Media*, vol. I (1837); vol. II (1841) (Longmans, Green and Co., 1885).

PART I   THE SEARCH FOR TRUTH

Chapter 1

1. Wis. vol. I. p. 88.
2. LD III, p. 276, note 2.
3. Ibid. p. 277.
4. Ibid.
5. Ibid. p. 276.
6. Wis. p. 119.
7. LD I, p. 4, note 1.
8. Maisie Ward: *Young Mr Newman* (Sheed and Ward, 1948), p. 2.
9. AW. p. 29.
10. Ward. p. 4.
11. Apol. p. 16.
12. Ibid. p. 17.
13. Ibid. p. 17.
14. Ibid. p. 20.
15. AW. p. 30.
16. Ibid.
17. LD I, p. 35.
18. Ibid.
19. Ibid.
20. LD I, p. 35.

21. Henry Tristram: *Newman and his Friends* (The Bodley Head, 1933), pp. 55–56.
22. Ibid.
23. LD I, pp. 37–38.
24. Ibid.
25. Ibid. p. 39.
26. Ibid. p. 43.
27. Ibid.
28. Ibid. p. 44.
29. Ibid. p. 46.
30. Ibid. p. 67.
31. AW. p. 149.
32. Ibid. p. 41.
33. Ibid. p. 46.
34. Ibid. p. 47.
35. Ibid. p. 48. LD I. p. 94.
36. LD I, p. 95.
37. Ibid. p. 85.

Chapter 2

1. LD I, p. 99.
2. Ibid.
3. *Memoranda of JHN*; quoted Seán O'Faoláin: *Newman's Way*, (Longmans, 1952), p. 57.
4. LD I, p. 119.
5. Ibid.
6. LD I, p. 122.
7. Ibid. p. 125.
8. J.M. Flood: *Cardinal Newman and Oxford* (Nicolson and Watson, 1933), p. 14.
9. Ibid.
10. AW. p. 62.
11. LD I, p. 139.
12. Tristram. p. 44.
13. Apol. p. 21.
14. LD I, p. 154.
15. Ibid. p. 166–67.
16. Ibid. p. 170.

17. AW. p. 200.
18. LD I, p. 152.
19. Ibid. p. 280.
20. Ibid. p. 282.
21. Ibid.
22. Apol. p. 29.
23. Flood. p. 51.
24. Walter Lock: *John Keble* (Methuen, 1893), p. 54.
25. LD II, p. 32.
26. Ibid. p. 36.
27. Ibid. p. 28.
28. Ibid. p. 37, note 1.
29. AW. p. 212. Quoted LD II, p. 37.
30. LD II, p. 42, note.
31. Ibid. p. 55.
32. Ibid. p. 47, note 1.
33. Ibid. p. 61.
34. Ibid. p. 69.
35. Ibid.
36. Ibid.
37. LD II, p. 70.

Chapter 3

1. Apol. p. 27.
2. LD II, p. 64.
3. Ibid. p. 108.
4. Ibid.
5. Ibid.
6. LD II, p. 68.
7. Ibid. p. 306.
8. Ibid.
9. LD II, p. 95.
10. Ibid. p. 105.
11. Ibid. pp. 118–19.
12. Ibid. pp. 119–20.
13. Ibid. p. 127.
14. Apol. p. 26.
15. LD II, p. 131, note 2.
16. Ibid. pp. 129–30.
17. Ibid. p. 140.
18. Ibid.
19. JHN: *Parochial and Plain Sermons*, vol. I

(Rivington, 1882); Sermon XV; pp. 190ff.
20. Ibid.
21. Ibid.
22. LD II, p. 163.
23. Ibid. p. 164.
24. Ibid.
25. Bernard Basset SJ: *Newman at Littlemore* (Friends of Newman), p. 13.
26. JHN: *Suggestions in behalf of the Church Missionary Society*. VM. vol. II, p. 2.
27. Ibid. p. 11.
28. Ibid. p. 15.
29. Ari: Advertisement, p. v.
30. Ibid.
31. Ibid. pp. 202–3.
32. Ibid. p. 373.
33. Ibid. pp. 268–69.
34. Ibid.

Chapter 4

1. LD III, p. 17.
2. Ibid. p. 25.
3. Ibid. p. 93.
4. Ibid. p. 125.
5. Ibid.
6. Ibid. p. 132.
7. Ibid. p. 106.
8. Ibid.
9. Ibid. p. 177.
10. Ibid. p. 178.
11. Ibid.
12. Ibid. p. 180.
13. Ibid. p. 188.
14. Ibid. p. 189.
15. Ibid.
16. Ibid. p. 209.
17. Ibid. p. 223.
18. Ibid. p. 219.
19. Ibid. p. 240.
20. Ibid. p. 232.

21. Ibid.
22. Ibid.
23. JHN: *The Good Samaritan. Verses on Various Occasions* (1867) (Longmans, Green and Co., 1912), p. 112.
24. LD II, p. 259.
25. Ibid.
26. LD III, pp. 265–66.
27. Ibid. p. 268.
28. Ibid.
29. Ibid. p. 280.
30. Ibid. p. 181.
31. Ibid. p. 282.

Chapter 5
1. LD III, p. 294.
2. Ibid. p. 302.
3. Ibid.
4. AW. p. 116.
5. LD III, p. 108.
6. JHN. *The Pillar of the Cloud. Verses on Various Occasions*, p. 114.
7. LD IV, p. 3.
8. LD III, p. 264.
9. AW. p. 125.
10. Lock, p. 28.
11. Dean Church: *The Oxford Movement* (Macmillan, 1897), p. 83.
12. Ibid. pp. 83–4.
13. Owen Chadwick: *The Victorian Church*, vol. I (A. & C. Black, 1966), p. 59.
14. Ibid.
15. LD IV, p. 30.
16. Ibid. p. 32.
17. Ibid. p. 33.
18. Ibid.
19. Ibid. p. 62.
20. Ibid. p. 17.
21. Ibid. p. 18.

22. Ibid. p. 17.
23. Ibid. p. 18.
24. LD IV, p. 10, note 2.
25. Ibid. p. 109.
26. Ibid. pp. 141–42.
27. Church, p. 99.
28. Ibid.
29. JHN: VM, vol. II, pp. 31–32.
30. Ibid.
31. Ibid.
32. LD IV, p. 183.
33. Ibid.
34. Chadwick, p. 76.
35. Ibid. p. 78.
36. LD IV, p. 290, note 2.
37. Ibid. p. 295.
38. Ibid. p. 293.
39. Ibid. pp. 297–98.
40. Ibid. p. 305, note 1.
41. Ibid. p. 327.
42. Ibid. p. 258.
43. Ibid.
44. Ibid. p. 273.

Chapter 6
1. O'Faoláin, p. 206.
2. Ibid.
3. LD IV, p. 132.
4. LD V, p. 7.
5. Ess. p. 116.
6. Ibid.
7. Thomas Mozley: *Reminiscences*, vol I, p. 380.
8. LD V. p, 151.
9. Ibid. p. 150.
10. Lock, p. 63.
11. LDV, p. 151.
12. Ibid. p. 239.
13. Ibid.
14. Ibid. p. 240.
15. Ibid. note 1.
16. Ibid. p. 242.
17. Ibid.
18. Ibid. pp. 242–43.

19. Ibid. p. 249.
20. Ibid.
21. Ibid. p. 246, note 2.
22. Ibid. p. 263.
23. Ibid. p. 293.
24. Ibid. p. 299.
25. Ibid.
26. Moz. vol. II, p. 196.
27. LD V, pp. 299–300.
28. LD VI, p. 18.
29. VM. vol. II, p. 95.
30. Ibid.
31. Wis. vol. I, p. 233.
32. LD V. p. 252.
33. Ibid. p. 290.
34. Ibid.
35. Nicholas Wiseman: *Lectures on the Doctrine and Practice of the Catholic Church* (Thomas Baker, 1888), p. 570.
36. Ibid.
37. Flood. p. 168.
38. Ibid. p. 166.
39. Ibid.
40. Apol. p. 65.
41. LD IV, pp. 163–64.
42. Ibid.

Chapter 7
1. LD VI, p. 145.
2. Ibid.
3. LD VI, p. 87.
4. Moz. p. 279.
5. LD VI, p. 282.
6. Ibid. p. 285.
7. Ibid. p. 324.
8. Ibid.
9. Christopher Dawson: *The Spirit of the Oxford Movement* (Sheed and Ward, 1945), p. 106.
10. Ibid.
11. Apol. p. 108 note.

12. LD VI, p. 254.
13. VM. vol. I, p. 42.
14. *Dublin Review*, October 1838.
15. Apol. p. 108.
16. Ibid. pp. 110–11.
17. Moz. vol. II, p. 286.
18. Cp. p. 41.
19. Ibid.
20. Cp. p. 44.
21. Cp. p. 43.
22. Cp. p. 46.
23. Ess. vol. II, p. 19.
24. Ibid. p. 70.
25. Ibid.
26. Ibid.
27. Ibid. p. 74. note to Essay (1888).
28. Ibid.
30. Ibid. p. 72.
31. Ibid. p. 73.
32. Apol. pp. 44–45.
33. HS. vol. II, p. 98.
34. Ibid. pp. 95–96.
35. Ibid. p. 98.
36. Basset. pp. 24–25.
37. Ibid.
38. Cp. vol. II, p. 305.
39. Ibid.
40. HS. vol. II, p. 99.
41. Apol. p. 113.
42. Moz. vol. II, p. 300.
43. Apol. p. 123.
44. Cp. p. 72.
45. VM. vol. II, p. 326.
46. Ibid. p. 352.
47. Ibid. pp. 347–48.
48. Cp. p. 326.
49. Ibid.
50. Cp. p. 329.
51. Ibid.
52. VM. vol. II, p. 362.
53. H. P. Liddon: *Life of Pusey*, vol. II, p. 185.
54. Cp. p. 103.

PART II THE OLD RELIGION

Chapter 8

1. Wis. vol I, p. 348.
2. Bernard Kelly: *Historical Notes on English Catholic Missions* (Kegan Paul, Trench, Trubner, 1907), p. 33.
3. Edwin Burton: *The Life and Times of Bishop Challoner* (Longmans, Green, and Co., 1909), Appendix K, pp. 307–8.
4. Ibid. pp. 280–81.
5. Ibid.
6. Bernard Ward: *The Dawn of the Catholic Revival* (Longmans, Green and Co., 1909) pp. 21–22.
7. Ibid.
8. Ibid. p. 28.
9. David Matthew: *Catholicism in England* (Eyre and Spottiswoode, 1955), p. 164.
10. Wis. vol. II, p. 314.
11. Wis. vol. I, p. 4.
12. Ibid. p. 7.
13. Ibid. p. 8.
14. Nicholas Cardinal Wiseman: *Recollections of Rome* (Burns Oates, 1936), pp. 3–4.
15. Ibid. p. 8.
16. Ibid. p. 14.
17. Ibid.
18. Ibid. p. 97.
19. Wis. p. 96.
20. Ibid. p. 100.
21. Revd Fr Pius: *The Life of Father Ignatius Spencer of St Paul* (James Duffy, 1866), p. 90.
22. Quoted in Denis Gwynn: *The Second Spring 1818–1852* (Catholic Book Club Edition, 1943), p. 77.
23. Ibid. p. 79.
24. Pius. p. 249.
25. Ibid. p. 253.
26. Ibid. p. 253–57.
27. Cp. p. 51.

Chapter 9

1. Wis. p. 375.
2. Ibid. p. 376.
3. Ibid. pp. 376–77.
4. Ibid. p. 378.
5. Ibid. pp. 386–87.
6. Cp. p. 120.
7. Ibid. p. 123.
8. Wis. p. 388.
9. Ibid.
10. Ibid. p. 391.
11. Ibid. p. 393.
12. Cp. pp. 124–25.
13. Ibid.
14. Apol. p. 178.
15. Quoted in John Moody: *John Henry Newman* (Sheed and Ward, 1946), p. 68.
16. Ibid. p. 69/Moz. p. 356.
17. Ibid.
18. Cp. p. 146.
19. Moz. p. 386.
20. Basset, p. 32.
21. Ibid. p. 34.
22. Ibid.
23. Ibid. p. 35.
24. Cp. p. 395.
25. Basset, p. 40.

26. Cp. p. 219.
27. Ibid. p. 248.
28. Ibid. p. 251.
29. Ibid. p. 262.
30. Ibid. p. 276.
31. Ibid. p. 278.
32. Ibid. p. 291.
33. Ibid. p. 293.
34. Ibid.
35. JHN: *Sermons bearing on Subjects of the Day* (Longmans, Green and Co., 1891), p. 396.
36. Ibid. p. 409.
37. Tristram. p. 224.

Chapter 10

1. Moz. vol. II, p. 412.
2. Cp. p. 322.
3. Ibid.
4. Ibid. p. 325.
5. Ibid. p. 326.
6. Ibid. p. 331.
7. Ibid. p. 332.
8. Ibid. p. 334.
9. Ibid.
10. Ibid. 336.
11. Ibid.
12. Church: *The Oxford Movement*, p. 385.
13. Apol. p. 205.
14. Church. p. 294.
15. Wis. p. 429.
16. Cp. p. 388.
17. Urban Young CP, *The Life and Letters of the Ven. Dominic Barberi* (Burns Oates, 1926), p. 258.
18. Ibid. p. 261.
19. Ibid. p. 259.
20. Ibid.
21. LD XI, p. 16.
22. Ibid.
23. Young, p. 265.
24. LD XI, p. 120.

25. Ibid. p. 124.
26. Ibid. p. 125.
27. Ibid. p. 126.
28. Ibid. p. 131.
29. Ibid. p. 127.
30. Ibid. pp. 127–28.
31. Ibid. p. 129.
32. Ibid.
33. Ibid. pp. 132–33.
34. Ibid.
35. Ibid. p. 135.
36. Ibid. pp. 135–36.
37. Ibid. pp. 139–40.

Chapter 11

1. Wis. p. 434.
2. Dev.
3. Ibid. p. 124.
4. Ibid.
5. Ibid. pp. 106–07.
6. Ibid. p. 106.
7. Ibid. p. 306.
8. Ibid.
9. Ibid.
10. Ibid.
11. Ibid.
12. LD XI, p. 251.
13. Ibid. p. 252.
14. Ibid. p. 253.
15. Ibid. p. 272.
16. Ibid. p. 275.
17. Ibid. p. 285.
18. Ibid. p. 294.
19. Ibid. p. 305.
20. LD XII, pp. 19–20.
21. Ibid. p. 22.
22. Ibid. pp. 22–25.
23. Ibid. p. 41
24. Ibid.
25. Ibid. p. 101.
26. Ibid. p. 107.
27. Ibid. p. 109.
28. Ibid. pp. 114–15.
29. Ibid. p. 141.

Chapter 12

1. LD XII, p. 140.
2. Ibid.

3. Ibid.
4. Ronald Chapman: *Father Faber* (Burns Oates, 1961), p. 170.
5. LD XII, p. 168.
6. Ibid.
7. LG. pp. 327–28.
8. Ibid.
9. LG. p. 116.
10. LD XII, p. 361.
11. LD XIII, p. 15.
12. Ibid.
13. Ibid. p. 27.
14. Ibid. p. 43.
15. Ibid. p. 29.
16. Ibid. p. 30.
17. Ibid. p. 31.
18. Frederick William Faber: *Selected Letters 1833–1863*, ed. Raleigh Addington (D. Brown and Sons, 1974), p. 196.
19. LD XIII.
20. Ibid. p. 167.
21. Faber: *Selected Letters*. p. 198.
22. Ibid.
23. Ibid.
24. Ibid. pp. 199–200.
25. Ibid. pp. 200–1.
26. Ibid.
27. LD XIII, p. 261.
28. Ibid. p. 259.
29. Ibid. p. 261.
30. Ibid.
31. Ibid. p. 101.
32. Ibid. p. 103.
33. Ibid. p. 266.
34. Ibid.
35. Ibid. p. 278.
36. Ibid.
37. LD XIII, p. 274.
38. Mix. p. 1.
39. Ibid.
40. Ibid.
41. LD XIII, p. 245.

42. Ibid. p. 260.
43. Ibid. p. 266.
44. Ibid. p. 465.
45. Ibid.

Chapter 13

1. Bernard Ward: *The Sequel to Catholic Emancipation 1840–1850* (Longmans, Green and Co., 1915), vol. II, p. 233.
2. Kathleen O'Meara: *Life of Thomas Grant* (W.H. Allen & Co., 1886), p. 65.
3. Diff. p. 156.
4. Quoted in Meriol Trevor: *The Pillar and the Cloud* (Macmillan, 1962). p. 518.
5. Shane Leslie: *Edward Henry Manning* (Burns Oates and Washbourne, 1921), p. 89.
6. Diff. p. 9.
7. Ibid.
8. Ibid.
9. Diff. pp. 4–6.
10. Ibid.
11. Ibid. p. 26.
12. Wis. p. 522.
13. Ibid.
14. Ibid.
15. Ibid. p. 526.
16. Ibid. p. 532.
17. Ibid.
18. Ibid.
19. Ibid. p. 535.
20. *Sermons Preached on Various Occasions,* Sermon IX: Christ Upon the Waters. p. 137.
21. Ibid. pp. 130–31.
22. Ibid. p. 135.
23. Ibid. pp. 136–37.
24. Ibid.
25. Ibid. p. 139.
26. Ibid.
27. Ibid. p. 141.
28. Ibid. pp. 142–43.
29. Ibid. pp. 143–44.
30. Ibid. p. 145.
31. Ibid. p. 144.
32. Ibid. p. 145.
33. Ibid. p. 146.
34. Ibid.
35. Ibid. p. 152.
36. Ibid. p. 153.
37. Ibid. p. 155.
38. Ibid. p. 156.
39. Ibid. p. 162.
40. Ibid.

Chapter 14

1. Wis. p. 554.
2. Ibid. p. 557.
3. Ibid. p. 568.
4. Ibid.
5. LD XIV, p. 125.
6. Ibid.
7. Wis. p. 548.
8. Ibid.
9. LD XIV, p. 156.
10. Ibid.
11. Ibid. p. 175.
13. Ibid.
14. Ibid.
15. LD XIV, p. 244.
16. Edmund Sheridan Purcell: *The Life of Cardinal Manning* (Macmillan, 1895), vol. I, p. 620.
17. LD XIV, p. 247.
18. Ibid. p. 185.
19. Ibid.
20. Ibid. p. 216.
21. Ibid.
22. Prepos. p. 1.
23. LD XIV, p. 310.
24. Prepos. p. 207.
25. Moody: p. 310.
26. Brian Fothergill: *Nicholas Wiseman* (Faber and Faber, 1963), p. 188.
27. Ibid.
28. Henry Manning: *The Pastoral Office*, p. 221.
29. JHN. *Sermons Preached on Various Occasions,* Sermon X: The Second Spring, p. 167.
30. Ibid. pp. 168–69.
31. Ibid. pp. 170–71.
32. Ibid. pp. 171–72.
33. Ibid. p. 173.
34. Ibid. p. 181.
35. Ibid. p. 182.
36. JHN: *Sayings of Cardinal Newman. On the Relations between Catholics and Protestants in England* (Burns & Oates), p. 48.
37. Ibid. p. 46.
38. Ibid. p. 50.
39. Ibid. p. 53.
40. Ibid. note.

Index

Index by Christine Shuttleworth